Background to Business

3rd Edition

Background to Business

3rd Edition

A. R. Leal
MA (Cantab) LLB Grad Cert Ed AMBIM
Chief Examiner for Background to Business in the
Secretarial Studies Certificate of the London
Chamber of Commerce
Head of Business Studies Department
Plymouth College of Further Education

Pitman

PITMAN PUBLISHING
128 Long Acre, London WC2E 9AN

A Division of Longman Group UK Limited

© A. R. Leal. 1987

First published in Great Britain 1987
Reprinted 1988, 1989

British Library Cataloguing in Publication Data
Leal, A.R.
  Background to business.–3rd ed.
  1. Commerce
  I. Title
  380.1   HF1008

ISBN 0 273 02762 X

All rights reserved; no part of this publication may be reproduced,
stored in a retrieval system, or transmitted, in any form or by any
other means, electronic, mechanical, photocopying, recording or
otherwise without either the prior written permission of the
Publishers or a licence permitting restricted copying in the United
Kingdom issued by the Copyright Licensing Agency Ltd, 33–34 Alfred
Place, London, WC1E 7DP. This book may not be lent, resold, hired
out or otherwise disposed of by way of trade in any form of binding or
cover other than that in which it is published, without the prior
consent of the Publishers.

Printed and bound in Singapore

Contents

Contents

Preface

This new third edition considerably updates the second edition and incorporates new chapters on Communications, The Office, Introducing the Electronic Office and Organisation and the Large Business, in order to cover the additional areas of the office function and organisation, communication, office machinery and use of electronic technology which are necessary to pass the Business Administration 1 paper. Students who commence studying for the Certificate in Secretarial Studies may later opt for the first certificate in Office Technology and the new chapters will eliminate the need for a new textbook.

The new book should prove equally satisfactory for students studying either the Background to Business or the Business Administration 1 papers in the group certificates.

Acknowledgements

We are indebted to the following for permission to reproduce copyright material:

Commercial Union Assurance for our Figs. 13.1, 13.2 and 13.3; Halifax Building Society for our Fig. 8.4; Lloyds Bank for our Figs. 8.1 and 8.2; and the London Chamber of Commerce for permission to quote questions from past examination papers and to incorporate past projects in the text.

We would also like to thank Dorothy E. Wooster for her advice.

There is a sixty-minute cassette tape, written by the Chief Examiner, accompanying this book. It expands on material in the main text and provides advice on examination techniques. The cassette, price £3.75, can be obtained by sending this form to

Barl Enterprises
Lake House
78 Radford Park Road
Plymstock
Plymouth
Devon
PL9 9DX

Please send . . . . . . copy/copies of the Background to Business cassette to

Name _____

Address _____

_____

I enclose a cheque for £ _____

Section A

Trade Unions

Chapter 1

Types of union

In the UK there are four distinct categories of union.

Craft unions

These are open to all the skilled craftsmen in an industry irrespective of the firms they work for. They are the oldest type of union but have become less important in recent years; changes in the nature of employment have resulted in falling membership and many craft unions now allow semi-skilled or even unskilled workers to join. The craft unions are, however, still very important within the printing industry but now their role is being challenged. News International decided to move their printing from Fleet Street to Wapping and to use modern printing technology that could be operated by electricians. This brought them into conflict with the print craft unions.*

General unions

Membership of these is open to all regardless of their skill or the industry in which they work. Two of the largest unions in this category are the Transport and General Workers' Union and the General and Municipal Workers' Union.

Industrial unions

As the name suggests this type of union is open to all the employees

*At the moment of writing the dispute was unresolved.

Murdoch I won't budge

Rupert Murdoch yesterday ruled out further talks with the Print Unions following their rejection of News International's £50m offer to settle the Wapping dispute. The 5,500 strikers have lost all chance of compensation, he said last night. "It was the final offer, make no mistake about that." Murdoch said that to talk further, "would destroy News International's credibility" – and Brenda Dean's, who had told her SOGAT members that the offer was final. His comments came as Dean's union executive committee met in Scarborough to discuss their next move in the dispute.

Murdoch said the company has made a generous offer to workers who had no legal right to anything after they went on strike. "The sad thing is that these people have now been misled twice: by going on strike in the first place; and now by rejecting this generous offer." The union leaders had failed to work for the "Yes" vote and the only voices the strikers heard were extremists. . . .

SOGAT, the NGA and the Amalgamated Engineering Union all voted on Friday to reject News International's offer of £50m compensation and the old *Sunday Times* printing plant in Grays Inn Road to end the bitter 4 month old dispute. Murdoch is now considering moving the printing premises to another location and selling the printing plant worth an estimated £12m. . . .

SOGAT's conference in Scarborough will be a crucial test of how much new support – if any – the striking London print workers will get from the rest of the union.

AEU forced to shed jobs and freeze pay

A wage freeze for all full-time staff and elected officials of the Amalgamated Engineering Union is being proposed by its leaders in an effort to head off a mounting financial crisis.

Sixty of more than 200 full-time elected officials are to be made redundant to try to save £2 million a year. The deficit on the general fund for this year is projected to stand at over £2.5 million.

The AEU, as a union with craft origins in manufacturing, has been badly hit by the recession and the switch of employment to services.

within one particular industry regardless of their skill or grade. They are typical in the USA and Germany but no true industrial unions exist in the UK. The nearest are the National Union of Mineworkers and the National Union of Railwaymen. Even they do not represent all their industries' employees; the NUR for example coexists with a craft union (Associated Society of Locomotive Engineers and Firemen) and a white-collar union (Transport Salaried Staff Association). Within the coal industry following a bitter industrial dispute a breakaway union (Union of Democratic Mineworkers) was formed. This division is an embarrassment for the TUC who do not recognise the UDR although unofficially they have attempted to act as conciliators between the two unions.

Bank jobs at risk

A report on the impact of new technology in banking suggests that up to 10 per cent of existing jobs could be lost by 1990. This means that 250,000 jobs are at risk around Europe. . . .

Barclays Bank is to close 150 banking offices, including 63 full branches as part of an ambitious reshaping of its network. This makes it the first of the big four banks to announce a streamlining of its branch system, at a time when rising costs and new electronic systems have raised big question marks over the future of the huge high-street networks.

The closures will be over two years and the downgrading of the 700 branches over five to seven years. There is no redundancy programme but 350 branch managers will be offered voluntary early retirement over the five-to seven-year period "to combat any adverse impact upon promotion prospects", the bank said.

Bank unions, which were told on Friday, expressed serious concern about the career prospects for members. A spokesman for the Banking Insurance and Finance Union said it was concerned about the jobs of managers being put at risk and promotion routes being blocked. Up to a third of managers in some grades were to go.

GA jobs to dry up

General Accident, the country's largest motor insurer, is today negotiating redundancies with the unions ASTMS and Apex. There is no indication of the number of job losses and General Accident hopes that most of the jobs will go by natural wastage and early redundancies.

White-collar unions

This is the fastest growing part of the trade-union movement for three reasons.

1. The loss of job security

Clerical occupations were, at one time, very secure and redundancy was unknown. Today the growth of modern technology has resulted in severe reductions in clerical areas.

The need to improve efficiency has also put pressure on clerical posts.

Shell HQ jobs go

Hundreds of jobs are to be lost among the 850 employees of Shell UK Oil who work in the Shell-Mex building in the Strand, in London.

Mr. Japp Klootwijk, the managing director of Shell's marketing and refining wing in Britain, has sent a letter to staff warning that "substantial and sustainable reductions in costs" must be achieved. He has ordered all managers in the building to find ways of cutting overheads in their departments by 40 per cent.

Employees, who mostly carry out administrative functions, fear that job cuts of around 30 per cent will be ordered. "A really large change in head-office costs can only be achieved by eliminating tasks, although well-performed and desirable, but which must be seen as not absolutely essential," Mr. Klootwijk said in his circular.

---

2. The growth of the 'office-factory'

Many clerical staff now work with machines (albeit sophisticated electronic ones) and this has caused a change in atmosphere which has been conducive to union recruitment.

3. The loss of 'status' of white-collar workers

During the 1950s and 1960s the industrial unions achieved large pay increases for their members, longer holidays and improved working conditions. The non-union office worker failed to achieve the same improvements. Many have joined unions as a result.

Membership of a white-collar union is open to staff in non-manual occupations such as teachers, computer programmers, civil servants, supervisors and clerical staff. The union may be organised around one occupation (teachers or banks) or cover a variety of occupations.

Once you start work you would be entitled to join a white-collar union. It therefore seems appropriate to examine the organisation structure of one such union (APEX – Association of Professional, Executive Clerical and Computer Staff).

Organisation of APEX

This is a medium-sized union with approximately 150,000 members and is organised along traditional union lines. Thus the body responsible for administering the union is the **Executive Council.** This consists of:

- Representatives elected by the membership. Two representatives are elected by national ballot of all the membership while each region (of which there are nine) can nominate one representative.
- Alongside the eleven lay representatives (i.e. members who have full-time jobs) there are the full-time union officials, the most important of whom is the general secretary. He is the union's chief spokesman and the secretaries of the main unions are national figures (e.g. Arthur Scargill of the NUM).

The executive council of APEX normally meets once a month in London and its function is to implement union policy. This is laid down at the union's **Annual Conference** by delegates from the branches of the union, each branch being entitled to send to it one delegate for each 50 of its members. Because branches have stronger representation at their conferences white-collar unions are considered more democratic than general unions.

Prior to the conference, proposals for consideration at it are submitted by branches to the executive council; such branch proposals are circulated to all branches to give them an opportunity to discuss them and to make recommendations on voting to their appointed delegates.

At conference the delegate's role is to discuss and debate the proposals on the agenda, bearing in mind the recommendations of their branch but often relying heavily upon the advice of the executive council and of full-time officials. Votes are taken and these are binding on the executive council.

Below the executive council are the geographical regions. One of these covers the West of England and it is administered by a lay regional council. Its role is mainly administrative, the effective power being wielded by the full-time paid official (the area secretary) who has his own full-time officials. His function is to serve the membership within his region and he is responsible to the general secretary of the union.

Role of the full-time local union officer

The full-time officers responsible to the area secretary would spend most of their time in the 'branches'. When visiting them the officer may:

1. Negotiate with management in instances where local representatives have been unsuccessful in resolving a specific grievance involving a union member. When this happens a 'failure to agree' is registered and the full-time official is called in to deal with the problem.
2. Negotiate with management over pay settlements. In some companies the **staff representative (shop steward)** negotiates on behalf of the members but frequently the negotiations are left to the full-time official.
3. Discuss union policy with members.
4. Attend meetings of staff representatives to talk about union objectives and the tactics they should use in pursuing these.
5. Recruit members.

The branch and unpaid officers

We have already mentioned the **Branch** in connection with the annual conference. Every union member belongs to a branch which is based either on one company or on companies in a small geographical area. The branch holds regular meetings (although attendance at such meetings is usually low) and elects a committee. Most branch committees are comprised of staff representatives (in some unions called 'shop stewards') who are appointed representatives of members working in local companies.

The staff representative is unpaid (although the firm may give time off to perform trade union functions) and is expected to deal with local union matters. Thus the official may:

- act as a negotiator with management;
- seek to increase union membership;
- act as a communications link between the members and the full-time officials;
- represent the union on committees;
- monitor health and safety standards (in many white-collar unions the function of staff representative and health and safety representative are separated);
- collect union dues.

Aims and objectives of a union

A union exists to represent its members and therefore its aims are those of its members. As the immediate priorities of members change so the short-term objectives of the union must change. Thus in the 1970s there was considerable discussion on industrial democracy; this means giving the work-force more say in the running of the company by perhaps having representatives on the board of directors. In the 1980s much less is heard about this as most unions seem preoccupied with pay and unemployment (which with unemployment figures in excess of 3,600,000 in 1986 is hardly surprising) as the following articles show.

In a switch of policy the General Municipal and Boilermakers' Union[1] conference next weekend will be asked to support the idea of a statutory minimum wage to underpin union attempts to eradicate low pay.

It stresses that sympathetic government action must be paralleled by a concerted commitment by unions to give low pay priority in their bargaining and organisational activities.

Note

1. This is a general union.

The executive of the Transport & General Workers' Union[1] voted yesterday to ban from March 1983 the importation of the Vauxhall "S" car, the new General Motors small model already being marketed on the Continent as the Opel Corsa.[2]

Mr. Moss Evans, the union's general secretary, said that it was taking a stand against imports which now accounted for 55 per cent of car sales in Britain.[3]

"No country can afford to import cars at the rate of 50 to 55 per cent," said Mr. Evans. "If the Government is not prepared to deal with a serious situation where the fabric of the motor vehicle industry is being destroyed, then we have got to do something. . . . We cannot afford to allow our members to be put on the dole. We have warned Vauxhall repeatedly but they have just ignored us".

Notes

1. The TGWU is a general union.
2. A ban on imports is a form of industrial action.
3. Imports now account for 55 per cent of car sales (refer to Ch. 9).

The changing priorities of union members can be explained by the work of Maslow who was an industrial psychologist.* He analysed individual needs and classified them into five groups as illustrated in Fig. 1.1.

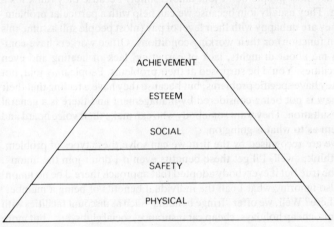

Fig. 1.1

According to Maslow an individual starts at the bottom of the triangle and seeks to satisfy physical needs. *Only* when these have been satisfied can there be a move up the triangle to 'safety'. Thus once a need is satisfied you move up to the next one. To put it simply, if you are starving you are solely preoccupied with finding food (physical) and don't care what your neighbours think of you (esteem).

Physical needs are self-explanatory; they include food and shelter. *Safety* needs could be described as security; office workers want to feel secure in their employment (no fear of redundancy, etc.). In the 1970s there was job security, wages were rising and promotion prospects were healthy. The bottom two needs in the triangle were satisfied and so individuals started to look at levels three, four and five. These are more difficult to explain but involve the employee feeling 'part of the organisation' with the capacity to 'achieve' something (to obtain job satisfaction). But the 1980s the fear of redundancy had increased to such an extent that employees' safety needs were unmet. The satisfac-

---

* The work of other industrial psychologists is discussed in the tape supplementing this book.

tion of these then became paramount and the work-force soon lost interest in the higher needs.

It follows therefore that the aims a union may pursue at a moment in time will vary. In the long term, however, it is possible to classify the main aims of unions. Before this is done let us eavesdrop on a meeting at which the local union official is trying to persuade clerical and secretarial staff to join APEX.

Official

'I accept that most people don't join unions simply because they think it's a good thing. They usually join because we can help with a particular problem. Perhaps they are unhappy with their level of pay (most people still assume this is our main function) or their working conditions. Office workers have complained to me about draughts, lack of carpeting, lack of heating and even canteen facilities. You'd be surprised at their problems. People may join, not because they have specific problems, but because they have a feeling that their point of view is not being considered by management and there is a general lack of consultation. They want somebody who can make their voice heard and inform them as to what is going on.

'Once we are recognised by the firm we can solve these types of problem. You may think, "well, I'll get these benefits even if I don't join the union". That may be true but if everybody adopted that approach there'd be no union! You are also ignoring what I call the individual benefits of being a member. What are these? Well, we offer "fringe benefits" such as discount facilities with various firms, cheap holidays, cheap car insurance, social clubs, etc., but more important we will provide you with "individual protection". Imagine you have an individual complaint or grievance. You may be afraid to mention it to your employer or lack the expertise to pursue it (especially if it involves the complex employment legislation). The union official has the expertise and also the access to senior management. You may have, even in the office, a problem with health and safety ranging from eye strain with visual display units to (surprisingly) potential risks with the use of certain chemicals. The union has extensive research facilities on office-related health and safety issues and is therefore in a position to give sound advice. Another individual benefit arises if you "get into trouble" and you are subject to disciplinary hearings. The union will represent you and while it might agree to your dismissal it will insist the appropriate procedures are followed.

'Being in a union is almost like taking out insurance in case a problem occurs. The union will even provide you with legal aid and advice; this is particularly important as regards accidents at work. If the management contest the case you will not be able to afford to take it to court. The union will, however, pay legal costs in approved cases.'

The above enables us to summarise the main aims of a union thus:

1. To improve conditions at work.
2. To improve job security.

3. To improve the working environment.

To achieve these aims unions negotiate with employers; they indulge in collective bargaining. Each seeks to obtain the best deal although both parties must of course work within the legal framework. Thus in some trades the employers cannot negotiate a lower wage than the statutory minimum (i.e. laid down in law) and all contracts must conform to Acts of Parliament such as the Contracts of Employment Act.

The white-collar unions generally are less militant than their industrial colleagues (white-collar unions do not use the term 'brother'!) arguing that they achieve success through logical argument rather than by industrial muscle. Occasionally, however, they do get involved in strikes.

Ford managers are to meet leaders of the white-collar union ASTMS in London today to try to resolve the strike by 550 foremen and supervisors which has prevented car production since Monday at the Halewood plant in Liverpool.

The dispute hinges on responsibility for training workers on the production line.[1] Ford says that the foreman's responsibilities include job instruction, with physical demonstration when required.

Note

1. This provides an illustration of on-the-job training (see Ch. 4)

The manual unions are more likely to be involved in industrial action (although this is not as common as would appear from media presentation). While the more common forms of industrial action can include strikes, sit-ins, and working-to-rule, other forms of industrial action can also be used.

Strikes

British Leyland's first crisis since the departure of Sir Michael Edwardes deepened yesterday when 1,700 men had to be sent home as a direct result of a strike by 5,000 workers at Cowley over the withdrawal of so-called "washing up time".

The dispute has come at an embarrassing time for BL, less than a month after the launch of the Maestro. This is a success in the showrooms, and some 6,200 Maestros have been sold in the last four weeks. However, 20,000 vehicles have been produced, so stockpiles are high. . . .

The strike, costing the company 800 vehicles a day in lost production, left management and unions with little common ground last night, and all the signs are that it will continue over the holiday period. . . .

The shop stewards continued to claim yesterday that the overwhelming votes in favour of a strike reflected not only dissatisfaction over the company's latest move but also anger over the way manning levels and work practices have been altered in the past year or so.

Sit-ins

Britain's world lead in flat TV screen technology is being jeopardised by the sit-in at the Timex Dundee plant. Clive Sinclair, the inventor of the best-selling personal computer, is close to cancelling the project if the dispute is not settled quickly.

Crisis talks take place in Glasgow today between Scottish industry minister Alex Fletcher and union leaders. Last night Fletcher, alarmed at the damage to Scotland's reputation as a high technology investment location, said: "The whole future of the Timex plant is under threat. Time is running out."

Fletcher called the union meeting after Sinclair – whose computer is made at the Timex factory – travelled to London last week to deliver what amounted to an ultimatum. The five-week-old sit-in, in protest over planned job losses by Timex management, is costing Sinclair £1 million a week. Despite desperate efforts by Sinclair managers, the Timex workers are refusing to allow work on the vital cathode ray tube for Sinclair's £50 mini-TV, due to be launched this summer. . . .

With the Japanese about to launch their own mini-TV, Sinclair believes that his lead is fast being eroded. "We can't afford to delay," said a spokesman for Sinclair last night. "We may have to drop the project altogether if we don't hit the market at the right time."

Work-to-rule

Warders' strike sparks 4-hour noise protest at Dartmoor

More than 500 prisoners in Dartmoor gaol staged a four-hour protest of banging tin mugs, whistling, singing, and shouting yesterday because of conditions caused by a prison officers' work-to-rule. . . .

Prisoners have had no exercise periods outdoors for nearly three weeks and no association with others. . . .

The amount of time spent in their cells, each of which is occupied by only one man, has also been substantially increased as a result of the "controlled unlocking" – any one prison officer will only unlock three prisoners at a time, when pre-viously about 30 would have been unlocked. . . .

Visits from outside are also believed to have been suspended almost completely, and all chapel visits cancelled. Workshop hours and visits to the canteen have been severely curtailed.

Mr. David Evans, general secretary of the Prison Officers Association, said that everything in the prison was taking several times as long, and prisoners were having to spend about 10 times as long in their cells each day. . . .

Prison officers were working according to regulations in protest at recent cuts in manning levels imposed by the Home Office.

Of course there are numerous other ways to disrupt a company.

Vauxhall men at Luton lift ban on Spanish car

Vauxhall's 7,500 workers at Luton voted yesterday to call off their ban on imports of the Spanish Nova in return for a resumption of night-shift production.

Yesterday's vote follows talks between national union officials and Vauxhall directors last week. The company has agreed to increase line production rates, leading to a return to double shifts at Luton in August. . . .

The package also includes agreements on early retirement and voluntary severance. The unions are hoping that enough of the older staff will volunteer for early retirement to guarantee jobs for apprentices at the end of their training.

"The unions' requirements for allowing the Spanish car in were a return to double shifting, which the company has conceded," said a spokeman for the Amalgamated Union of Engineering Workers. "Our recommendation was to accept the outcome of the talks between our national officials and the company directors."

Industrial action should be the last resort and where the employers and unions cannot agree they may request the assistance of a third party to help solve the dispute.

Ford yesterday accepted an independent inquiry finding that Mr. Paul Kelly, an assembly worker at the Halewood, Liverpool, plant should not have been dismissed for allegedly deliberately damaging a bracket. He should instead have been suspended for 10 days without pay, given written warning, and transferred to another section.

The dismissal in March led to a strike by 5,000 Halewood workers. Mr. Kelly, who has been suspended on basic pay, will now be offered a new job. . . .

The inquiry, which was headed by Mr. John Wood, chairman of the Central Arbitration Committee clearly felt the bending of a bracket should become a sackable offence only after a written warning.

The value of having assistance from an independent third party was recognised by the creation in 1974 of the Advisory, Conciliation and Arbitration Service (ACAS).

ACAS

As its name suggests it has three main functions. It advises employers and unions on any matters concerned with industrial relations; this service is free. The conciliation service involves persuading the parties to a dispute to talk to each other; it has been defined as 'the act of promoting goodwill between people'. It is hoped that by persuading the parties to discuss their problem in a friendly atmosphere a solution is more likely. Arbitration usually occurs when both sides disagree and cannot see any possibility of a solution. It arises when they ask a third party (ACAS) to make a decision which both sides will accept. (ACAS does not itself arbitrate but nominates a third party.)

ACAS to mediate in vandal strike

The three-week old strike at Ford's Halewood plant over allegations of vandalism by an assembly worker is to go to ACAS for arbitration, the company and unions agreed yesterday.

The above article refers to the dispute outlined earlier where the arbitrator was chairman of the Central Arbitration Committee.

If the parties are not prepared to accept binding arbitration ACAS can arrange mediation. This involves getting the two parties together with a third party who puts forward proposals for discussion or acceptance. The parties are, however, free to ignore any recommendations he makes, unlike arbitration.

Trades Union Congress

Almost every union belongs to the TUC. Just as employees benefit by joining together so the unions benefit by having one body representing all the unions in negotiations with employers and the government. The head of the TUC is the general secretary but, although he exercises considerable influence, he is bound by the policy laid down by the Annual Congress. Delegates to this represent all the affiliated unions and apart from determining policy elect the General Council who are responsible for implementing policy. It works through committees (supported by full-time staff) on which members of the council sit; details of the main committees are given below. See if you can insert the names of their chairmen.

Finance & General Purposes Committee Chairman..............

Economic Committee Chairman..............................

Employment Committee Chairman ....

International Committee Chairman ....

The committees are responsible for the day-to-day work and report on their progress to the regular council meetings.

The TUC can intervene in industrial disputes involving member unions; these are not always union *v.* employer as is shown in the following articles.

The TUC has been asked to intervene in a bitter inter-union conflict over who should represent more than 5,000 managers in ICI and other top chemical firms. One of the most savage white-collar recruitment wars of recent years has come to a head with a complaint by Frank Chapple's electricians' union against ASTMS.

McGahey seeks peace with UDM

Mr Mick McGahey, the veteran miners' leader, emerged last night as the driving force behind a move within the National Union of Mineworkers to seek a reconciliation with the breakaway Union of Democratic Mineworkers. As leader of the NUM's Scottish area, he has secured widespread support from left and right within the union for an attempt to unify both organisations as soon as possible.

The delegates to the NUM's annual conference, which opens today at Tenby in Wales, last night welcomed a Scottish resolution instructing the NUM leaders to seek "national unity".

At the centre of the plan is a suggestion that a third party, either the TUC or the Labour Party, could assist in the reconciliation.

The members of the Council sit on various bodies, such as the NEDC, as well as being involved in less formal discussions with employers and government. At regular intervals the TUC will produce papers outlining policies they would like to see implemented.

TUC in million jobs campaign

TUC leaders will today put the finishing touches to an ambitious project to cut unemployment by 1m in 2 years. They say the scheme could knock £5b off the £20b jobless bill. . . .

TUC leaders have costed the exercise at £4b in the first year and £9.8b in the second year. They anticipate criticism of the cost by saying that the project would have to be paid for by changing the balance of existing spending plans. This would be achieved by diverting resources from other sectors, including defence, by raising the taxes of high-income earners, and by increased government borrowing.

Confederation of British Industry

This is the employers' counterpart of the TUC and acts as industry's spokesman. You will note that in many of the press clippings the views of the CBI are mentioned.

Postscript

Female workers tend not to be unionised. Could that be the reason for
the figures shown in Table 1.1?

Table 1.1. Women's pay as %
of men's pay (Europe)

Country	%
Sweden	87.3
Denmark	85.5
Italy	81.5
Norway	79.8
France	75.7
Netherlands	75.0
Finland	74.3
West Germany	72.3
Belgium	71.0
Great Britain	70.0
Switzerland	66.1

Examination questions

1.

Trades Union Congress
|
Executive Committees
|
District Committees
|
Branches
|
Shop stewards
|
Members

(a) Briefly explain this simplified diagram of trade union organisation.
(b) Explain the essential differences between the following types of unions:
   (i) Craft union
  (ii) Industrial union
 (iii) White-collar unions
 (iv) General unions

(Q. 10 1977)

2. What are the main functions of shop stewards?

(Q. 3 1975)

3. A newspaper article commented that 'white-collar workers will exercise greater economic strength in the future'. Who are the white-collar workers?

   (Q. 1(c) 1974)

4. Give **two** examples of issues which might be the subject of 'collective bargaining'.

   (Q. 1(j) 1977)

5. What is the meaning of the terms:
   (*a*) conciliation
   (*b*) arbitration?

   (Q. 1(f) 1975)

6. Describe the main objectives of a trade union and explain which you would consider most important at the present time.

   (Q. g 1982)

7. Other than strikes, state two forms of disruptive action.

   (Q. 1(f) 1983)

8. A large engineering concern is forced to make part of its work-force redundant.
   (*a*) What is meant by redundancy?
   (*b*) Explain the ways in which a union might respond to this.
   (*c*) Where might the redundant staff retrain or learn new employment skills?

   (Q. 8 1983)

9. Describe two industrial disputes that have arisen whilst you have been on your course. Explain how the unions pursued their claims.

   (Q. 4 1984)

10. At Comlon International plc many of the office staff belong to a white-collar union. What advantages are there in belonging to a union and why has recruitment to white-collar unions increased?

    (Q. 6 1986)

Communications – methods
Chapter 2

Good communications are essential for the effective operation of any business.

A supermarket manager(ess) needs to let the staff know their lunchtime rotas; the business person will need to place orders and travellers abroad will need to obtain foreign currency. Unless they can effectively communicate their instructions to their subordinates, there will be problems. Communications do not just flow from management to staff, they need to flow the other way. How else can the managers find out what is happening? The supermarket manager(ess) needs to know which lines are selling before the store can be laid out; the office supervisor needs to know which staff are absent before work can be allocated. At the highest level, the board of directors need to know how the business is performing before they can make the correct policy decisions.

Communications is, however, not merely a matter of transmitting information. It is a process which, used properly, can help management to motivate the staff, but used wrongly it can result in strikes, sit-ins and other forms of industrial action. This aspect of communications is often overlooked but we will examine it in a later chapter.

We do not need equipment to communicate orally but it does help! How could you talk to your friends after college without the telephone? You are probably familiar with the 'common household telephone' (over 80 per cent of homes in the UK have one) but are you aware of the sophisticated telephone services available to the business user?

Telephone systems are built around switchboards. The traditional system, which you'll see in many of the old black and white movies (Private Branch Exchange – PBX), was controlled by a switchboard operator within the firm who often doubled as receptionist. This switchboard has been replaced in most large organisations by a Private Automatic Branch Exchange (PABX) which enables clients and customers to dial directly in and for external calls to be made without the services of an operator. It is cheaper, quicker and more like using the 'phone you have at home.

Advances in micro-electronic technology have, however, enabled further advances to be made. The most sophisticated switchboard currently available (the call-connect system) allows you to make telephone calls (of course!) but has numerous other facilities which, if used properly, mean greater efficiency and hence profitability for the business user. These facilities include the following.

Short code dialling

Long numbers dialled regularly can be replaced by a short code so that instead of having to dial 01033143303394 you can dial 616. This saves time, and time is money. Dialling time can also be saved if you use a 'callmaker'. This enables up to 400 pre-selected numbers to be automatically called without dialling and is useful when certain numbers are regularly called, especially if they involve long dialling codes. The 'callmaker' has an attachment which looks like a telephone pad where 400 addresses can be stored and pressing the button next to the address causes the appropriate number to be called.

Automatic call back

The ability to 'camp on' means you don't have to keep re-dialling engaged numbers; you can 'camp on' so that when the receiver is put down, the telephone will ring and connect you – another time saver!

Diversion service

Nothing is more frustrating for a caller than the unanswered or engaged telephone. This service can avoid that frustration; it puts callers in a better mood and makes it easier to deal with them. The service enables a business person to transfer all calls to another extension; the transfer can be immediate so that the 'phone never rings, after a 'phone has rung a set number of times or only if it is engaged. This facility is especially useful if you are interviewing and do not wish to be disturbed or are out at a meeting or lunch. It means the incoming caller can speak to someone. An alternative is to use an answering machine but many people find leaving messages on such machines difficult and unsatisfactory. However, such a system will still be necessary in the small business where there are no other extensions on to which the call can be transferred. The caller is greeted by a message (usually letting them know the other party is out) which invites them to leave their message.

Loudspeaker

Often several people will need to be involved in a decision and by incorporating a loudspeaker into the system they can all hear the information being provided by the caller. Even when there is only one party involved, the system has its advantages where you want to make notes. It is easier than trying to cradle the telephone on your shoulder! Your notes are likely to be fuller and more accurate and that makes later reference to them more satisfactory.

Three-party service

This enables a three-way conversation on the telephone. It saves time. Without it you need to relay the conversation to a third party and then refer back for comments. How much simpler for all three of you to be able to talk as you would if you were together in one office.

As a bonus this telephone system can be linked in with computer terminals and therefore used in the transmission of text and graphical data.

Of course, nowadays you do not have to have access to a traditional telephone to be able to use the telephone system. Some people, by the very nature of their jobs, cannot always be close to a telephone although they still need to be in contact with other people to work efficiently. Such individuals may carry a radio-pager; this is a light-weight receiver which will fit into a handbag or pocket. When the receiver bleeps, the carrier knows he/she must 'phone the office. If he/she has more than one office, the bleeper can have a different tone for each. Bleepers are often used within large organisations such as hospitals, hotels or airports where previously the paging system would have simply been a loudspeaker.

The pager still means that, once bleeped, you must find a non-vandalised telephone, which can result in delays. To avoid this and to be instantly available, executives might choose to have a radiophone installed in their cars. This enables them to call anyone on the 'phone in the UK (and several countries overseas) while on the move. A radiophone looks and operates like an ordinary telephone. This type of 'phone is not to be confused with the 'cordless' 'phone found in many domestic households as the latter can only be used up to 200 metres away from the office or home.

If you have staff such as sales representatives, who make numerous calls while out of the office, you can provide them with a credit card. This enables them to make calls from any telephone box in the UK or abroad without payment; the cost is charged to your (the firm's) account. This system eliminates the possibility of staff claiming for calls that have not been made and renders expense claims unnecessary thereby saving the time of both the representatives and the accounts office.

Telephones and telephone lines are no longer just used for communicating orally; they can be used to send written messages and, as we will see in chapter 6, are an essential ingredient of the electronic office. In addition, British Telecom provide 'services' specifically aimed at the business community. Recorded information on certain specified topics can be obtained by dialling the appropriate numbers. Traveline, for example, gives information on rail, road, air and sea services while *Financial Times* city line, which is updated seven times each day, provides details of the stock market and other items of business news.

Another service, frequently used by the business community, is 'freephone'. Freephone callers ask the operator to connect them to the freephone number they require and there is no charge to the caller as the freephone subscriber pays the bills. This service is frequently used by firms as part of their promotional activities (see Fig. 2.1).

The telephone provides an instantaneous method of communication but for legal, security and other reasons many communications need to be written. The ordinary post is adequate unless speed is important. An order may be vital: a bookseller may require textbooks before term starts. If they do not arrive on time, sales will be lost and the books will be left in stock. Profit is lost and money is unnecessarily tied up in stock. A spare part may be required for a machine otherwise production may be delayed and the orders lost to competitors. Many firms will not accept oral orders because they lack the authority of the written word and so you must find a method of instantaneous written communication. One such system is telex.

Fig. 2.1

Telex

A telex machine (teleprinter) can send written messages to any other telex subscriber anywhere in the world at any time of the night or day. Like most office machines, the teleprinter has benefited enormously from the development of the 'chip'. It now has a VDU on to which all the message can be typed (or into which a word processor can 'send' the message, hence eliminating the need to type it again), checked and, if necessary, stored. The machine can then be instructed to send the message at the appropriate time, and if the recipient's machine is engaged it will keep trying until it gets through.

Sending the message is easy. Just give the machine the recipient's number. The machine will then send the message, check that it has been received (using the 'answerback' system) and provide a copy for your file. It is even easier to receive a message. Just ensure your machine has enough stationery and leave it switched on. It will work throughout the night, weekend and holidays; when you return to work you will find a pile of messages or documents that have been sent to you.

Teleprinters cost money and may be too expensive for small businesses; an alternative cheaper method of transmitting a written message quickly is the telemessage. The caller gives her message (maximum 35 lines of text) to the operator and it is sent electronically to a Royal Mail sorting office near the destination. There it is printed out and delivered the next day. Providing it is sent before 10 p.m., next day delivery is guaranteed; no delivery and you get a refund. A business reply service is provided where a postage-paid window envelope can be included so that the recipient can reply. While telex is the most common form of electronic text transmission, there are a number of competing services.

Electronic mail systems, e.g. Teletex

Teletex (not to be confused with teletext which is the service allowing adapted television sets to receive pages of text via Ceefax or Oracle – see page 63) is part of the communications system of the future. While it provides a message transfer service like telex and unfortunately sounds similar, the two services have fundamental differences. Telex requires special equipment whereas you can use existing equipment from simple electronic typewriters with teletex adapters through word processors, to a range of business computers for teletex terminals. Teletex is 30 times quicker than telex; it takes approximately 10 seconds to transmit an A4 document. The hard copy produced by a telex terminal has limitations whereas teletex can produce upper- and lower-case letters and all the symbols on a typewriter keyboard.

A teletex terminal has, of course, all the features of a teleprinter; it can receive incoming messages or send prepared material without disturbing current message preparation; prepared messages can be stored and sent when appropriate; the terminal can automatically recall engaged numbers and each message is headed by a call identification line which includes the identification of both parties' teletex number, time and date of transmission.

When this system eventually becomes worldwide, a secretary will prepare a letter on a typewriter or word processor and, by pressing the right buttons, send it over the telecommunications link to the necessary addresses. No envelopes, no stamping, no posting, no delays! In a fully integrated electronic office, teletex will be linked in with Prestel and handle graphic transmission through facsimile copy thus allowing diagrams and technical drawings to be sent. There will be a system of electronic mail without using a postal service.

Facsimile

Sometimes the information which you have to transmit is visual, such as graphs and charts. You might be on a North Sea exploration oil rig and wish to send a graph to London to be evaluated in head office before you continue. As time is money, you will want London to see it as soon as possible. Flying it down can mean a delay of many hours, and it is possible to send it instantaneously by using an automatic telecopier. This system, known as FAX, enables replicas of documents to be sent any distance by utilising the speed of the telephone with the reproduction facility of the office copier. The FAX device is connected to a telephone; the original document is scanned and the information transmitted down the telephone lines. There is a machine at the other end which can 'read' the information and reproduce the original document in hard copy: it takes about a minute. However, the recipient must have equipment compatible with the sender.

The machines that transmit are automatic and can be programmed to transmit the information at any time. This is profitable for the business because it means information can be sent at cheap times such as evenings or weekends and, of course, the machine keeps a record of all transmissions. FAX is often regarded as a companion to the telex service but it possesses the advantage that it can transmit large quantities of information very quickly in their original form and, because the input material does not have to be prepared, it can save secretarial time (although modern teleprinters can be inputted directly from word processors).

Data transmission

This is the process of allowing computers in different places to 'talk' to each other. If you visit your local travel agent, you may see an example of data transmission in practice. There will be a VDU and computer in the travel agents which are linked to a central airline computer. By using the VDU, the travel agent can gain instant access to the airline computer to find out flight availability and, by making a booking on the VDU, this information can be immediately transferred to the airline computer so that the seat is booked and not offered to another client. You may see another example in your local supermarket. Many supermarket tills are now computerised and the bar codes on items can be automatically read; the data concerning the price and type of item can be transmitted to a central computer so that the day's sales, stock levels etc. are available to management at the end of each day. Having access to all the information means better decision-making and ultimately more profit. In the near future it will be possible for customers' bank accounts to be directly debited from checkouts in shops!

For computers to use existing telephone lines it is necessary for the equipment at both ends to have a modem attached. This converts computer language into a form that can travel down the telephone lines and then transfer it back into a form that the computer at the other end can understand. By enabling computers to communicate with each other, it enables staff, wherever they are located, to have access to the information on the central computer. Better-informed staff means more efficient staff and that means more profits.

In much of the above, we have talked about the role of electronic equipment and computers in communication, but a word of warning. We have been communicating for centuries without such sophisticated equipment and, indeed, one of the most efficient methods of communication is one of the oldest, speech. Communication simply means getting your information or message across and sophisticated equipment is only a tool to be used. Within an organisation it may be unnecessary (and therefore a waste of money) to use it. You may be able to put your message across in a simpler form, by speech, memorandum or in another form. Imagine that you need to present a list of figures to your colleagues at a meeting. You might find it easier to get your message across by using graphs, charts or diagrams. A list of figures can be transmitted electronically but just because the other party has the figures it does not mean they understand them.

The method chosen to represent information depends on the person or persons who are to receive it and the degree of accuracy required. If you wish to present precise information, you are more likely to provide the actual figures; but where it is enough to create an impression, a graph or chart is probably better. Statistical evidence is much more easily grasped if presented in this manner and, because the information is so clearly displayed and understood, it is more easily remembered.

If you wish to present information in a 'visual' form, you have a variety of choices.

Line graphs

These are especially useful in showing comparisons or trends. The graphs in Fig. 2.2 relate to change in the *Financial Times* share index, i.e. share prices and changes in the exchange rate between the pound and dollars, and are taken from a daily newspaper. You will notice that each graph is titled and each of the axes clearly labelled. The graphs shows quite clearly that share prices slumped in August but rose in September and that the £ has been rising and falling against the $.

Pie charts

This is a circle, representing the whole, divided into parts and is a

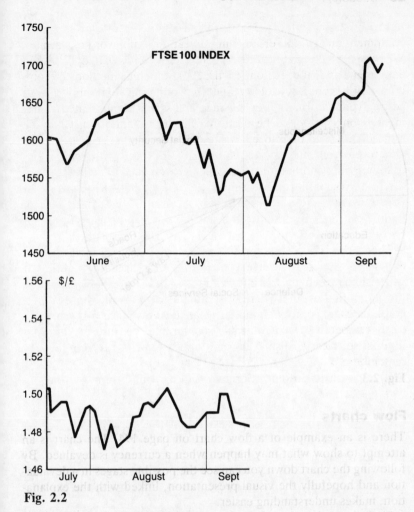

Fig. 2.2

useful way of presenting statistics which show how something is made up, for example expenditure of UK government. The pie chart in Fig. 2.3 presents the same information as on page 188. Which do you think is easier?

Bar charts

These have individual bars which represent figures and are useful for showing comparisons or trends where line graphs would be inappropriate (see Fig. 2.4).

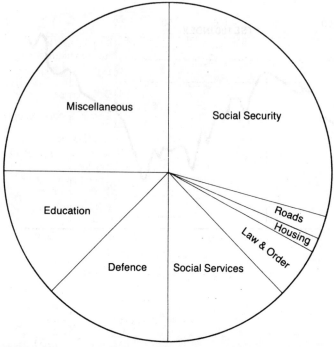

Fig. 2.3

Flow charts

There is an example of a flow chart on page 194. The chart is an attempt to show what may happen when a currency is devalued. By following the chart down you can see the possible stages in a devaluation and hopefully the visual presentation, linked with the explanation, makes understanding easier.

Flow charts therefore show the progress of an idea or a document. Organisation and methods may be investigating a firm's documentation to see whether it may be reduced. This involves tracing the passage of a document (plus copies) through the organisation; this passage can be easily shown by means of a flow chart.

Flow charts are also used by computer programmers when designing software.

Diagrams

These can present information ranging from the position of stands at an exhibition, wiring diagrams, to plans of a store layout (Fig. 2.5).

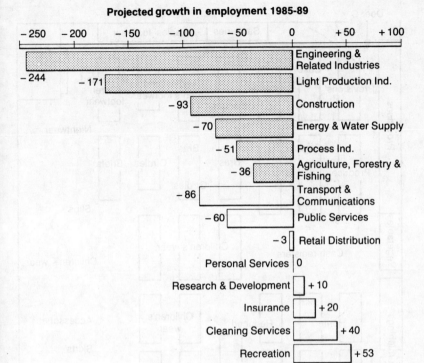

Projected growth in employment 1985-89

Fig. 2.4

Legend:
- Non Services
- Services

Selection of appropriate media

You should now be aware of the main methods by which you can communicate and the possible repercussions that the choice may have on the morale of staff. It is only by combining both areas of knowledge that you can select the appropriate media; sometimes the choice is easy but sometimes . . . some of the considerations are contained in the acronym UNDER, as follows.

Urgency

Is the communication required urgently?

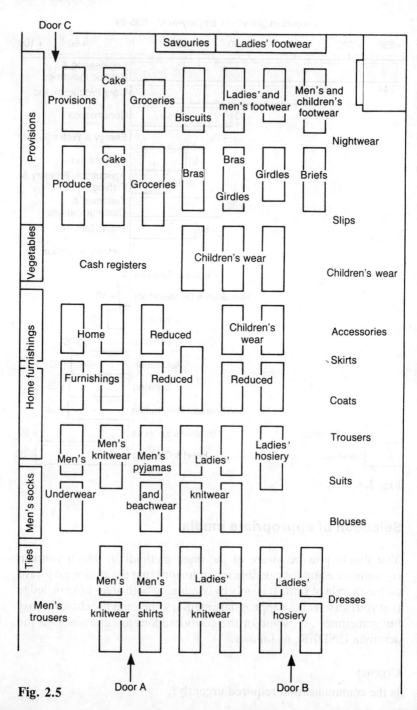

Fig. 2.5

Nature

If the document to be transmitted is a photograph, this will limit your choice, as will a document's complexity. Some documents, especially of a legal nature, also have to be in writing and sometimes there is the aspect of confidentiality to consider.

Distance

Is the communication going to the secretary in the next office or to an executive in another country?

Emotional

Remember the impact the news may have on the other party (loss of a job perhaps) or how its presentation may affect the morale of the individual or individuals receiving it.

Record

Do you require a record? If you are given an oral instruction, at a later date it can be difficult to prove such an instruction was given!

Of course, it is no good choosing to send a telex if you don't have a teleprinter or someone who can use it; and remember, whatever method you choose, your boss will have to pay the cost!

Examination questions

1. How is the 'Freephone' system operated?

(4 marks)

2. What is FAX?

(4 marks)

3. Outline two British Telecom services aimed at the business community.

(4 marks)

4. Distinguish between pie charts and bar charts.

(4 marks)

5. What is the main difference between a radiophone and a cordless telephone.

(4 marks)

6. What is a modem used for?

(4 marks)

32 Section A

7. Dialling long telephone numbers can be time-consuming. What time-saving facilities exist?
   Describe these fully.

   (20 marks)

8. In what ways do Telex and Teletext differ?

   (20 marks)

9. Show the following information by means of a chart or graph:

   SALES – JAN to APRIL

   Jan – 502
   Feb – 608
   Mch – 415
   Apl – 500

Using a different method, show the following information:

Jan:	Overseas sales	–	EEC	300
	Overseas sales	–	other	102
	Home sales	–		100
Feb:	Overseas sales	–	EEC	300
	Overseas sales	–	other	150
	Home sales	–		158
March:	Overseas sales	–	EEC	200
	Overseas sales	–	other	110
	Home sales	–		105
April:	Overseas sales	–	EEC	300
	Overseas sales	–	other	75
	Home sales	–		125

(20 marks)

Communications – motivation

Chapter 3

If my secretary produces a letter from the shorthand notes which I have dictated, this could be quoted as an example of effective communications. That is: I have communicated the content of the letter to my secretary who responded by producing a mailable letter. If this were all that 'communications' involved, the subject would hardly merit the attention it receives on management training courses. Being an effective communicator, however, involves more than the mere ability to transmit information to another party.

In training somebody to be an efficient communicator (i.e. able to transmit information) the tutor's first task is to persuade the student to answer the question, 'what does the other party (e.g. staff) need to know?' This will enable them to determine the content of the communication. The first essential in communicating is therefore to decide on the information you need to give the other party.

- If you are seeking a quotation for the installation of computers in your office, then you must tell the supplier the number of terminals you require, the memory capability, the job they must perform, etc. A letter simply asking for a quote for a computer system would be meaningless.
- If I want my secretary to type a letter with two copies, then I must say so.
- If I want a report typed in double spacing so as to allow correction, then I must inform the typist, otherwise it will be typed with normal spacing.
- If I give the operator a document for the word processor, he/she will need to be told about the number of copies I want and whether I require the document to be stored on a 'floppy disk'.
- If a new piece of equipment arrives, then before I ask staff to use it, they must receive clear instructions on how to operate it.

A lecturer must decide what information he/she is going to give the students during the lesson, and has to answer the question, 'What do the students need to know to pass their examinations?' At some time during your schooling you will probably have left a class having failed to understand the lesson. There has been a failure in communication. It may have occurred because your teacher tried to tell you too much. In business it is equally important not to 'overload' the staff with information, as the sheer volume of it may only serve to confuse them. The more you tell someone the more they are likely to forget something. For this reason when communicating try to be precise and to the point (without being so brief you don't make sense). You must therefore be careful not to give information which is irrelevant. If a new computer arrives in the office, then a brief description of its functions will probably suffice. No purpose is served in explaining how the computer operates with detailed descriptions of its circuitry.

Having given the information, you must check that the recipient has understood it. The college lecturer will check that the students have understood the lesson by asking them questions or perhaps getting them to write an essay. In business you cannot ask the staff to write an essay but you can ask them to repeat the instructions or, if you have instructed them how to operate a new piece of equipment, you can watch them use it the first time.

The above deals with the 'mechanical' side of communications but an effective communicator can use skills to **'motivate'** the staff. The communications process can be used to make staff feel part of the organisation; they will respond by working harder. What is communicated and **how** it is communicated can be important in motivating staff. My secretary will type a letter whether I say 'type that letter' or 'please type that letter'. The choice of instruction will, however, affect the secretary's attitude and commitment to the business.

The key to motivating staff is to remember that they are human. They have feelings and provided you respect these you will gain their respect. Therefore:

1. Explain to your staff why
It is part of human nature to want to know why things happen or why an instruction has been given. Suppose the letter dictated, which was mentioned in the earlier example, said:

Dear Mr Johnson,
Thank you for your application for the recently advertised post. I regret to inform you that on this occasion you have not been successful.
Yours faithfully

Successfully dictating the letter means successful communication, but it is hardly going to motivate the secretary. A good employer may therefore discuss the reason for the decision with the secretary after dictating the letter, and may explain that the person was too old or perhaps insufficiently qualified. The secretary now knows the reason for the decision and this will help broaden his/her experience.

I may want the caretaker to move two additional typing desks into a classroom. If, after the request, I say '**because** our classes are 22 instead of the 20 we planned', the caretaker knows the reason for the request. If when you give an order (or preferably make a request – 'please would you . . .') you always say **because**, you will satisfy the other person's desire to know why.

2. When communicating use the most appropriate method or medium
When the communicator concerned with motivation decides on the method of communicating he/she must appreciate:

(a) *The difference between one-way and two-way communications.* The latter allows a response from the employee whereas the former does not. **One-way** communication such as a notice board or a firm's weekly bulletin is therefore useful for giving out information such as the time of a meeting, a staff dance, winner of a competition or the basic facts on a new product. Where, however, the staff are likely to want to ask questions, it is better to use **two-way** communications such as an interview or a meeting. If an employer wants to ask his office staff to work late for a week to produce the accounts, then the request is much better done at a meeting where the staff can ask questions. If the request is simply put on a notice board, then such questions cannot be answered and this leads to speculation and the development of a 'grapevine'.

(b) *The formal channels of communication.* Most organisations possess a formal channel of communications. Thus if I want a junior member of my office staff to perform a task I would be expected to go through the office manager and not go directly to the person concerned. People tend to get upset if they are bypassed; it can suggest a lack of confidence in them, and this affects their morale.

In many organisations the formal channels of communication can be found by examining the **organisation chart.**

Communication within a typical College of Further Education could be along the lines shown in Fig. 3.1.

The figure shows that it is the Head of Department who is responsible for passing information from the Principal to the staff, but would, however, be expected in most cases to do this via the Section Leaders.

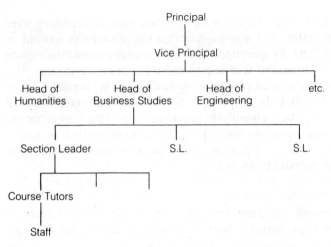

Fig. 3.1

It is they who are the link between the Head and the staff. In theory, a link therefore exists between the Principal and the staff.

If a Section Leader in Humanities wanted to discuss a problem with a counterpart in Business Studies (perhaps over the teaching of communications) then, using the channels in the chart, it would be mentioned to the Head who would talk to the Head of Business Studies. This process would be cumbersome. In the organisation there will therefore be a formal system of **lateral (sideways)** communication so that Section Leaders can communicate directly with each other.

We have seen that a one-way communication, such as a noticeboard, will be inappropriate when the staff may have questions. In deciding the method of communication we were considering the **'needs'** of the staff. The **'feelings'** of a member of staff may also be relevant in determining the way we communicate.

Some information of a private or confidential nature is best dealt with on a one-to-one basis.

My secretary might arrive ten minutes late for work on several occasions. I may feel the need to talk to her. Our interview is best conducted in private. An interview will be chosen because the secretary may wish to say something and it will be held in private because criticism in front of colleagues is likely to lead to resentment and a lowering of morale. This could ultimately lead to a less effective secretary.

3. Think how your staff will react
Important letters should not be dictated immediately after the Christmas office party! Your secretary's shorthand may be rather

shaky. Seriously, the timing is important because it can affect the staff response. Returning to an earlier example, I want my office staff to put in some overtime. I decide quite correctly that the request should be made at a meeting and choose Friday at 4.15 p.m., fifteen minutes before they go home. The previous week has been difficult, because of pressure of work, and by 4.15 p.m. on Friday staff are anxious to go home. It would therefore not be surprising if my request for overtime received an unfavourable reply.

My secretary may have improved considerably since the interview we had regarding poor time-keeping, and being a good employer I may wish to congratulate him/her. I inform the secretary on Friday at 4.30 p.m. just as he/she is about to leave that I wish to see him/her in my office on Monday at 9.00 a.m. What is the effect of this piece of information? My secretary is likely to spend the weekend worrying about the reason and may feel that there is going to be another critical interview. By choosing an inappropriate time to notify him/her of the interview, I have created tension for him/her over the weekend and illustrated a lack of awareness of staff feelings. If you wish to see a member of staff, it is much better to make an appointment for the same day.

It was mentioned earlier that you must check that your communication has been understood, perhaps by asking questions. This involves you **listening** to the reply. The ability to listen is also vital in motivating staff. If staff come to you with their problems they want to feel you are listening to them. The manager who is too busy or appears to be thinking of other more important matters while staff are talking is likely to give them the impression that they are unimportant. This will hardly improve their performance in the office. What this means is that if you are genuinely interested in your staff they are more likely to respond by working harder. If your secretary asks for time off to take his/her daughter to the dentist an enquiry the next day as to how the visit went may result in a better relationship with your secretary.

You should also be prepared to listen when staff have ideas about improving the business. If you apparently ignore them they will feel you consider their views unimportant.

As a good communicator you will realise how important your staff are and go out of your way to reassure them of their importance. You will say 'thank you' when they do something well and be lavish in your praise. Individuals love to be praised and it generally produces a good reaction from them. You should be slow to criticise but quick to praise, and if possible call them by their name. (If you have any doubts on the wisdom of this just think how you feel when your lecturer praises you!)

The above may seem simple but in reality poor communications exist throughout large parts of British industry. Just read the following article.

British Leyland Cars last night claimed that 3,000 men who voted for a strike which stopped all production, including the Maestro, at Cowley had been misled by union officials.

The men walked out after being told at a mass meeting that management was adamant that "washing up periods" had to be swallowed by the working day to allow production lines to be kept running to the end of each shift. This would add another 66 minutes or 100 cars to the working week.

BL claimed that the men had been misled because the three minutes, twice a day in the morning and the evening, and a total of nine minutes a day on the night shift, customarily taken off so that workers could wash themselves, had no official basis.

The workers see the move as another change in working practices, of which they claim they have had to endure many during the past two years. Mr. Bobby Fryer, a senior shop steward of the Transport and General Workers'

Union said: "The decision shows just how Cowley workers are fed up with the way they have been treated."

Management said yesterday that Cowley, which produces 4,000 cars a week, including models such as the Maestro, the Acclaim and the Ambassador, was merely being brought into line with other BL car plants in the UK.

In its statement the company said: "There is no need or justification for employees of the Cowley assembly plant to be on strike. Indeed, it is very doubtful that such a decision would have been taken if they had not been advised wrongly at the mass meeting that the issue was some sort of attack on basic trade union rights. The facts are that the workers are paid to work right up to the proper finishing time. Early finishing is entirely an unofficial practice."

BL last night urged shop stewards to call another mass meeting for today saying that a proper return to work was vital to secure Cowley's future.

Two reasons why communication can be poor are given next.

1. Size of the organisation

As organisations grow in size so the number of layers of management between the top management and the staff at the bottom grows. If a college gets very large there may be Faculty Heads between the Vice Principal and the Heads of Department; there may be Course Leaders. Each layer of management means one more level through which a communication must pass. This increases the chance of distortion and the possibility that the communication will not get passed on. If a student's parent telephones the Principal with a message it is most unlikely the student will receive it, given the number of people it must pass through! This is probably one of the reasons for the communication problem at British Leyland. One remedy for this is to create committees on which individuals from each of the layers of management sit. Another possibility is to divide an organisation into autonomous (separate) parts, each being of a more manageable size.

This may be preferable to the 'committee' solution because smaller units make motivation easier. In larger organisations employees can become isolated from management and this makes motivation more difficult. Communications tend to be through memos, noticeboards and magazines which, apart from being one-way communications, are impersonal. Verbal communications tend to be 'friendlier' than cold bits of paper.

2. Attitudes

To be a good motivator you must care about your staff (or persuade them that you do). Where staff have the wrong attitude the motivator's communications are more likely to create resentment than motivate. I can recall one manager who said 'Good morning' in such a way that it sounded like a question or a challenge! We have already seen how a request is far more effective than an order.

A superior who is incapable of assessing staff reaction is likely to use words his or her staff do not understand and will not appreciate how the staff will react to the message. Realising that staff prejudices and assumptions affect how they receive the message is one factor which determines how you put your message across. For instance, you might tell one manager that an order has been cancelled and his/her reaction will be to look for replacement orders. If the same information is given to another manager, who is less confident, he/she may interpret this as a hint that he/she is about to be made redundant.

Informal communication

Where problems exist within the formal structure because of the organisation's size or the attitude of the communicators, then there is likely to be a growth in informal channels. The most significant and perhaps the most distrusted of these is the **'grapevine'** which consists of part rumour, part gossip and occasionally part truth. Management dislike the grapevine because they cannot control it and information can become distorted. Where staff are kept fully informed there is no need for a grapevine, but where management are reluctant to tell their staff what is happening, then it is inevitable that they will speculate. If a word processor is being introduced into an office it is inevitable that staff will be concerned about possible redundancies. Managers who are aware of the problem will have a meeting with the staff to explain the impact of the word processor and reassure them. If, however, they do not bother to communicate this information with them, then the grapevine will turn the introduction of the word processor into a number of redundancies. The managers then have a problem which has arisen simply because of their failure to be aware of the importance of communication.

Examination questions

1. The larger the organisation the more difficult effective communications become. Why should this be so? What steps might be taken to minimise the risk of ineffective communications in the large organisation?

   (*Q. 9 1977*)

2. We often read in newspapers about 'breakdown of communications between management and workers'. What methods might be employed to improve such communications?

   (*Q. 9 1976*)

3. In communications what do you understand by the 'grapevine'.

   (*Q. 1(f) 1983*)

4. Your Personnel Department has been asked by the Board of Management to run courses for supervisors on 'effective communication'.
   (*a*) What might be included in the course?
   (*b*) Apart from training, list the other functions of a Personnel Department.

   (*Q. 3 1983*)

5. Give an example of one-way communication and explain when it could be used.

   (*Q. 1(a) 1982*)

6. The following are examples of poor communication. A manager:
   (a) criticising someone in front of colleagues;

(b) informing staff about redundancies through a notice on the noticeboard;

(c) discussing any changes with staff without informing their supervisor;

(d) telling staff what to do without explaining why.

Using two of the above, explain why they are examples of poor communication and describe the possible reaction of the staff involved.

(Q. 6 1984)

7. Describe a correct and an incorrect method of communicating the following information to staff, indicating the possible effect each choice might have on the motivation of staff:

(a) Personal criticism of a member of staff

(b) A request to work late

(c) The loss of a major export order

(d) The date of a staff dance.

(Q. 8 1985)

Training
Chapter 4

Almost everyone in employment has undergone some form of training. This ranges from several years for a solicitor or accountant to a few days or even hours for Saturday staff in a large store. The amount of training you require to obtain the necessary skills, and the way in which you acquire these skills depends on the nature of your job and the type of organisation you work for.

This is illustrated if we examine the training requirements of the members of an imaginary family. Apart from the parents, Ken and Marie, there are four children, all of whom are about to leave full-time education. The eldest, Andrea, has just graduated from university with a degree in Business Studies. The other three are triplets, Derek has obtained four good GCSE grades. Evelyn achieved three GCSE grade C's while Justine jailed to pass any examinations, being more preoccupied with members of the opposite sex in her last year at school. Let us now consider each of these.

Andrea

Having obtained her degree she has decided to qualify as a Chartered Accountant. This involves further examinations (although her degree exempts her from some of the examinations). How can she obtain the tuition she needs to pass these?

Many professions (and skilled trades) insist that new entrants possess both theoretical and practical knowledge. The former can be tested through examinations but practical knowledge comes only through experience. The Institute of Chartered Accountants will therefore insist that Andrea works for a member firm (to obtain the practical knowledge) while she prepared herself for the final examinations. She will work under the close supervision of a qualified accountant who will be able to relate her theoretical knowledge to practical problems. As she will be working full-time tuition for a prospective Chartered Accountant is only available in two forms:

(a) Day release

Some organisations are prepared to release their employees for one day a week to attend a relevant course (often at a local college). This is common with professions such as bankers. This method is expensive to employers as they are losing their employees for one day per week while still paying their wages.

(b) Correspondence course

This avoids the above problem as the staff do not require time off to follow a correspondence course. Andrea can enrol with one of the many 'correspondence colleges' who will send her books and notes with a schedule of work. She will complete her assignments and return them to the 'college'. Their staff will mark them and return them to Andrea. This method is popular with employers but less popular with employees because it involves giving up their own time in the evenings. To 'share the burden' of tuition some employees allow staff an afternoon off to attend college provided the staff attend on an evening in their own time.

Derek

He has applied for, and been successful in obtaining, an 'electronics apprenticeship' with a local firm. Like Andrea he needs to obtain both practical and theoretical knowledge but he is fortunate in that apprenticeships traditionally incorporate **off-the-job training,** usually day release at the local college. When we use the term 'off-the-job' training this indicates that training occurs away from the normal working environment. This could be at the local college or in the firm's own training establishment which could be just one room set aside for training within the factory (shop or office).

Being trained away from the work-place means he can learn in a more relaxed environment without the noise and bustle which occurs there. It is also easier for his tutor who is free to concentrate on teaching; where training is given in the work-place the employee responsible for passing on the skills has his/her own job to perform and may resent the time needed to help the trainee. The employee may also be a poor teacher, perhaps lacking the communications skills. Lecturers are chosen for their skills and so should be more effective!

As far as Derek is concerned, he will attend a college for one day a week to learn his theory and will spend the other four days at work gaining practical knowledge.

At the end of his apprenticeship he acquires 'craft' status; he is now a tradesman (he can become a 'full' member of the appropriate craft union).

Evelyn

She intends to become a secretary and her parents have considered both a full-time college course and a job as an office junior/receptionist.

Some skills can be taught **on-the-job;** this means an employee learns to do her job during the ordinary working day. On-the-job training would be suitable for a receptionist who was being taught to use the firm's switchboard (provided, of course, it was fairly simple and she had correct telephone techniques). Suppose you gain employment as a receptionist at your local radio station. Experience on their switchboard would be necessary. Your training on the first day would consist of three parts:

(a) You would watch the existing receptionist operate the switchboard who would explain its operation to you.
(b) You would then use the switchboard under the supervision of the receptionist.
(c) Having successfully operated the switchboard under supervision, you would be left to use it on your own.

This area is suitable for on-the-job training because the new employee needs to learn on the firm's equipment and it would be costly to duplicate this facility in a training room.

Some skills cannot be learnt on the job. Consider typing. Can you imagine learning to type while watching a secretary? How could you work (i.e. type) and learn to type at the same time? If this sounds impossible, imagine learning shorthand in anything other than a class-room environment. Evelyn's parents have decided that shorthand is still essential if their daughter is to obtain a worthwhile job with good promotion prospects and so they opt for a college course. This is full-time and has been designed following consultation with many of the local employers. This should ensure that students are, at the end of the course, employable. For this reason it includes both word- and infor-mation-processing. There is no cost to Evelyn's parents as education is provided by the Local Education Authority (which is primarily financed through rates paid on property and from government grants). It is unlikely that Evelyn will receive a grant to attend college (unlike

Andrea who automatically received a grant at University) unless there is financial hardship within the family as might occur if her parents were unemployed, or it was a 'single-parent' family.

Evelyn could opt for a full-time course at a private college. This exists, unlike local authority colleges, to make a profit and she will therefore have to pay fees. In the UK private colleges can be found in areas other than secretarial; they exist in accountancy, data processing and teaching English to overseas students.

Justine

She has realised her mistake in choosing boys rather than books and is keen to make amends. She also applied to the local college but because of her poor school record she has been rejected. Employers have also turned down her job applications for the same reason. She is one of the unemployed.

All the political parties agree that some educational and training provision should be available to those who fail to obtain employment or a place in full-time education. In 1982 the government therefore set up a **Youth Training Scheme** (YTS). This lasts for two years and those entering it receive a training allowance; this is more than they would receive if they were on unemployment benefit but is below current wage levels. During the period of training the 'trainees' are 'employed' by a firm (the 'sponsors') and released for a period of approximately sixty-five days 'off-the-job' training. In some areas firms are using the YTS scheme to replace their first-year apprenticeship (because the government pays the cost of training and the trainees' 'wages'). At the end of the two years' training the trainees may be taken on by the firm but in most cases they will leave and, unless they can find a full-time job, join the number of unemployed.

Justine has obtained a position with her local council. During her off-the-job training she is being taught to type, and receives a very basic grounding in computers, communications and numeracy. This is being done by the council in their own training suite although it could use the facilities provided by the local college of further education private colleges in the area or open distance learning (see page 81).

Marie

Now the children have left home their mother has decided to return to work, but having last worked 23 years ago (before she had Andrea) she requires retraining. She cannot use the local college because, being over 19, she would have to pay tuition fees and it is unlikely she would receive a grant to cover these and her living expenses.

This is a typical problem for 'mature' people wishing to retrain either because they have not worked for a long time or because they wish to acquire new skills to improve their promotion prospects. Mature students often have financial commitments and cannot afford to leave jobs to gain new skills. To overcome these problems the government has become involved in retraining. In some areas the retraining is carried out in government skill-centres where the trainee attends for a short concentrated course. Like Justine they receive a weekly wage; it is, however, higher than Justine's allowance and reflects the maturity of their entrants. Some retraining is carried out in Skill Centres under the **Job Training Scheme**, especially in the 'service area'. These include clerical and commercial courses and hotel and catering. In all government retraining there are no fees to trainees.

Marie has been selected for a clerk-typing course at the local college on which she will learn typing and word processing.

Ken

He is now 47 and has been working for the same firm since he was 16 when he joined their apprenticeship scheme. Although his apprenticeship was completed when he was 21 this was not the end of his training. Being a keen and enthusiastic worker he has been promoted, eventually becoming a supervisor.

At this point in his career he discovered that his initial training was insufficient. The skills he learnt as an apprentice were inadequate for a supervisor; he now needed to learn management skills. In many large firms such training would be carried out within the organisation by the training department (usually part of the personnel function) but a small firm may decide to give the employee time off to attend a college or polytechnic. Alternatively, Ken may be forced to attend evening classes.

Retraining

The need for retraining so as to acquire new skills is growing because of the development of modern technology (in Ken's case, because of modern management techniques). In the office the typist needs to learn about electronic typewriters and word processors – the accountant and solicitor need to familiarise themselves with computers.

Computer breakthrough

Down on the South Coast a firm of solicitors has set up a link with a computer 4,000 miles away in Dayton, Ohio, giving it access to a huge electronic "library".

Lexis, the legal information service, has 40bn words in its data bank. A further 3m are added each week with reports on criminal tax and industrial law in Britain, the US and France.

It is controlled from Dayton by Mead Data's central mighty computer and in Britain by the law publisher, Butterworth.

Lexis claims to be the world's biggest full-text data retrieval service. "It gives the solicitors far wider access to information at great speed."

The Lexis users in Britain are connected to Dayton via a telephone line. So far, about 5,000 of Britain's 40,000 lawyers use the service. Bosworth is a bit cagey about giving the exact number of law firms on Lexis (he is wary about rivals like Eurolex), but does admit that all the top 12 City firms, all government department and 50 of the 55 law schools are linked up.

Computerised financial services with information on share prices, currencies and commodities, are growing fast, with firms like Extel, Datastream and Reuters making the running. Twenty years ago only 40% of Reuters' revenue came from financial services. Now it is 90%, a shift which has revived Reuters' fortunes. Last year it made £36m profit on £179m turnover against 1979's £3m profit on turnover of £76m.

The breakthrough for Reuters came in 1973 with its Monitor service. There are now about 50 separate Monitor services, and 13,000 subscribers using 34,000 terminals in 78 countries.

Reuters' next step is into information processing. Later this year it starts its Data Network, which will offer subscribers a package of sophisticated information to help them deal in the complex world currency markets.

These new skills should be incorporated into training courses for entrants to the professions, while more 'mature' members will need to update theirs.

All the facilities outlined above (colleges, within the firm, etc.) are available for training but the firm selling electronic office equipment will often provide a period of free training for the purchaser's staff. This has the advantage of familiarising the employee with the actual equipment being used.

A company runs courses to update staff on new developments and also to improve efficiency within specified area. In the former category come courses to help staff cope with the changes brought about by Health and Safety regulations or the advent of a new system of sick pay. Improved efficiency would stem from courses in safety (to reduce accidents) or sessions in a supermarket to reduce shoplifting and pilfering; courses in this area can cover a variety of topics as indicated in the following article:

BR turns on the charm

CHARM schools for railwaymen, to encourage diplomacy and good manners in dealing with customers, are being run in Scotland and some parts of England to boost the image of rail travel in the face of severe competition from buses and the airlines.

By the end of the year, 6,000 rail staff who are regularly in contact with the public will have taken a one-day course in Edinburgh or Glasgow which encourages them to seek out customers with problems rather than waiting to be approached. A similar scheme is being tried out in other regions, and the results are being monitored.

The system has already led to a distinct drop in the level of complaints from customers and a measurable increase in passengers in Scotland, although the full effects are not expected to become apparent for some time.

Induction courses

One training course which is common to any job is the **induction course.** This occurs, or should occur, when anybody joins a new organisation whether it be a business or a college. Although it is a form of training it is perhaps more important as a process of welcoming newcomers and making them familiar with their new employer and their new job. As an employee is paid from the first day it is in the firm's interest to get the employee working efficiently as soon as possible. Induction tries to do this, and a guide to systematic induction is set out in Fig. 4.1.

An induction course has three main features.

Inductor to initial when covered
Trainee to initial – instructions received.

Introduction to Co-ops
Structure of P.S.D. Co-op
Departmental structure

Society regulations
Conditions of employment
Wages
Health & Safety
Security
Legal requirements
Hygiene – Personal/General
Tour of building

Typing letters
Typing reports
Typing statements
Stencil making & duplication
The filing system
Using the photocopier
Using the word processor

Fig. 4.1. Sample induction course

1. The *personal* part of the programme

This introduces the new employee to colleagues and place of work and deals with company policy. In a college this would involve meeting your new lecturers and being shown around the college. You would see the classrooms, the toilets, the canteen and the library. If there is a students' union you may have a talk from one of the committee. You will be told about college policy on lateness, sickness, fire drills, etc., and finally you will probably be told that if you have any problems at college you should see your course tutor.

In a company the pattern is similar although a different union will be involved and the course tutor is replaced by the personnel department. In addition to company policy on sickness and fire drills the new employee will be informed about holiday entitlement, pension schemes, contracts of employment and payment schemes (i.e. methods of calculating pay). Payment systems vary according to the job, and are illustrated by the examples given below.

Andrea

Once she qualifies as an accountant Andrea is likely to be paid a **fixed wage** (salary) regardless of the number of hours she works. It is unlikely that she will be paid overtime. Her wage will be periodically reviewed and as she becomes more experienced it will probably increase. This system is common in the professions and senior management.

Derek

There are various payment systems for manual and blue-collar (skilled) employees. He is paid for **attendance;** this means the union has agreed with the management a basic working week of perhaps 35 hours. A basic hourly rate is agreed (say £5) and each employee receives £175 per week (i.e. 35×£5). Any hours worked in excess of 35 hours are called overtime and these hours are paid for separately, usually at above the basic rate (e.g. £7 per hour). The hours worked and the basic hourly rate are the subject of annual negotiations with the union.

Evelyn

At the end of her course she obtains employment in a bank. She will be paid on an **incremental system.** This means her wage is fixed but each year it automatically rises by one increment until she reaches the top of her scale.

Her starting point on the scale and the scale (A or B) will depend on her age and qualifications but if she remains with the bank long enough she will be paid £5,600 if she is on scale A. She may of course be promoted in which case she would move across on to a higher scale (i.e. B). The scales will be re-adjusted annually because of inflation.

Scale A (£)		Scale B (£)
	10	6,400
	9	6,200
	8	6,000
	7	5,800
10 5,600	6	5,600
9 5,400	5	5,400
8 5,200	4	5,200
7 5,000	3	5,000
6 4,800	2	4,800
5 4,600	1	4,600
4 4,400		
3 4,200		
2 4,000		
1 3,800		
0 3,600		

Justine

Although she has finished the YTS course she has been unable to obtain employment in an office and has started work on the production line in a local factory. She is paid by **piece-work.** This means she is paid a fixed amount for each item produced; the more she makes the more she is paid.

Ken

Now he is a supervisor he receives a salary (fixed wage) but he also receives a commission (**payment by results**) which is based on the number of orders his section obtains and processes. The payment-by-results method is commonly used for salesmen and is based on the orders they obtain.

To supplement wages many firms offer 'perks'. These will also be explained to staff. They range from free social club, subsidised canteen through to the company car and expense account.

2. The *company*

To motivate staff you will recall that you should make them feel part of the company. You can start this process on their first day by telling them about the company. This involves its history, its products and perhaps the future. In many organisations new office staff are given a tour around the factory to give them an insight into the company (Wedgwood office staff are sent to Stoke), although this may not occur until they have been with the firm for a certain time.

3. The job

This involves telling new employees what is expected of them at work. It may include demonstrations on new machinery and instructions on how the firm wants its letters typed.

Examination questions

1. Many organisations give employees induction training. What do you consider to be the main aspects that should be covered in an induction programme?

(*Q. 12 1977*)

2. Explain with an example the difference between 'on-the-job training' and 'off-the-job training'.

(*Q. 1(k) 1975*)

3. Explain with examples:
   (*a*) Those aspects of the job of a secretary which can be learned on a college-based course.
   AND
   (*b*) Those which can only be learned from experience at the work place.

(*Q. 4 1980*)

4. A Training Officer is anxious to give his new office staff time off each week to attend a local college. The Managing Director says they can learn to do the job and use the equipment under supervision of experienced staff. What points might the Training Officer use to persuade the directors to accept off-the-job training?

(*Q. 6 1982*)

5. (a) Ken works in the Accounts Department at Comlon International plc and wants to acquire further qualifications. He is told he may be sponsored for study by means of a correspondence course or attendance at a day-release course. Explain each of these to him. Give examples.
   (b) What things are suitable for learning *effectively* 'on-the-job'? Explain your choice.

(*Q. 4 1985*)

6. Give examples of staff who would be paid:
   (i) piece rates
   (ii) a commission
   (iii) on the incremental scale

(*Q. 11 1985*)

7. In wage payment systems what is meant by an increment?

(*Q. 1(d) 1985*)

8. The workforce employed by the installation division are paid piece-rates and it is believed this is leading to poor work. Why might this be so?

(*Q. 1(c) 1986*)

The office
Chapter 5

We have already seen in chapters 2 and 3 that good communications are vital if a business wishes to succeed and one of the essential services of an office is to ensure the smooth flow of communications, both inside and outside the business. A primary function is therefore to handle and process all forms of communication. Just as a manufacturing business is only successful if it provides the right goods at the right time and at the right price, so a successful office must ensure that the right information is available at the right time and at the right price (more about the cost of 'the office' later).

Subsidiary to its main purpose, the office is also responsible for ensuring the company's legal and financial obligations are met; it protects the company from breaking the law. Protection also extends to effecting insurance and designing systems and procedures for safeguarding the company's assets.

In a traditional office, these activities usually result in mountains of paperwork. Correspondence, from both inside and outside the organisation, need distributing to the relevant individuals who will then take the necessary actions. This invariably results in more paperwork; letters are typed, documents photocopied, reports prepared and then sent to someone else. The preparation of all this requires numerous office staff ranging from clerks and secretaries to telex operators; it uses equipment; it takes up office space; the storage of all this paper requires filing cabinets taking up yet more space. All this space has to be rented, rates have to be paid, the area needs heating and lighting and staff cost money (and good staff cost even more money!) and so the service provided by the office can be expensive and, given the volume of paper, at times slow and inefficient. Documents can be misfiled; one person's filing system can be another's nightmare. Staff need time to process, circulate or retrieve information and sometimes the time is just not available. Sometimes the delays are not the responsibility of the office; letters get lost or delayed in the post. Whatever the cause of the delay, it creates frustration and results in a less efficient system.

The above problems, coupled with the realisation that information is vital for success, has led to the introduction of 'electronic office equipment'. In recent years technology has moved so fast that the traditional office with its filing systems, memoranda and letters may soon be a relic of the past. In the 'paper' office there will be staff records held in the personnel office. These will include the personal details of staff, their salaries, absences and holiday entitlements. Just imagine the work in updating the files when someone gets married or everybody is awarded a 4 per cent cost of living increase. If all the staff records are on a computer, then all the updating can be done at a computer terminal and one single instruction can result in everybody's records being amended to show the 4 per cent increase.

We now have the necessary technology and more staff with the backgrounds to fully utilise it (hence your study of word and information processing). Just as word processors have replaced manual typewriters, so the electronic office will replace the paper one, but just as with word processors, the pace of change will vary from organisation to organisation. There are still some offices with manual typewriters!

The new electronic office will enable information to be processed more rapidly, and because of the ability of the equipment to perform numerous tasks fewer staff will be required. They will be employed more efficiently. They will not need to walk to and from sets of files; the information can be called to their terminal. Large areas of office space can be released for other use. Costs will fall in the long term but there will need to be considerable staff training as some jobs will disappear and functions previously regarded as separate will merge. Word processing, report writing, data processing will all be carried out from the same terminal; if these become common within a firm anybody will be able to retrieve information at the press of a key.

Instead of providing a seemingly unrelated list of electronic equipment, we will examine the two key functions in the office to see how they are performed in a traditional and in an integrated electronic office of the near future. With the pace of technological change it is possible you will start work in the 'office of the future'.

The two main office functions are information storage, retrieval and updating, and communicating.

1. Information storage, retrieval and updating

In the paper office, information is generally input using either keyboards or reprographic equipment. Even in the traditional office you will find electronic equipment but its role is very different from similar equipment in a fully integrated electronic office.

The electronic typewriter has now generally replaced the manual typewriter as a means of inputting information. Such typewriters may have a limited memory and although less sophisticated than word processors they have a number of labour-saving functions, such as:

indenting   right hand justification of text
centring
merging
repeater key   multi-pitch selection
automatic decimal
tabulation   automatic tabulation
automatic underscore

On non-display electronic typewriters, if the typist makes a mistake it will be printed, but on the display models up to one line of typing can be displayed on the screen so that the typist may correct any mistakes before printing. The growing popularity of electronic typewriters has resulted in many manufacturers offering to upgrade their machines with VDUs, so converting the typewriter into a basic word processor.

Once a machine has more than 2K of permanent memory it becomes a word processor. Apart from the keyboard, these consist of a VDU, a computer with some form of storage capacity plus a printer. In a traditional office, a stand-alone system is common. This is a self-contained unit consisting of all the above; it can be a dedicated word processor (it only does word processing) or it can be a microprocessor capable of numerous functions (such as accounts) which is capable, with the appropriate software, of being utilised as a word processor. With the stand-alone system it is possible to install communication links with other equipment and that facility will be reviewed later.

Although the final document for filing may have been typed, the 'source' document can range from the scribbled note to the audio tape. Most audio machines now use mini-cassettes and the most efficient machines can be used by the dictator and then, by exchanging the microphone for a foot pedal, by the audio typist. A cheaper unit would not possess the recording facility but might be suitable where the executive is out of the office and uses a small portable recorder. He can produce the cassettes on this and can then send them to his secretary for transcription.

Where copies of plans or drawings are required, there is a choice of reprographic equipment. Although some organisations still use duplicating (this involves preparing intermediate devices from which the ultimate copies are produced), the improvements in technology have resulted in most offices being equipped with photocopiers. These enable copies to be taken directly from the original thereby eliminating the need to produce a master.

Photocopiers are relatively easy to operate although some of the more sophisticated models which are capable of reduction, collating and automatic feed require a few hours' basic training. This is normally on-the-job and consists of tuition provided by the distributors of the machine.

The information can now be 'stored'. At some later date, however, it will need to be retrieved. In the paper office this is the reason for filing. If your employer is suddenly called to a meeting and needs a copy of a document, he/she will automatically assume you can find it immediately, and an efficient secretary can. Filing may be regarded as one of the less rewarding office jobs, and it certainly does not receive the appreciation from employers that it deserves, but if you tell your employer you cannot find an important document, just watch the reaction!

There are many systems of filing and the most appropriate for any office will depend on the nature of the work involved. Alphabetical filing where the documents are filed according to the first letter of the name may be appropriate for correspondence or staff records but subject filing may be more appropriate if your office deals with topics rather than individuals. Whatever the system chosen, whether it be alphabetical, subject, numerical or geographical, it needs to be simple to operate so that the documents are quickly and easily retrievable.

In the fully integrated electronic office the information storage function will be performed very differently. Information (words, charts, diagrams etc.) can be put into the filing system by various methods. The first of these is the word processor but using it very differently from the secretary in the more traditional office. There we assumed a stand-alone machine would be used, but the secretary in the electronic office would be using a shared logic or a distributed logic system.

With the former, there are a number of terminals (which can be used among other things for word processing) all run by a large central computer on which all the data is stored. Any terminal can access this data but they can all work independently of each other. There is a limit to the number of work stations any one computer can support but with improvements in hardware (such as Winchester disks) the numbers have increased. The work station (or terminals) are totally dependent on the central computer and should there be any malfunction the whole system will cease to operate. With a distributed logic system, while there is a central computer, the terminals possess their own computing power so that while the system possesses all the advantages of a shared logic system it can still function in the event of a central computer malfunction. (As we shall see later, because the word processing units/terminals are not stand-alone they have an important role in the electronic office.)

The electronic office is, however, characterised by the other input devices; it is these that provide the distinctive flavour of the modern office.

(i) Optical character recognition (OCR)

If a terminal or word processor is connected to an OCR reader, then documents can be fed into the OCR which reads them and automatically transfers all the information into the terminal/word processor. The operator does not have to key in the information and, of course, once into the word processor on a shared or distributed logic system, it can be transferred into the database of the central computer to which all the other terminals have access. Future OCRs will also be able to read and transfer handwritten documents!

(ii) Magnetic ink character recognition (MICR)

This form of direct input is used by banks to 'read' cheques; each character is magnetised and gives off a different electric current. This can be read by the special reader which then transfers the information into the database.

(iii) Computer input from microfilm (CIM)

Documents can now be microfilmed and transferred directly into a central computer for subsequent processing.

There is little double that in the future data will be input directly from speech or handwritten documents which will completely eliminate the need to input through a keyboard.

The information is now in the system, but how do you retrieve it?

Before providing the answer, a few words of warning. First, although computers do everything faster than humans, they cannot remedy the errors. If your manual filing system is chaotic, then putting it on to a computer will not solve the problem. Secondly, having an electronic filing system costs money and the benefits which such a system will undoubtedly provide must be balanced against this cost. At present a small office may feel the costs are too high, but with falling prices and improved software the position requires constant reviewing, especially as more staff are trained in the new technology.

The software required to establish an electronic filing system is called a 'database management system' and there are numerous such packages on the market. They permit staff to create, update and manipulate files; documents stored within an electronic filing system can be easily retrieved so that changes can be made and, given current developments, there is virtually no restriction on the amount that may be filed. Storage capacity of computers has increased while the cost of storage has fallen. Improvements in the software mean that staff can search for files by punching in key words, and as software becomes more user-friendly it has become unnecessary to employ specialist staff to retrieve information. Soon all staff with access to a terminal will be able to sort records and then have the information displayed on their VDU to be printed if a permanent record is required.

The choice of printer reflects the needs of the organisation, but the commonest ones are the impact printers (golf-ball, daisy-wheel, dot matrix) in which a key strikes the type ribbon to form a character. For good-quality copy, a daisy-wheel is usually preferred while dot matrix is useful for long runs of information used internally. The non-impact printers (thermal, electro-sensitive, ink jet and laser) are more expensive and are unlikely to be found in the average business. Laser printers, for example, can produce 20,000 lines per minute!

2. Communicating (inside and outside the organisation)

In the 'paper office' most communications will either be oral or written. In the former category there will be telephone calls, meetings, ranging from the board meetings attended by directors through departmental meetings to working parties and committees established to solve particular problems. There may be managerial briefings for executives (many of whom may have to travel to the meetings) or even large conferences where perhaps the sales director is going to address all the sales force.

Where oral communications are inappropriate for reasons outlined in Chapter 2, communications will be through memorandums or letters. Reports may have to be written and it may be necessary to send drawings or plans to supplement these.

With all the paper going into and coming out of the business, some of the office staff may be assigned to the mail room. Just consider the equipment they will need if they are to cope efficiently with large quantities of mail.

The incoming mail needs opening and possibly date stamping. Apart from the small items such as date stamps and scissors, a large office might need to invest in a letter-opening machine. To cope with outgoing mail you will require small items such as staplers, letter and parcel scales and string, but again the larger business might find it necessary to install more expensive equipment so that the staff can get the mail out on time. If the mail room has to despatch documents, such as reports or price lists which run into several pages and require sorting and pinning in sets, they might require a collating machine. Letters will require folding before they are put into envelopes; there are electric folding machines. Once folded, the letters will need to be put into envelopes which then require sealing; there are inserting and sealing machines. The envelopes will require addressing; there are addressing machines. Finally, the envelopes need stamping; there are franking machines.

All this activity costs money. Staff wages have to be paid, accommodation provided and the equipment needs to be purchased and maintained. It is all time-consuming.

The materials required in the paper office also have to be purchased. As paper is used, it needs replacing. It is the function of the stationery department to ensure that the necessary stationery supplies are available, and in good condition when required. Just consider the items of stationery the paper office will use:

headed paper (in various sizes)	memo paper
typing paper (in various sizes and quantities)	envelopes (in various sizes and quantities)
postcards	lined writing paper
unlined writing paper	compliment slips
shorthand notebooks	typewriter ribbons
carbon paper	desk blotters
photocopy paper	ink
petty cash vouchers	files and folders

plus a whole range of other miscellaneous items such as Sellotape, paper clips and string.

In addition to these items, the stationery department may be responsible for the other office accessories and aids:

guillotines	collating machines
paper punches	staplers
shredding machines	letter-opening machines
date stamps	folding machines
inserting and sealing machines	addressing machines
franking machines	postal scales
roller and sponge dampers	letter trays
waste paper bins	ashtrays

The office may need to obtain information from outside the business. A secretary finalising travel arrangements will need train timetables, air timetables, etc. and it may be necessary for the business to possess up-to-date information on the stock market or government legislation. The secretary can obtain this information through reference books, telephone calls (often using the special services outlined on page 22) or by visits.

Even within the traditional office, technology has a role to play. We have already mentioned the stand-alone word processor, but many offices will also use telex where, unlike letters, the written communication is almost instantaneous and, because of the answerback system, there is no risk of the communication being lost.

In a fully integrated electronic office, however, the telex system will be incorporated within the system of electronic communications. The ability to communicate electronically has been greatly facilitated by two developments: Local Area Networks (LANs) and modems. A LAN is a cable into which all the electronic equipment is linked. Messages can be sent from one piece of equipment to another through the cable; the message is 'addressed' to a piece of equipment, and then travels around the system until it reaches the appropriate equipment. This means that all equipment linked to the circuit can communicate directly; any terminal can communicate with any printer linked into the cable and this eliminates the need for each terminal to possess its own printer. Where a LAN is inappropriate because of cost or the distances involved and it is necessary for two machines to communicate, then the parties will use a modem and the ordinary telephone line (see page 25). By using either of these two systems it is possible for computer equipment to communicate directly.

When communicating orally, such devices are unnecessary. The telephone system is itself a network in that each telephone can directly communicate with another. In the electronic office, however, by using a call-connect system, the user has facilities not available with the ordinary telephone system. You will recall from Chapter 2 that this system connects all internal telephones together while giving some access to outside lines. After instituting such a system, additional facilities are available as previously outlined.

We referred above to meetings and conferences at which interested parties are present and the travel costs (and time) sometimes involved. These costs can be avoided by using 'conferencing' facilities which brings together people in different locations. The conferencing system offered by British Telecom is called 'confravision' and at present, to use it, you need to attend special studios, but in the near future terminals will be available which will allow this facility to be available in the office. It will therefore be possible to have meetings and conferences without the parties leaving their offices, and with support services it will be possible for them to exchange documents and plans during the conference.

Electronic mail means that a business can send text messages (written or graphic) from one location to another; paper communications are therefore eliminated because machines will be able to 'talk' to each other. To transfer written documents and messages, we can use telex, teletex or FAX (see page 24) but a fully integrated electronic office will require an 'electronic mail box'. The system used by British Telecom is called 'Telecom Gold' and an extract from the sales literature is shown below.

How often do you find that the facts you need are trapped in the postal system, or the people you need to contact are not available when you 'phone? And when you're on the move how do others reach you? The lifeblood of business is information. Circulating that information to the vital organs of a corporate body is essential to the productivity of an organisation.

The answer is brilliantly simple in concept and remarkably efficient in practice; it's a mail box. An electronic mail box that you – and only you – can open and for which messages can be sent or retrieved 24 hours a day. A reliable, secure system which enables you to read your 'mail', deal with urgent issues, act on information received or ask more questions of the sender.

From any telephone . . . you can communicate instantly with another mailbox in the next room, the next town, with one or with thousands across the country or anywhere in your business world irrespective of time zones.

So where do you start?

You need a telephone, a terminal and a Telecom Gold mailbox.

To participate in this scheme you need a terminal (micro-computer, word processor or any other VDU) which is linked to the telephone system via a modem. The terminal can receive messages from and insert messages into the system and is linked to a computer in London. If users wish to know if there are any messages for them, they will key in their password; they are then connected to their mail box. The messages will be displayed on the screen and they can be printed out if necessary. Anyone can send messages to your mail box but only you have access to the box. Messages can be transmitted to anyone with a box and can be sent to one box or up to 500. Once it has been received, the message is stored in the memory until the box is opened and the contents checked. Such a service can be used internally within a company thereby dispensing with internal memos. Each individual or department having a mail box will be able to communicate with anybody in the company having access to a box. The system may be even more beneficial where there is a head office with regional offices or where a retail group has a head office which needs to communicate with several hundred stores.

Although the electronic mail box will be used for external communications as well, it may be inappropriate where it is necessary to verify the sender. Such communications (for example, orders) can be sent through teletex because at the beginning and end of each message there is an answerback system so that the sender and receiver know they are dealing with the appropriate businesses.

As an indication of the potential of the electronic system, 44 pages of A4 can be transmitted in one second.

In an electronic office utilising electronic mail, the diminishing importance of 'paper' is reflected in the roles of the mailroom and stationery store. If all mail were transmitted electronically there would be no need for date stamps, letter-opening machines, electric folding machines, inserting and sealing machines and addressing and franking machines. In fact, there would be no need for a separate mailroom with the consequent savings in staff and accommodation.

The reduced role in the electronic office for traditional stationery means a reduced role for the stationery department. Re-examine the list on page 60 to see which items the office would no longer require but remember you will need to also add some items such as daisy-wheels and computing paper (and remember the stationery for hand copies).

If a secretary in the new office requires information such as travel timetables, it can be obtained by simply using a terminal and linking into Videotex. There are two separate systems, viewdata and teletext.

Viewdata

Prestel, which is the British Telecom viewdata system, allows anyone with an adapted television or micro-computer to access a computer-based information system through an ordinary telephone line. The information on Prestel is organised into pages and the user has a special key pad to call up any one of its 250,000 pages. Many of these are specially designed for business users containing, for example, details on investment statistics, company information, export information or tax guides. In addition, Prestel provides a modified form of electronic mail service as users can send messages through the system to other users.

The intelligent viewdata terminal is capable of storing viewdata programs known as telesoftware. This enables the user to copy pages from Prestel for future reference.

Teletext

The two services available in the UK are Ceefax (BBC) and Oracle (IBA) and subscribers can have information transmitted direct to their television screens once they have a modified aerial. It is more expensive than ordinary television but cheaper than Prestel, which is not surprising as it is not a two-way system and only has 900 pages of text.

Of course, one function that remains unchanged is the buying, distributing and controlling of stationery used by the business. The stationery itself may change; as communications become increasingly electronic there will be fewer envelopes, but paper will still be required for hard copies and daisy-wheels will be ordered instead of typewriter ribbons. In some organisations the cost of stationery and office sundries justifies the establishment of a centralised stationery department. It has the responsibility for ensuring adequate supplies of stationery are available, stored correctly (in a cabinet or store-room) and that an effective system of stock control exists. For this reason, stock will only be issued against a requisition signed by an authorised person. In an electronic office where numerous staff have access to terminals and printers it may be necessary to implement a more decentralised system and, while this may make control more difficult, the benefits of the electronic system will more than compensate.

In the office of the future it should be possible to have access to all the information that is needed to do the job without leaving the workstation and the same can be said of facilities for passing on information in almost any form. The office worker of the future will need to develop different skills from those used at present.

BT aims to link Prestel with Telecom Gold

British Telecommunications expects next year to introduce an improvement that allows subscribers to exchange information with users of Telecom Gold, the no-frills communications network that links personal computers. The move is designed to make its Prestel electronic information system more attractive to business and private customers.

An electronic connection between the two systems, which at present are incompatible with each other, will allow electronic messages created on one network to be received on the other. The computerized linkage is now being tested, according to a BT spokesman.

Prestel, introduced in 1979, offers customers the possibility of displaying text and graphics in colour on a specially-modified television set connected to a telephone line; Telecom Gold is a system that allows computers to send messages over telephone circuits, but without offering colour or graphics.

Despite its sophistication, and its acceptance by the travel industry as a reservation and information system, Prestel has failed to live up to expectations. Although it is profitable, it has only 70,000 users and is growing at a rate of only a few hundred customers a week. BT, in an effort to emulate its success in the travel industry, has sought to target Prestel on additional specific business and consumer information market needs. But few new information providers are making use of the system.

Telecom Gold, which is four years old, already has 50,000 users and with the addition of 1,000 customers a week, is expected to double its customer base in the next year.

In a further move to bolster Prestel, BT also hopes to link it to the French Minitel system, which has more than 2 million users and is the world's largest system for giving the public access to electronic message services and information banks.

Minitel, originally launched by the French telecommunications administration as a replacement for telephone directories, has expanded to include hundreds of information services, including several which specialize in offering sexually-explicit messages and graphics. Unlike Prestel terminals, which cost about £800, Minitel terminals are being distributed free to French telephone customers.

When it was introduced, BT hoped that Prestel would quickly appeal to hundreds of thousands of users and dominate what was seen as a worldwide market. But Prestel failed to gain a foothold in the vital American market.

Telecom Gold, introduced as a simple electronic mail network, lacks the capability of Prestel to display graphics and information in colour, but is nevertheless enjoying a measure of success that has taken BT by surprise.

There will be very little writing in the electronic office; most work will involve keyboard and reading skills and much more direct voice contact with colleagues and customers over the telephone. There might even be visual contact through the view phone or extended video conferencing facilities. Quite what effects this new environment will have on office workers is not yet known, however much of the repetition of paper filing, collecting and copying information will be gone forever, and who knows, one day office workers may never go to work but conduct their jobs from their electronic workstations at home.

Thomson to scrap phone link

Travel agents will soon be unable to make telephone bookings with Thomson Holidays. The package tour group has decided to rely totally on its computer network from December.

Thomson began using the British invention of Videotex to automate its business four years ago, and today 85 per cent of all bookings are handled by computer.

Videotex uses ordinary television sets, souped up with a few microchips, to communicate with central computers down the telephone line. The idea was pioneered by British Telecom but France has used and developed it more widely than Britain.

Mr Colin Palmer, Thomson's deputy managing director in charge of computer development, said yesterday that Videotex has given the group "a tremendous competitive edge." This year Thomson was carrying 2.5 million passengers – three times the number in 1979 but with no increase in staff. "And this year we can plough some of the increased productivity into price."

Thomson has spent about £2.5 million a year since 1982 on developing its computer network and this year investment has been increased to £6 million. Mr Palmer said this gave the group "the largest private Videotex system in the world" – 650 entry "ports" at 37 computer points serving 5,500 travel agents. Eight hundred further ports would be added by December.

As a result, Thomson had increased its market share from 20 per cent to nearly 30 per cent in a year.

Mr Palmer said that abandoning telephone booking would not mean any Thomson redundancies. About 500 travel agents were still using the phone, but half of those were investing the necessary £300 a year in Videotex equipment. The rest were firms mainly concerned with business travel.

Examination questions

1. What distinguishes a word processor from an electronic typewriter?

   (*4 marks*)

2. What do you understand by the term 'shared logic system'?

   (*4 marks*)

3. What is 'confravision'?

   (*4 marks*)

4. What is the difference between duplicating and photocopying?

   (*4 marks*)

5. Name *three* systems of filing.

   (*4 marks*)

6. Sate *two* methods used for inputting information in an electronic office.

   (*4 marks*)

7. What advantages does the 'electronic' office have over the 'traditional' office?

   (*20 marks*)

8. Give a full explanation of one of the functions of an office.

   (*20 marks*)

9. What do you understand by the following terms:
   (a) LANs
   (b) Modems
   (c) Optical character recognition?

   (*20 marks*)

10. Describe how a Telecom Gold Mailbox can be used.

    (*20 marks*)

11. How could a 'database management system' be used in an office?

    (*20 marks*)

Introducing an electronic office
Chapter 6

Before a business can convert from a traditional to a fully integrated electronic office, there are a number of questions to be answered. First, the tasks in the office must be analysed to see if they can be performed more efficiently in an electronic office. Will this greater efficiency justify the cost of the new equipment? Electronic equipment, although becoming cheaper, is still expensive and an electronic office should only be introduced if ultimately it will result in the business saving money.

This task may be given to the organisation and methods staff within the firm. They are the office equivalent of the work study officers in the factory. Just as the latter study production methods with a view to their improvement, so organisation and methods will appraise office systems with a view to their streamlining. In a traditional office they may suggest mechanisation of the accounts, centralised filing or the re-organisation of systems and procedures. They are the exponents of rationalisation and modernisation and as the introduction of an electronic office is just this they are ideally suited to assessing its effectiveness.

If management decides to go ahead, then should the new system be centralised or decentralised? In the traditional office, a centralised system is one where the services are organised and controlled from a central point; services are located in one area such as a typing pool or word processing area. Such a system provides management with better administrative control and, with the improved supervision, better utilisation of staff and equipment is possible by spreading out the workload. Reduction of staffing levels means reduction in accommodation and both of these produce falling costs. Centralised systems can, however, be inflexible, and can cause delays while material is being sent to the centralised point.

Centralisation of electronic equipment involves different considerations. A centralised system means having one central computer with no terminals spread throughout the building and this was the system used when computers were first introduced. Documents were collected in batches and then sent to a centralised data processing department where they were fed into the computer. A decentralised system involves having computer terminals spread throughout an organisation, all capable of inputting and accessing information from the central computer. As you will realise having read Chapter 5, the electronic office must be decentralised if the advantages of such a system are to be gained. By having terminals in each department or section, all staff have immediate access to all the information in the main computer which improves decision-making; internal electronic mail is also only possible if each section or department possesses its own terminal. Therefore if management operates a centralised office system it needs to consider how to decentralise it.

Having decided to introduce a decentralised electronic office, the third problem is to select equipment which meets the immediate and future needs of the business. Management must purchase a computer to store data; software (programs) to tell the computer how to use the data; VDUs and keyboards to enable the staff to input and manipulate the data; printers to enable a paper printout of the data; and, finally, external storage devices such as disks or tapes. As we shall see later in the chapter, operating such equipment can cause physical and psychological problems and so equipment purchased must satisfy safety and design standards as well as being functional. There are numerous manufacturers, and the competition and advances in technology means that new models are frequently being launched; as these are not always compatible with existing equipment, the first purchase may be vital. Once you are 'into' a particular system it is often difficult and expensive to modify it.

The most difficult purchasing decision is the software; these are the programs that will 'do' your accounts, filing, stock control or word processing. Once you have decided on the software, it is then a matter of purchasing computers that can 'run' (use) it. If possible, you should try to buy a computer that will run a range of software programs (including the ones you have chosen!) – if the machines are 'IBM compatible' this increases the range of software which can be used. Suppliers are always prepared to demonstrate their software either at your firm or within their organisations; the former is better. When receiving a demonstration, insist on 'seeing' and make certain it does exactly what you want; never take the demonstrator's word. Expensive mistakes have been made that way! Modifying software is invariably very expensive and so it is important when you purchase it that it performs the tasks you want – nearly is not good enough.

Even the electronic office needs humans to operate it and its successful introduction requires the support of the staff and union. It is therefore important that management can answer any questions they raise, and there will be questions as evidenced by the article on pp. 70–1.

The main health hazards relating to VDUs are:

(i) headache, eyestrain, back, shoulder and arm problems
(ii) stress and boredom
(iii) possible danger from radiation

If there was a meeting between management and unions prior to the introduction of the electronic office, the main agenda might be as follows:

AGENDA
1 Safety
– equipment
– office environment
– operators
– working practices
2 Security and Confidentiality of Data
3 Training and Retraining Programmes
4 Redundancies
5 Any other business

Let us therefore eavesdrop on certain parts of the meeting.

1. Safety

UNION: Before we look at the specific items on the agenda, what's the general position regarding safety?
MANAGEMENT: Well, if anybody is injured at work because of the company's carelessness then we have, by law, to pay them damages to compensate them for their injuries.
UNION: That's all very well but money can't really compensate. Prevention is better than cure. Can't we do anything before someone is injured?
MANAGEMENT: Compensation is only paid if someone is injured but we are all now under a duty to see that premises are safe under the Health and Safety at Work Act which came into force in 1975.
UNION: What does it say?
MANAGEMENT: The idea behind the Act, as I said, is to make premises safe so that accidents do not happen.
UNION: How does it work?

Health, fitness and VDU screens

One might think that sitting in front of a computer screen all day is about as safe a life as one could wish for, but according to a large body of opinion, you would be wrong. The seemingly harmless VDU is being blamed for all sorts of maladies, ranging from eye strain and headaches to aching arms, frozen shoulders, dud backs and miscarriages.

Sorting out the truth from the imaginings of people who might be suffering from those problems anyway is a difficult matter at the best of times, and is compounded by the near-impossibility of doing comparative studies. An American government department called the National Institute for Occupational Safety & Health is working on a study (which won't be ready until 1987) looking at how exposure to computer screens can affect pregnant women, but it is having difficulty in finding two large groups of people doing similar work in every respect, except that one group is doing it on computer terminals and one isn't. (If it's the sort of work that can best be done on computers, we've reached the stage now where everyone *will* be doing it on computers . . . and if it isn't, they won't.)

It's a difficult subject for the layman to get to grips with, simply because of the lack of worthwhile data. Essentially, there are two fears: first, the long-term exposure to radiation emitted from the computer screen can cause harmful effects (this is the worry uppermost in Britain and the United States); and second, that the constant bashing away at a computer keyboard can lead to chronic aches and pains. This is dignified with the term 'repetitive stress injury' (RSI), and is the main ground for concern in Australia.

RSI is, as it were, currently doing better than radiation. It's taken hold in Australia with RSI now accepted as an official industrial injury, and with large numbers of employees (many genuine, some undoubtedly utterly bogus but who have swotted up the symptoms) running for compensation.

But it is the radiation worries which could ultimately prove the more devastatingly real. One US risk management expert has said that 'we may be looking at a sleeping asbestosis problem.'

The computer lobby opposes the claims staunchly – you would hardly expect it to do anything else. But the picture is confused: first, although some radiation is undoubtedly emitted from a computer VDU due to the sheer fact that a beam of electrons is striking a phosphorescent screen on the other side of the glass, the level of emission is extremely small.

One American doctor told me: 'If you ask me officially about VDU radiation, I would say: "Sure, this could be a problem, and thus it requires careful and rigorous investigation." If you ask me off the record, though, I'd say: "Hell, these things give off a great deal less radiation than a colour television, and if you've got someone who is spending eight hours at work in front of a VDU, then going home and spending five hours in front of the TV, with occasional trips to heat up a pizza in the microwave, I know where he's more at risk from radiation."'

It may turn out that the radiation question is a wild goose chase on both sides. The most dramatic of the problems being blamed on computer terminal work is that of spontaneous abortions, with some American figures suggesting a significant rise in abortions among women exposed to VDU screens in the first three months of pregnancy. But opinion is divided over the interpretation of the figures, with some experts saying that they do not move outside the normal range for any given population.

But what if the figures *are* abnormal? 'Again,' says the doctor, 'officially, maybe. Unofficially, you don't need radiation to produce abortions, and if those figures are beyond normal variance – which I doubt, personally – you'd be better off looking for some other, more likely cause. Stress, for example, can cause a number of physiological processes which you can link with problems like abortion. And that makes more sense; you can say: "Stress causes reaction A, which produces a high blood level of substance B, which we know can cause the sort of reaction C which might lead to a miscarriage."

'I would look at stress, every time.'

One might not think that entering data from a keyboard is particularly stressful. But such work does have many of the qualities of stress-inducing work. It is fast, repetitive, demands high accuracy, is done from a fixed posture and requires a fixed gaze. All of which can be just as stressful as the popular idea of the stressed executive, all hell let loose around him, forcing his way through against huge odds, and all the rest of the popular mythology which has made stress a badge of business success and the stress-cure industry a lucrative proposition. Too bad for the executives, who wear their stress like a Broadway agent wears his ulcer, if it went downmarket and became the prerogative of clerks as well as chairman. But that's what seems likely.

What can a company do to protect its employees – and, less nobly, to protect itself in the event of a claim for VDU-related compensation? American insurers advise a number of points which are already common practice in Europe, but are worth re-stating:

- Encourage people not to sit bashing away and staring at the screen for hours on end, but to take regular breaks, get up, walk around, break the gaze and so forth.
- Use keyboards which are detached from the screen so that the employee can move the equipment to a comfortable position. Make sure that the screens can be tilted or swivelled to provide a decent angle of view.
- Check lighting and ventilation in the office – stuffy offices can bring on a headache, which is then made worse by focusing on a VDU.
- Give pregnant women the option of transferring to work which doesn't involve sitting at a terminal.

None of this can guarantee that nobody starts to display unfortunate symptoms. But at least for the time being you can say you have done your best.

MANAGEMENT: The Act lays down duties on employers to [and here he reads from the Act]

(i) 'ensure so far as is reasonably practicable, the health, safety and welfare of his employees at work.
(ii) 'to maintain plant and systems of work that are . . . safe and without risks to health.
(iii) 'provide a safe working environment'

and so on. There are other duties but I think you now get the idea.

UNION: Does the Act involve us?

MANAGEMENT: All staff must be provided with a written statement of the company's safety policy and procedures and employees are entitled to have a safety committee. In addition, each union has the right to appoint a safety representative with whom we can consult.

UNION: It's only right that the staff should be consulted.

MANAGEMENT: Agreed, but the Act also lays down certain general duties for employees. There are three. First, employees must take reasonable care for their own health and safety and of that of their colleagues. Secondly, they must co-operate with their employers when they are implementing their safety policy, and finally they must not interfere with items provided in the interests of health and safety.

UNION: Does that mean if someone plays about with a fire extinguisher they've committed a criminal offence?

MANAGEMENT: I'm afraid so.

UNION: OK. The law says that premises must be safe and you have to consult with the staff and unions. Suppose we think the premises are unsafe and you refuse to do anything about it. What actions can we take?

MANAGEMENT: I'm sure if you had found something wrong we would remedy it but if we didn't you could go to the inspectorate.

UNION: Who are they?

MANAGEMENT: The Health and Safety Executive employ inspectors to ensure the Act is not broken. They have wide powers of entry and inspection and can start criminal proceedings against offenders.

UNION: But that doesn't necessarily make premises safe.

MANAGEMENT: Legal proceedings are considered to be the last resort. Before then the inspectors will probably issue either an improvement or a prohibition notice. The first gives an employer so many days to remedy the situation; the inspector is really saying you've broken the law but I'm giving you 30 days to put it right. If the premises are really dangerous and involve risk of personal injury, the inspector can issue a prohibition notice which effectively shuts you down until you put matters right.

UNION: Suppose you ignore the inspectorate?

MANAGEMENT: That's hardly advisable because failure to comply can lead to a prosecution in the Magistrates Court or even Crown Court, where you can receive an unlimited fine and/or imprisonment for up to two years.

UNION: I think we'll comply [they all laugh]. As far as our members are concerned the really important thing is that they will be consulted and we'll have a safety committee and safety reps to monitor safety standards.

MANAGEMENT: That's right.

UNION: Well that seems satisfactory. Can we now look at the specific items on the agenda? Let's look at equipment.

MANAGEMENT: The piece of equipment most likely to cause problems appears to be the VDU. To avoid these arising those purchased will be able to tilt and swivel and the operators will be able to change the contrast of the screen to obtain the right balance between the brightness of the characters and the background. This should help eliminate eyestrain and muscle problem.

UNION: What about the size of screens?

MANAGEMENT: We will review the amount of text a screen holds; the more it holds the smaller the characters and so the greater the strain. We hope to find a suitable compromise. . . . The keyboards will be separate from the unit so staff can move them to a comfortable position to avoid backstrain and we are providing document holders at eye level to reduce neck and eye problems.

UNION: Can't you get back problems if you have the wrong type of chairs?

MANAGEMENT: Yes, you can and that's why our chairs will have adjustable seat heights and there will be foot rests. The desks will also be at the right height so the staff don't have to sit hunched over them.

UNION: I've just thought of something. We might buy the right VDUs but what if they go wrong?

MANAGEMENT: There will be regular maintenance and service checks. If there's any display instability (character jumping or jitter) on the screen, then the machine will be closed down until it's repaired.
. . .

UNION: The second special item was the office environment and the use of the equipment. What our members want to know is whether the office will be re-organised and will the working environment be changed.

MANAGEMENT: This is obviously an important topic because it affects staff morale and productivity. Perhaps I can deal with the question under several headings.

Layout – Here we have a choice between individual offices (which you have now) and open-plan offices. We know staff prefer individual offices because they feel open plan is too noisy, not private enough and they can't adjust the heating and lighting to suit themselves. Of course, if we had open plan we'd have better supervision and it's more economical on accommodation but to utilise the full capabilities of the electronic equipment we'll need to keep individual offices and workstations so the staff needn't worry on that score.

Lighting – We've always accepted that office staff need good lighting and this is even more vital with VDUs because of the need to eliminate glare and reflection on the screen. We'll ensure there are no unshielded fluorescent tubes and that the VDUs are positioned between rather than under a row of lighting.

Design of work space – Staff already have modern furniture – some of which wouldn't be out of place in their own homes – which has been specially designed for their needs. As I said earlier, the furniture used will help staff to adopt the right posture to minimise problems of backstrain. The space allocated to each member of staff will be greater than that laid down by the Offices, Shops, Railways Premises Act 1963 (that is 40 square feet).

Noise – The new printers are noisy and we are looking at the possibility of putting them into a separate sound-proof room. If this isn't possible we will ensure they all have acoustic shields.

Temperature – Again we'll comply with the 1963 Act and ensure the temperature is 16°C after one hour but we regard that as a minimum and I know you all expect it to be higher. Because the machines and lights can make life hot we've had individually adjusted ventilation installed by each workstation.

Decor – This covers walls, floors, curtains and blinds. Obviously we cannot satisfy everyone because this is really a matter of personal taste but rooms will be decorated in relaxing colours and there will be a contract with an outside firm to provide plants to give the VDU operators something more relaxing to look at.

UNION: You seem to have thought about everything there. Our members are perhaps more concerned about who is to operate the machines and the possibilities of redundancies.

MANAGEMENT: If we can leave redundancies until we reach it on the agenda, I hope your worries will be dispelled. Who's going to use the machines? Well we hope everyone, and not just traditional office staff. We do however appreciate that certain individuals may find it difficult to work with VDUs.

UNION: Can you give examples?

MANAGEMENT: Anyone who finds it difficult to read the screen, those with a history of epilepsy and pregnant women.

UNION: They won't have to use the VDUs?

MANAGEMENT: No, or anyone else who is vulnerable.

UNION: What will happen to them?

MANAGEMENT: Let's wait until we reach that item on the agenda, shall we?

Fortunately for management the coffee arrives and there is a break before discussions continue.

MANAGEMENT: If we've exhausted that topic perhaps we can move on to working practices [there are no comments and so management continues]. We recognise that VDU work needs continuous concentration and therefore there will be a rest break of 10 minutes in every hour. This will be taken away from the screen and we also suggest that no operator should use a VDU for more than 2 hours in any one day. This follows the recommendation of the British Health and Safety Executive. We also accept the principle of numerous short breaks rather than longer occasional breaks and we are prepared to ensure that all staff have a good mix of VDU and non-VDU-based work.

UNION: That's acceptable to us. Shall we now move on to the next item?

MANAGEMENT: Item 2. Security and Confidentiality of Data.

UNION: One of the justifications for 'going electronic' is that all staff records can go onto the computer which will make updating easier.

MANAGEMENT: That's right.

UNION: But you also say that anyone with a terminal can 'access' information in the computer. That means anyone can get staff data out of the computer. I don't think my members will stand for that.

MANAGEMENT: In theory what you say is true, but in practice it won't happen. If it did we'd be committing a criminal offence.

UNION: You'd be breaking the law?

MANAGEMENT: Yes, the Data Protection Act regulates the use of personal data held on computers.

UNION: I've not heard of that.

MANAGEMENT: That's not surprising as it only came into force in September 1987.

UNION: Well how does it protect my members?

MANAGEMENT: Your members are 'data subjects'.

UNION: [interrupting] What?

MANAGEMENT: That just means they're people about whom data is held. The company, because it holds personal data on a computer, is a 'data user' and that means we must register with the Registrar. If we didn't register with him we'd also be committing a criminal offence.

UNION: I don't see how registering will help protect my members.

MANAGEMENT: In order to register we have to agree to keep the eight data processing principles [he hands the union a list of these – Fig. 6.1] and also tell the Registrar what data we're holding, where we got it from, what we're going to use it for and, perhaps most important for your members, to whom the data will be disclosed. In addition we're obliged, on request, to tell anyone what data we have on them.

(a) Personal data must be obtained fairly and lawfully;

(b) Personal data must be held only for one or more lawful purposes specified in the data user's register entry;

(c) Personal data must be used or disclosed only in accordance with the data user's register entry;

(d) Personal data must be adequate, relevant and not excessive for those purposes;

(e) Personal data must be accurate and where necessary up-to-date;

(f) Personal data must not be kept longer than necessary for the specific purposes;

(g) Personal data must be made available to data subjects on request;

(h) Personal data must be properly protected against loss or disclosure.

Fig. 6.1. The eight data protection principles

UNION: I'll read the eight principles later but if I understand what you're saying, any of our members can ask you what you have on the computer.

MANAGEMENT: About them, yes.

UNION: Supposing they don't agree with it?

MANAGEMENT: If the data is wrong they can have it corrected or erased.

UNION: But it might be too late. They might have suffered some damage.

MANAGEMENT: If they have, they still have the right to have their details corrected or erased but in addition they are entitled to compensation. The same is true if we fail to properly protect the data and it gets into the wrong hands.

UNION: We all know you won't break the law [laughter] but just suppose you did?

MANAGEMENT: Apart from committing a criminal offence, we're going to find ourselves investigated by the Data Protection Registrar, who will investigate all complaints and can enforce the Act through three types of notice. The first is an enforcement notice. This tells us which of the eight principles we are breaking and how long we have to put matters right.

UNION: What happens if you don't comply?

MANAGEMENT: Then we've committed a criminal offence and we still have to put matters right otherwise the Registrar might issue a deregistration notice. This removes us from the register and, as you must be registered if you're using a computer for personal data, it will mean we can't use our computers without committing another offence.

UNION: You said there were three types of notice.

MANAGEMENT: The third isn't really relevant to us. It's a transfer notice and it stops you transferring information overseas if that contravenes the Act. As we don't have overseas subsidiaries, there are no problems here.

There are some further technical discussions on how the data is protected and then they move on to the next item on the agenda.

MANAGEMENT: Item 3 is the Training and Retraining of existing staff.

UNION: Do you accept there will be a need to train or retrain staff?

MANAGEMENT: Yes, I don't think there's any doubt about that. Staff will need to be thoroughly trained in the new systems for inputting and retrieving information and on the vairous specific packages that we'll buy on wages, stock control and the various accounting functions. Remember, of course, that the change won't just affect the clerical staff such as secretaries or typists, we're going to have to retrain the administrative staff who are acting in a supervisory capacity and the whole exercise would be pointless if management didn't understand the potential of the system. There'll be training courses at that level although, of course, they'll be slightly different from the ones we provide for the secretarial staff.

UNION: That's reassuring but what you've said is very general. How will existing staff be affected? What, for example, about the private secretaries? At the moment they have a wide range of duties; they prepare a lot of the documentation, perform confidential work as well as supervising other junior members of staff.

MANAGEMENT: As far as the private secretaries are concerned, I don't think they have much to worry about. After all, we insist when they are appointed that they have a good general education, especially in English. These are just the qualities that are going to be needed to work with the new technology and you'll find the other skills they have in typing, shorthand and general secretarial procedures will still be needed. They'll still have to arrange meetings like this one, prepare minutes and keep diaries but they'll be able to use the electronic equipment to help them. The system we are introducing will provide, among other things, an electronic diary so that the secretaries will be able to check the electronic diaries of other staff, making it easier to arrange meetings and appointments. It eliminates all that telephoning around. Of course, they'll need a training course to familiarise them with the new equipment but then we would hope they would be able to spend less time on routine tasks which the equipment can perform, leaving them free to take on more junior management functions. They are doing a lot of this at the moment; they have to handle figures and work with the minimum of supervision. All that will happen is that they'll have more of this work which we hope will make their jobs more interesting. Given the qualities of the secretarial staff we appoint, we don't see any problems in their making the transition.

UNION: The private secretaries appear to be OK but what about some of the less well academically qualified staff like copy typists?

MANAGEMENT: We could have had a problem there because their main role was the accurate production of typewritten material plus other general office duties such as filing. Clearly within the new electronic system much of this work will disappear and, given the importance of proof-reading, many of the staff we would have employed as clerk typists would no longer be suitable. It shouldn't, however, pose too much of a problem within our organisation because we've had word processing in the office for several years and so as our old clerk typists have left, we've recruited staff capable of using the word processors and they shouldn't have any problem in transferring to the new equipment.

UNION: Well I suppose that's lucky.

MANAGEMENT: Or perhaps we had some foresight.

UNION: Well, anyway, it doesn't appear to be a problem but we do have lots of shorthand and audio typists employed. What about them?

MANAGEMENT: There will still be a need for staff who can take shorthand dictation and transcribe accurately and the usual secretarial duties will still need performing albeit with the assistance of electronic equipment. Similarly, we shall need staff who can accurately transcribe from audio cassettes. With both shorthand and audio typists, we only recruit staff with good English qualifications because of the need to transcribe and therefore both should be able to work with the new technology. It's true there will be less demand for shorthand and audio typists and we may have to retrain some of them as word processor operators.

UNION: And what would their jobs involve?

MANAGEMENT: Their main duty will be to prepare material either from paper or from audio tapes using the word processor. They'll need to be able to use all the main functions on the word processor, including storage and retrieval of data, but as I mentioned a bit earlier, for safety reasons no-one will spend more than 2 hours a day on the word processor and for the rest of the time they'll be performing normal office duties.

UNION: We seem to have talked a lot about word processing but, as I understand it, the electronic office will be used for a variety of office functions. Aren't we even using computers to control the telephone system? Doesn't that affect the jobs of telephonists and ordinary clerical staff who are involved with things like wages and accounts? What's to become of them?

MANAGEMENT: Many of their duties will still need to be performed but the staff in those areas will be using electronic equipment and will therefore need keyboard skills which will involve some element of retraining. Of course, one of the reasons for introducing the electronic office is to save on staff costs and we would anticipate staff savings will be made in this area. The same applies to the telephonist. A few will still be required but with the new call connect system we will again be looking for staff savings in this area which is no doubt why you put redundancies on the agenda.

UNION: Of course. How will the new technology affect the receptionist?

MANAGEMENT: You will recall in the old days that the receptionist 'doubled up' as one of the switchboard operators. When we changed the system, the receptionist was no longer needed on the switchboard so we provided an electronic typewriter for work during the slack periods. We're now going to replace that with a terminal which can communicate with the main computer or any other terminal.

UNION: Will the receptionist still be in the foyer?

MANAGEMENT: We won't move reception. It's obviously got to be the first place visitors see. The receptionist's role won't really change and eventually the computer will be available to help him/her. At present, the receptionist keeps a written register of appointments with the visitor's name, date and time of visit and other relevant details. Eventually all that information will be available on the database.

UNION: What's the advantage of that?

MANAGEMENT: Anybody in the business would be able to 'access' this information which would avoid duplication of visits and that sort of thing.

UNION: Will the receptionist use the terminal for anything else?

MANAGEMENT: At times when reception is quiet the word processing supervisor will no doubt find the receptionist work to do.

UNION: We'll need to monitor that to ensure that he/she doesn't do more than 2 hours a day because of the health risk. . . .

MANAGEMENT: One post that will disappear is that of the secretarial services supervisor – now that we're having to decentralise our secretarial services. When everything was centralised, the supervisor was responsible for the overall schedule and work co-ordination and as such was responsible for everything from selecting the staff for a particular job to checking the final result, and where there were problems dealing with them or liaising with the personnel department to provide the appropriate training courses. Given the way the work will be organised in the future, we just don't need anyone and the position is in fact redundant.

UNION: You mean the supervisor will lose her job?

MANAGEMENT: Well, certainly that one but providing the supervisor is prepared to retrain, we're prepared to offer the job of word processing supervisor on the same conditions of service. The supervisor has the right background for the job, has keyboarding skills and a supervisory qualification, and is used to making decisions, delegating where necessary and being responsible for other staff. We also know the supervisor can work under pressure and is adaptable. All that is lacking is some technical knowledge within the electronic field and we'll offer the relevant training. Once settled into the new post, we would expect the supervisor to get involved in the setting up and implementing of that area of the electronic office. There'll still be scheduling and co-ordinating work, checking to ensure that the right standards are maintained, and previous experience with training will be invaluable. Given the possible safety problems with VDUs, it might be an idea if the supervisor was on the safety committee.

UNION: That's a good idea. We'll look into that. I suppose that's all the staff.

MANAGEMENT: Not quite. We're going to need a new post in management because of all the changes.

UNION: Typical. More chiefs and fewer Indians! What's the new post to be?

MANAGEMENT: Office manager.

UNION: And what will that involve?

MANAGEMENT: Basically, the office manager will be responsible for all the office functions. Now we're going electronic, the person appointed will have to devise suitable systems and procedures and advise us on new equipment; once that is done, there'll be a need to help plan the training of staff.

UNION: I thought that was personnel's job?

MANAGEMENT: It is, but the office manager has overall responsibility for all office personnel and will be in charge, although no doubt some of the functions will be delegated to the new word processing supervisor. Again, while within the word processing area, the office manager will be responsible for seeing the work is completed to a satisfactory standard, the person will be ultimately responsible for ensuring that all the office functions are running smoothly, and will also be responsible for ensuring safety standards are maintained within the office areas. . . .

UNION: Apart from redundancies which is next on the agenda, I can't see any major problems, but obviously the training programmes are very important. Just what had you in mind?

MANAGEMENT: We're looking at five different courses. The first will be on keyboard skills. A lot of staff using the electronic equipment have no keyboard experience but, given the numbers involved and the difficulty of freeing them all at the same time for a course, we decided to use Open Distance Learning.

UNION: That's a new one on me. What is it?

MANAGEMENT: With Open Distance Learning you buy in a package which may consist of a manual or a kit or, in this case, a computer program. Any individual can then learn at his or her own pace, by using the package whenever it is convenient. The advantage for us, of course, is that it causes the minimum disruption to the work here.

UNION: Wouldn't the staff be better off going to college?

MANAGEMENT: Not necessarily. With this type of learning the

employees can work at their own pace. Those who find it easy can go through the package quickly, but if you want to go more slowly you can. If the topic being studied was more difficult, then there would be back-up tutorials at the college but this isn't necessary on the keyboard package.

Any more questions? [There are none so management continues] The second course will be on the new equipment. Within the price we're negotiating with the suppliers, they will provide all staff with a two-day course before the equipment arrives and then they will have their own staff in the firm during the first two weeks of its operation to provide on-the-job training.

UNION: I can see the point of on-the-job training here. It would be a bit pointless sending them to college to learn on different equipment.

MANAGEMENT: Precisely. The third course will be on the Security and Confidentiality of Data held on the computer.

UNION: I thought 'Confidentiality' was covered in the induction course.

MANAGEMENT: It is to an extent. All the secretaries know that confidentiality marked documents must be kept locked and that they must supervise any photocopying and exercise extreme care with carbon copies and their destruction. With computers, it's a bit different. There aren't any suitable packages for Open Distance Learning and so we're sending all the staff involved to a two-day short course at the College of Further Education.

The fourth and fifth courses are on the care and maintenance of equipment and safety. Both of these topics are covered on the induction course but we felt it would be useful to have a refresher course which can then relate what staff know to the new equipment. We thought we'd carry out these courses in-house with some one-hour training sessions. This will enable us to give practical demonstrations on the equipment.

UNION: How does care and maintenance of the new equipment differ from that of the existing equipment?

MANAGEMENT: The same principles apply.

UNION: Let's see if I can remember them. They should be regularly cleaned; a servicing programme should exist; they should be turned off and covered when not in use.

MANAGEMENT: Full marks! Electronic equipment is more susceptible to dirt and the disks are especially vulnerable to greasy fingers and we'll have to emphasise that.

UNION: It's rather like the old 78 records.

MANAGEMENT: That dates you! [Everyone laughs] Again with safety it's only really repeating what they were told on the induction course.

UNION: Now I can't remember all that.

MANAGEMENT: You don't have to now. After the course, we provide our members with a safety checklist [the union representative is shown a copy – see Fig. 6.2].

---

1 Always use equipment as instructed.
2 Switch off machinery and remove plug when not in use.
3 Always use step stools or ladders to reach items positioned high up. Do not use swivel chairs.
4 Avoid trailing flexes. People fall over them.
5 Keep all gangways and corridors free from obstruction.
6 Do not lift heavy weights (such as typewriters) on your own. Obtain assistance.
7 Disinfect audio plugs regularly.
8 Do not smoke in the office wherever there is a risk of fire. If you do smoke, use ashtrays and not waste bins.
9 Do not remove guards from machinery.
10 Check machinery, electric flexes, cables and plugs regularly and maintain a faults book.
11 If there is a problem, seek advice. Do not meddle.
12 Store all flammable liquid in a safe place.
13 Do not leave filing cabinet drawers protruding into gangways and be careful how you load the drawers.
14 Know where your first-aid box is kept.
15 Know the safety procedures and fire drills.
16 Be conscious of safety at all times.

Fig. 6.2. Safety in the office

[The chairman then comes to the final item on the Agenda, Redundancies.]

UNION: We'd like to know what management plans are on these.

MANAGEMENT: As you're aware, the point of going electronic is to speed up the flow of information while reducing office costs. Inevitably this means fewer staff. As I've explained, many of the staff will be transferred to new posts following retraining, but after the retraining programme has been completed there will be surplus staff to our requirements. We would be entitled to make these staff redundant but in view of the good working relationship we have with the union, the firm will continue to employ them on the same conditions of service. Once, however, staff leave, they will not be replaced. That way we'll obtain the size of workforce we want through natural wastage rather than redundancies.

The Union agree to consider this proposition and as there is no Any Other Business the meeting concludes.

Examination questions

1. What responsibility does the Health and Safety at Work Act place upon employees?

(4 marks)

2. Explain the terms 'software' and 'hardware'.

(4 marks)

3. What is meant by open distance learning?

(4 marks)

4. State *two* advantages of a centralised office system.

(4 marks)

5. Who enforces the Data Protection Act?

(4 marks)

6. What steps can be taken to deal with a potentially unsafe environment under the Health and Safety at Work Act?

(20 marks)

7. What health hazards are currently being linked to the use of VDUs and what steps are suggested in order to overcome these hazards?

(20 marks)

8. Under the Data Protection Act, what protection is afforded to 'Data Subjects'?

(20 marks)

9. What do you understand by the term 'Open Plan Office'? Discuss the advantages and disadvantages of such offices.

(20 marks)

10. Describe the duties of *two* of the following:
    (a) private secretary
    (b) word processing supervisor
    (c) office manager

(20 marks)

11. You have just attended a short course on 'safety in the office'. Write a summary on what you learnt on the course.

(20 marks)

12. If a firm were moving from a traditional to an electronic office, what effect might it have on the jobs of
    (1) a private secretary
    (2) a copy typist
    (3) an audio typist

(20 marks)

Employing staff

Chapter 7

Employing the right staff is important for the employer who is in business to make a profit and therefore needs efficient staff. The employer will, of course, train them but this will be much easier if staff are initially selected with the appropriate skills and attitudes.

Engaging staff consists of recruitment, selection, and interviews.

Recruitment

This has a specific meaning and covers the first stages of employing staff. The employer must initially: (a) decide what is wanted; (b) attract suitable applicants.

(a) Deciding what the employer wants

What tasks will the employer want the new employee to perform? This question is best answered by producing a 'job description' which, as the name suggests, simply describes the job. The format of a job description varies but a typical one might state the title of the job and then describe the major objectives, followed by a more detailed list of the tasks and duties involved in the job. A few examples may help.

Example 1

JOB TITLE	Departmental Assistant to Head of Business Studies.
PURPOSE OF JOB	To assist Head in day-to-day running of departments.
DUTIES	To type all departmental correspondence.
	To take minutes at departmental meetings.
	To keep records of departmental expenditure.
	To deal with telephone enquiries.
	To keep departmental records, etc

Example 2

JOB TITLE   Receptionist – School of Chiropody.

PURPOSE OF JOB   To act as receptionist/clerical officer.

DUTIES   The receptionist will be responsible to the Chief Administrative Officer and Head of School.

Reception and booking arrangements within the School.

The issue of appointments to patients and dealing with relevant telephone and personal enquiries together with general assistance to patients.

Collection and receipt of fees for non-priority category patients.

Balancing of income and necessary payments to the Finance Office.

Maintenance of patients' records and files – Paramount and Rotadex systems are in operation.

Providing statistical information for internal and external bodies as required.

Input of simple data through a computer terminal.

Example 3

JOB TITLE   Clerk/Typist

Responsibilities and duties

Responsibility will be to the Typing Pool Supervisor.

Duties will include

1. A wide range of audio and copy-typing
2. The use of word-processing equipment
3. Clerical duties

Example 4

JOB TITLE   Junior Secretary

DUTIES

As Example 4 is similar to the type of job you may be applying for, try to complete the above yourself.

Once the job description has been completed, then the employer must decide on the personal attributes required of the new staff. I do not smoke; therefore, as I share an office with my secretary, I would require a non-smoker.

Once the employer has compiled the list, then he or she should draw up a chart listing the qualities required under two headings, 'Essential' and 'Desirable'.

Again let us consider some examples.

Example 5

JOB TITLE   Departmental Assistant

QUALITY	ESSENTIAL	DESIRABLE
Type	RSA 111 typing	RSA 11 audio
Keep minutes	80 wpm shorthand	
Skill with figures	Numerate	GCSE Maths
Telephone manner	Well spoken	
Keeping records	Organisational skill	Experience in secretarial capacity
	Non-smoker	
	Smart appearance	
	Good time keeper	
	Work without supervision	
	etc	

Example 6

JOB TITLE   Receptionist

QUALITY	ESSENTIAL	DESIRABLE
Reception	Smart and well spoken	
Booking arrangements	Efficient organiser	
Assisting patients	Sympathetic manner	
Collection of fees	Numerate	GCSE or above in Maths
Input of data	Ability to use a keyboard	RSA 1 typing
		Experience of computer
	etc	

Example 7

JOB TITLE   Junior Secretarial

QUALITY	ESSENTIAL	DESIRABLE

What qualities do you think your future employer will be looking for at your interview? Write them in on Example 7 and then ask yourself what you need to do to acquire them.

(b) Attracting suitable applicants

This means bringing the vacancy to the attention of suitably qualified people. They may already exist within your organisation waiting to be promoted. They can be notified through an internal newsletter or on staff notice boards.

Many appointments are, however, made from outside the company.

If a firm is seeking a junior secretary it may not advertise the post, preferring to use contacts in either the local College of Further Education or the Careers Service. The former is frequently used because, apart from being free, the college is likely to send along only suitable applicants, whereas anybody can reply to an advertisement.

Where the employer requires an experienced secretary, then the College or the Careers Service would be inappropriate and the Job Centre or a private agency might be used instead. The latter is very expensive.

The most common method of publicising a vacancy is, however, the newspaper advertisement, either in the local or national press. If we restrict our discussions to office staff, then a national advertisement is unnecessary as we would expect to attract sufficient suitably qualified applicants from our locality. In order to obtain a suitable response from the advertisement (i.e. getting people to apply) the employer must ensure that the advertisement's content is right and that it appears at the right time (i.e. when the prospective employee is likely to read the paper.)

A suitable advertisement should provide sufficient information to enable the reader to decide if they want to apply, e.g.

- details of company and location of job
- details of job
- qualifications required
- salary payable (this is often omitted, especially where it is low!)
- procedure for applying.

Once the advertisement is drafted, then the type of advertisement must be decided. Should it be classified or displayed? (See Fig. 7.1.)

Having made that decision the day or days of the week on which it will be inserted must be agreed. Friday evening seems to be a favoured time.

Selection

This covers the remaining stages in engaging staff. The application procedure specified in the advertisement may have included providing a curriculum vitae (c.v.) with a letter of application or the completion of an application form to be returned to the prospective employer. A short list of suitable candidates can then be prepared based on the information supplied. The curriculum vitae can be particularly important as it may provide additional information not covered by a letter of application or an application form. It might help to secure an inter-

CLASSIFIED

SOLICITORS require an Operator for a Word Processor. Training will be provided but previous experience an advantage. Applicants must have legal experience preferably in Conveyancing. 4 weeks annual holiday. Salary according to experience.–Apply in writing to . . .

JUNIOR Clerk Typist required for general office duties. Typing essential. 37½-hour week to include Saturday morning. Preferred resident in Plympton area.–Apply in writing only with details of age and qualifications to . . .

AUDIO Typist required for busy Plymouth Estate Agents. Must have experience with electric machines. Most demanding and responsible position.– Apply Box No. . . . .
. . . .

DARTINGTON. Secretary, salary to £5,600 p.a. There is a vacancy for a full time secretary to the Department of Art and Design at Dartington College of Arts. The work includes acting as secretary to the Head of Department and doing administrative and typing work for the rest of the department. – Letter of application with CV by 25th March to the Senior Administrative Officer, ...
. . . .

SECRETARY required for Powderham Estate Office, some experience, audio typing. Accommodation available. – Apply in writing with c.v., to . . . .
. . . .

WANTED Audio Secretary for Solicitors, North Hill area, conveyancing experience essential, salary £3,600, possible flexibility of hours. – Telephone Plymouth
. . . .

DISPLAY

SECRETARIAL APPOINTMENT

Local branch office of leading Life Assurance Company requires Shorthand Typist.

Pleasant working environment, five day week, luncheon vouchers, salary from £3,876, dependent upon age and qualifications. Position would ideally suit applicants in age range of 18 to 25 with proficient shorthand and typing abilities.

Please telephone or write to . . . .
. . . .
. . . .

COLLEGE OF
ST. MARK & ST. JOHN
PLYMOUTH
SECRETARY/
CLERICAL ASSISTANT

for a very busy office. Salary A.P.T. plus C. (£5,014, under review). Annual contract for the Mode A Youth Training Programme, capable of supporting a hard-working team. Good secretarial skills required. Letters to application and curriculum vitae to:

P.A./SECRETARY
to Company Secretary.

A vacancy exists for an agile minded accounts office experienced person of 21 years or more with abilities in shorthand and typing to assist the Company Director in his administrative and financial roles. Starting salary £4,250 p.a.
Applications in writing with full c.v. to:

Fig. 7.1

<table>
<tr><td>

**VIDEO PA/
SECRETARY**

Longman Video's small marketing team need PA with plenty of initiative and flexibility. Good secretarial and organisational skills to handle customer relations involvement in marketing activity and sales admin systems. Salary range £5,500 – £6,700 plus £1 per day L.V's.
Tel: ....
....

</td><td>

**SECRETARY P.A.
c£7,000**

For the senior partner of a small firm of Computer Consultants with responsibility for personnel and some administration. Speeds 90/50wpm, willingness to learn W.P. Ability to organise essential – scope for great involvement in an expanding company:
For further details please contact:

</td></tr>
</table>

Fig. 7.1 (*continued*)

view. (Two c.v.s produced by SSC students can be found in Figs 7.2 and 7.3.)

The application forms and c.v.s are then assessed and compared against the essential and desirable characteristics chart. Anybody lacking the former will not be short-listed; assuming there is still a choice, the best three to six will be short-listed and invited for interview.

The final selection can be by interview or by interview and test. For a secretarial position the test might consist of a dictation exercise with a typed transcript. With most posts the interviewer will, however, accept external exmination certificates as proof of competence and so the job selection depends on the interview.

Interview

The student about to apply for a first post needs to know something about the interview process because this knowledge may help to avoid some of the pitfalls and give an advantage over the other applicants.

No matter how competent you are, you will not obtain employment unless you impress at an interview. Your interview performance must improve if you know what the interviewer is looking for, as this helps you give the right answers!

What therefore does the interviewer look for? The interviewer begins by checking the information on your application and then seeks to assess your suitability for the post, by asking questions. When asking these the interviewer should follow certain rules; these include:

1. Don't ask questions that can be answered YES/NO. This type of question will not provide much information about the candidate.
2. Don't lead the candidate by 'suggesting' the appropriate answer in the question. (What would be your answer to the question, 'I believe in punctuality, don't you?')

Curriculum vitae

SURNAME   Cooper

FORENAME(S)   Sheila

ADDRESS   Southway, Plymouth, Devon

DATE OF BIRTH   23 March 1970   AGE: 17

STATUS   Single

SCHOOLS   Plymstock Comprehensive (1981–82)
                    Crownhill Secondary Modern (1982–86)
                    College of Further Education (1986–87)

EDUCATIONAL QUALIFICATIONS   **GCSE**
                    English Language   Grade B
                    English Literature   Grade C
                    Biology   Grade D
                    History   Grade E
                    Mathematics   Grade G
                    French   Grade G

VOCATIONAL QUALIFICATIONS EXPECTED
                    Shorthand   LCC 70/80
                    Typing   RSA II, III
                                                LCC Intermediate
                                                LCC Higher

                                                LCC Certificate in
                                                Secretarial studies
                    English Language   RSA II
                    Audio Typing   RSA II
                    Oral Communications   ESB (Elementary)

HOBBIES AND INTERESTS

Disco dancing, reading, swimming, going to discos, travelling, jogging, listening to
records and learning to drive, meeting people and walking.

REFEREES

Mr A. R. Leal   Ms. B. Jones
Head of Business Studies   56 Rushfield
College of Further Education   Sawbridgeworth
Paradise Road   Herts
Devonport

Fig. 7.2. Example of a c.v.

Curriculum vitae

SURNAME	Holt
FORENAME(S)	Jennifer
ADDRESS	Southway, Plymouth, Devon
DATE OF BIRTH	9 February 1970 AGE: 17
STATUS	Single
SCHOOLS	Plympton Secondary (1981–85)
	College of Further Education (1985–86)

EDUCATIONAL QUALIFICATIONS   **GCSE**

English Language	Grade B
English Language	Grade D
English Literature	Grade E
Geography	Grade D
Rural Science	Grade D
History	Grade D

VOCATIONAL QUALIFICATIONS

Typewriting	Grade E

VOCATIONAL QUALIFICATIONS EXPECTED

Shorthand	LCC 90/100
	LCC 70/80
	RSA 80
Typewriting	RSA II
	LCC Intermediate
	LCC Higher
	LCC Certificate in
	Secretarial Studies
English Language	RSA I
Audio Typing	RSA II
Oral Communications	ESB (Elementary)

HOBBIES AND INTERESTS

Gliding, swimming, badminton, roller skating, music, playing the guitar.

PREVIOUS EXPERIENCE

Working in secretary's office at a Primary School.

REFEREES

Mr A. R. Leal	Miss A. Smith
Head of Business Studies	Dene House
College of Further Education	Lower Road
Paradise Road	Lichfield
DEVONPORT	Staffs.

Fig. 7.3. Example of a c.v.

3. Do ask follow-up questions. This means that answers should be probed. The interviewer might ask, 'What sort of experience have you had?' The reply might be, 'As a secretary to an estate agent.' This does not provide much information to the interviewer so she must probe further by asking, 'What did your duties involve as secretary?'

As the person being interviewed, what rules should you follow? First, remember you are trying to show the employer you possess the qualities being looked for. You should know what these are (you listed them for a junior secretarial post in Example 7). At the interview, you must 'get these qualities across'.

Many of the personal qualities can be illustrated before the interview. Turn up early, dress smartly and don't chew gum! At the actual interview it is up to you to prove you are right for the job. A good interviewer will help by asking the right questions but the onus is always on you to present your case. Suppose an interviewer asked, 'Do you want this job?' Admittedly it is a poor question because you can answer Yes. Don't! Use the answer to give the interviewer information you feel will help your case. You might reply, 'Yes because I know this is a good company to work for. I discussed it with my Course Tutor at College. . . .' Your answer now tells the interviewer you have thought about the job. A plus for you.

You may have taken part in the Duke of Edinburgh scheme. Try to get this information across because it will impress. The interviewer may ask you if you have a Saturday job. You might not have worked on Saturday. Rather than simply tell her that, you can continue by pointing out that your weekends were involved doing the scheme. You have again scored a plus.

To summarise. A good interviewee works out what the interviewer will be looking for and decides what information to give and at the interview tries to pass on as much of this information as possible.*

At the end of the interview the candidate leaves and the interviewer should make written notes about the performance. This should be done before the next candidate arrives. At the end of the interviews, these notes will help ensure that the best candidate is appointed.

References are usually obtained before the interview but must be treated with scepticism. They are often only another person's view of the candidate and may therefore be biased; a reference should be a guide to the interviewer and should not be the sole criteria for selection.

*More information on interviews is included on the cassette tape which supplements this book.

Examination questions

1. The director in charge of finance has appointed a junior secretary to help his Personal Assistant. Describe the stages in the recruitment selection process.

   (Q. 2 1985)

2. What steps should a candidate take before attending an interview? Why are they necessary?

   (Q. 4 1986)

3. What is a 'curriculum vitae'?

   (Q. 1(a) 1986)

4. When recruiting staff what is meant by the term 'short list'?

   (Q. 1(e) 1984)

Sources of consumer finance
Chapter 8

On your first day at work you will normally attend an induction course. During it you are informed that the firm will arrange for your wages to be paid directly into your bank account. This is advantageous for the firm because:

1. *It is secure:* the transactions are made by a computer which transfers money from the firm's account into yours. This removes the need to transfer large sums of money from the bank to the firm, and hence avoids the necessity of hiring a security firm to transfer it.
2. *It is cheaper:* Apart from the 'security' aspect savings are also made in staffing. The firm no longer has to employ staff to make up wage packets, i.e. put the correct amount of cash into each packet.
3. *The firm's cash remains in the bank longer:* Money can earn interest in a bank. If the firm has to make up wage packets then it must withdraw money on Wednesday if it is to have wage packets ready on Friday. Paying directly into your account means the money is transferred out of the firm's account on Friday; the firm obtains two more days' interest each time wages are paid. In a large firm with a substantial wage bill the interest earned can be considerable.

Imagine that to explain the advantages to the staff the firm have invited the local bank manager to answer questions.

Q. *If my wages are paid directly into my account how do I get cash?*
A. The money is paid into what we call a **current account.** Once this is opened you are given a cheque book. If you want to draw out money you write out a cheque, bring it into the bank and my staff will give you cash for it.
Q. *But I work Monday to Friday and can't get into a bank.*
A. Don't worry, we've thought of that. You will also be issued with a cash card [an example is shown in Fig. 8.1]; this enables you to draw cash from a point outside the bank (called a 'cash dispenser') at any time, including evenings and weekends. All you do is put in

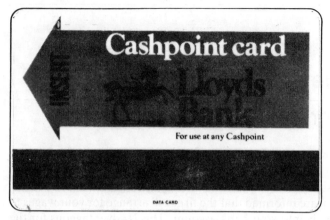

Fig. 8.1

the card, key in your personal code number (which only you know) and the amount you want and the cash will be delivered to you. I don't recommend you carry large sums of cash because of the spate of bag snatching. Just use your cheque book to buy things, only use cash for small items like bus fares.

Q. *Won't some businesses refuse to accept cheques?*

A. This used to be a problem because shops couldn't be sure that you had enough money in your account to cover the cheque. We've solved that by issuing our customers with a **cheque card** [see Fig. 8.2]. This guarantees payment of any cheque you write providing it

Fig. 8.2

is for less than £50. The bank will honour (that is pay) the cheque even if you have no funds in your account; you will, of course, have to repay the bank and if you keep over-drawing your account we may withdraw the card.

Q. *This sounds all very well but what's it going to cost me?*

A. That's a good question. It does cost the bank a lot of money to handle cheques but unless you go into the red, in other words need an overdraft, we will provide all services free.

Q. *That seems very reasonable.*

A. It is, because apart from cheque books there are other services that are available to you. I mentioned earlier that you could pay your bills by cheque. The bank has a system called a '**standing order**' which enables us to pay regular bills for you without you having to remind us. If you have an annual subscription to a club or a monthly payment for rates, rent, mortgage etc. all you have to do is to inform the bank when the payments are due and how much. We will automatically transfer the amount from your account to the other party. You don't have to do anything.

Q. *Won't I have to tell you if the amount changes?*

A. Yes. This is why we recommend standing orders for regular payments of fixed sums. If you pay different sums at fixed intervals then I suggest you use a **direct debit.** This enables the people to whom you owe money to contact the bank and tell us how much you owe them. The bank will then automatically transfer this sum from your account to theirs.

Q. *How do I know you're not paying them too much?*

A. Occasionally, monthly if you like, the bank will send you a bank statement [see Fig. 8.3] which lists all the transactions on your account. You can check all the transactions (both in and out) and if you're not satisfied just come into the bank and we will check them for you.

Q. *Can I pay several bills with one cheque?*

A. Yes. You use a **credit transfer.** One cheque is written for the whole amount with instructions as to its division among your various creditors. The bank will then arrange for them to be paid.

Q. *That seems good value. If I actually have money in my account do I get interest?*

A. We're looking into that and it may be possible in the future but at present we do not pay interest on current accounts. What I suggest is that you open a **deposit account.** We will pay you interest on this but you can't write cheques on it. If you want to withdraw money from this account we will require notice although if it's for small sums we will waive the notice. What we can do is to transfer

| | | ACCOUNT NUMBER | | In account with | SHEET 5 |
| | | ACCOUNT HOLDERS NAME | | **National Westminster Bank PLC** | |

1983   PLYMSTOCK BRANCH

Date	Details		Debits	Credits	Balance
14APR	Balance Forward				100.00
15APR		000061	106.20		
	.REV AUTO TRF		74.59		
	AUTOMATIC TRANSFER TR			180.79	100.00
18APR	.REV AUTO TF		180.79		80.79 %
21APR	MBIS INSURANCE PRM DD		2.50		83.29 %
25APR	D.C.C. SALARIES	–		1,250.38	1,167.09
26APR		000065	5.90		
	STANDARD LIFE A CO DD		35.10		1,126.09
27APR		000063	121.13		
		000069	35.00		
	CASH/CHEQUES			97.50	1,067.46
28APR		000066	20.00		
		000067	12.23		
		000071	267.00		768.23
29APR	.CASH/CHEQUES			124.07	892.30
3MAY		000072	17.65		
	HALIFAX B/S	50	149.24		
	PLYMOUTH CITY CNCL SO		52.26		673.15
4MAY		000068	18.24		
		000070	3.70		651.21
6MAY		000064	3.00		
		000073	15.00		
	CASH/CHEQUES			5.00	638.21
9MAY		000075	15.00		623.21
13MAY	LONGMAN ROYALTIES	–		996.71	1,619.92
16MAY		000077	17.85		1,602.07
18MAY		000074	13.47		
		000076	9.92		1,578.68
23MAY	MBIS INSURANCE PRM DD		2.50		1,576.18
24MAY	NORWICH UNION LIFE DD		21.25		1,554.93

Abbreviations CD Cash Dispensed DV Dividend TR Transfer O D indicates an
DD Direct Debit SO Standing Order Overdrawn Balance

Fig. 8.3

automatically part of your salary into the deposit account each month. As a bonus if your current account ever gets into the red we can arrange for an automatic transfer from your deposit account. This way you'll never pay bank charges.

Q. *We've just been told by personnel that we get paid at the end of each month. How am I to live until I receive my first month's salary?*

A. The bank appreciates that you may have cash problems when you start work so we'll give you **overdraft** facilities.

Q. *What's that?*

A. Basically it means we will let you write cheques up to a certain amount on your current account when it has no money in it. We will, of course, have to charge interest on the sum overdrawn and you will have to repay it over a certain period.

Q. *I'm not sure I understand. Could you give me an example?*

A. Certainly. Suppose your account has £100 in it. You want to buy items which will cost £200. We will let you have overdraft facilities of £100. Now you can write out a cheque for £200. You owe us £100 which you must pay back in £10 monthly instalments of £10. You pay interest on £100 for the first month, on £90 for the second, on £80 for the third and so on.

There are no more questions and the talk ends.

Budget accounts

As you are starting work you decide the clothes you wore at college are no longer suitable. You need smarter ones. You could use your overdraft facility but you will have to pay interest. Instead you decide to buy your clothes at a local store where they advertise 'budget accounts'.

When you enter the store you visit the Accounts department who explain how the system works. You agree to pay a fixed monthly sum regardless of purchases. Once you have paid the first sum this means that you can automatically spend 24 times this amount. Thus if you agree to pay £10 you can automatically purchase £240 worth of clothes. If you spend £240 this means your credit is exhausted but it will rise by £10 each month (the sum you pay) minus, of course, any other purchases you make. (See Table 8.1.)

Table 8.1

Month	Payment	Purchases	Outstanding credit
1	10	220	20
2	10	—	30
3	10	—	40
4	10	—	50
5	10	—	60
6	10	—	*
7	10	—	*
8	10	30	*

*fill in the blank figures

After several years at work you get married and decide to purchase a house. Both banks and building societies give loans (mortgages) to purchase property, and the rate of interest they charge is very similar (unlike a few years ago when building societies were cheaper). As your partner has had a savings account with a building society for many years, you decide to apply to them for a mortgage.

Building societies

In 1987 the Building Societies Act was passed which allowed building societies to expand their business activities. It is now legally possible for them to become estate agents, insurance brokers and mini banks, but at the current time their main role is to lend money for one main purpose: the purchase of property or its improvement. That operation falls into two parts.

1. Raising money

Individuals or institutions (such as pension funds) have surplus cash on which they want to earn interest. They can safely invest it in various ways, e.g.:

- Deposit accounts at banks
- Gilt-edge securities
- Building society accounts

The choice of investment is primarily determined by the rate of interest. You will invest your funds where they will obtain the highest return (providing the risk is acceptable). The banks and building societies (and to a lesser extent the government) are in competition for your money and each seeks to persuade you that they offer the best terms.

This competition for funds naturally benefits the investor and has led to a wide range of schemes being offered. The building societies offer an account which combines the advantages of both the current and deposit accounts of the bank. You can write cheques on it; money can be withdrawn immediately (unless the sum is very large, then a short period of notice is required) and it gains interest though at the lowest of the rates offered by the society. Additionally the societies have sought to make their facilities more attractive by opening on Saturdays and issuing cash cards.

You will recall that not all these facilities are available to holders of deposit accounts at banks, nor do all banks open on Saturday. However, some banks have retaliated. At least one is experimenting with Saturday morning opening, and some are considering paying interest on current accounts. This whole area is changing rapidly and students are advised to watch for developments; an easy way of doing this is to watch television adverts, as both banks and building societies use this medium to advise the public of their services.

The building societies have also tried to attract funds by offering additional interest to investors who are prepared to leave their cash in the societies for a minimum period (this competes with the government's national savings scheme). The schemes offered by all the societies are so numerous (and often complicated) that one society simplified its schemes and promoted them with the slogan 'find your way through the money maze by . . .'. As with the above this is an area of rapid change and students are advised to visit a couple of their local societies to gather leaflets on the schemes available. You will then be capable of answering topical questions.

You will probably find that the accounts offered to investors fall into three main categories.

(a) *Paid-up share accounts* (this is their equivalent of the deposit accounts). The rate of interest at the time of writing is 5¼ per cent.
(b) *A regular investment account.* A higher rate of interest is offered if you agree to deposit a fixed sum each month for a set period. The societies like this type of account because once you have committed yourself you cannot withdraw the funds if you discover there is a better rate of interest available elsewhere. The interest rate at the time of writing is 7 per cent.
(c) If you invest a lump sum (there is usually a minimum figure) and agree to leave it in the society for a fixed period this also achieves a high rate of interest. If you withdraw it before the agreed time you usually lose part of the interest. The rate of interest at the time of writing is 7¼ per cent.

You have probably realised that when building societies fix the interest rates payable to investors they must take into account the interest available at, for example, banks. If building societies' rates are lower than those operating elsewhere, then fewer people will invest with them. Conversely, as we will see in a moment, the interest rates payable by borrowers are determined by the rates paid to investors. It follows that the lower the rates paid to investors the lower the rates borrowers will have to pay. The societies therefore attempt to set rates at which the money investors pay in equals the amount customers want to borrow.

Example
Rate to investors 10 per cent: amount invested £100 m.
Rate to borrowers 13 per cent: amount borrowed £140 m.
   The building societies cannot satisfy all potential borrowers, they are £40 m. short.
Therefore:
Rate to investors 10½ per cent: amount invested £120 m.
Rate to borrowers 13½ per cent: amount borrowed £120 m.

The additional ½ per cent paid to investors has increased the inflow of funds (investors now find it more profitable at building societies) while the additional ½ per cent has discouraged a number of potential borrowers. If, therefore, the inflow of funds falls in any month (and this figure is reported in the press) there could be a 'mortgage famine' or 'mortgage queue'. If you see this type of headline in a newspaper it could mean a rise in mortgage rates to enable a higher rate to be paid to investors.

All interest rates may rise or fall as a result of government policy for reasons which are explained elsewhere.

2. Lending money

When building societies lend money to enable the purchase of property they are said to be granting a **mortgage.** A prospective borrower (who is called the mortgagor on receiving the loan) will approach a building society with a request for a mortgage. If the society has sufficient funds it will ask the borrower to fill in a mortgage application form (Fig. 8.4). (If there is a shortage of funds a building society will 'ration' mortgages and probably give priority to its own investors; this is a good reason for saving with a society.)

The amount of the mortgage depends on two factors. The first is the income of the applicant (and if married, the spouse). The society has a responsibility to its investors (whose money they are lending) to lend sensibly and it must therefore try to ensure mortgagors have sufficient income to be able to repay the loan. For this reason societies usually only lend 2½ to 3 times the income of the applicant.

Example
Income £10,000: max loan £25,000–£30,000
Income £15,000: max loan £37,500–£45,000.

The second factor is the value of the property. As stated above, the society is responsible for safeguarding investors' funds and so it must guard against the possibility that the mortgagor will not be able to repay the loan (i.e. **default**). This might arise because of redundancy or possibly death. The mortgage is therefore 'secured' on the property. In the event of default the society can sell the house, recoup the amount of the mortgage and hand over any surplus from the sale to the mortgagor. Obviously, then, the society will not lend more than the value of the house. In determining a house's value a society will take a pessimistic view; it is valued at the lowest price a society could get assuming there was a slump in the housing market. Thus you might buy

CONFIDENTIAL

FULL NAME (PLEASE USE BLOCK CAPITALS)

Title   Surname

Forenames

Married or Single _____   Date of Birth _____

Number of dependent children _____   Their ages _____

PRESENT RESIDENCE

Address

Town

County   Post Code

If this is rented accommodation please give details of the rent paid per week. £ _____

If the property is mortgaged please give the account or roll number. _____

Please give the name and address of your Landlord or Mortgagee (Lender).

If you are not a Tenant or Mortgagor please give details.

If your present residence is not in mortgage have you or your spouse had a mortgage on any property during the last

five years? _____ If so please give details. _____

INVESTMENTS

If you have any investments with the Society please give the account numbers.

BANKRUPTCY

Have you ever been bankrupt or entered into any arrangement with creditors or is there any judgement for debt

outstanding? _____

If so please give details. _____

Form 1 50005 6 (10 82)   Please turn over

Fig. 8.4

EMPLOYMENT - EMPLOYEE

If you are an employee please give the name and address of your employer.

_____

_____

_____

Your present position there. _____

Annual income:-

      Basic earnings. £ _____

      Overtime. £ _____

      Bonus. £ _____

      Commission. £ _____

      Total. £ _____

How long have you been in your present employment? _____

The Society will normally require confirmation of the above details from your employer. Please therefore state:-

The Department to which reference should be made (if applicable). _____

The Name and position of the person to whom reference should be made (if known).

_____

Your Works or Staff Number (if applicable). _____

Please state the amount of any additional income apart from that shown above £ _____ per year.

From what source is it derived? _____

EMPLOYMENT - SELF EMPLOYED

If you are self employed please state the nature of your business.

_____

Name and address of your business. _____

_____

Name and address of your accountants _____

_____

How long has the business been established? _____

Your **annual** income derived from it. £ _____

Please supply copies of audited accounts for the last three years or failing these, income tax assessments for the same period.

Please state the amount of any additional income apart from that shown above £ _____ per year.

From what source is it derived? _____

Please state the name and address of your bank. _____

_____ Account No. L__I__I__I__I__I__I__I

AUTHORITY

I authorise the Society to refer to my Accountants/Employer/Landlord/Mortgagee/Bankers if necessary.

I agree to the information on this form being supplied to the Insurance Company/Local Authority if at my request the Society makes application for a guarantee with this loan.

Signed _____ Date _____

Fig. 8.4 (*continued*)

APPLICATION FOR LOAN

Please give the information in the spaces provided or tick the appropriate box.
Please use BLOCK CAPITALS.

A   THE APPLICANTS

	(Forenames)	(Surname)
010		
011		
012		
013		

Note: The names written here must be identical with the names of the purchaser(s) of the property, e.g. if the property is held or is to be held in the joint names of husband and wife, both names should be given.

B   THE PROPERTY

Full Postal Address of the Property.

100		
101		
102	Town	
103	County	Post Code

1   DESCRIPTION

Tick the kind of property. ▶

104	House	Bungalow	Converted Flat or Maisonette	Purpose Built Flat or Maisonette	Other
	0	1	2	3	4

If OTHER please give details.

Is the Property ▶

105	Semi-Detached	Detached	Terraced	Other
	0	1	2	3

If a FLAT or MAISONETTE
How many storeys are there in the block? ▶

106	

Are there any business premises in the block? ▶

107	Yes	No
	1	0

If YES please give details.

If the flat is subject to an annual service charge, please show the current amount payable. ▶ £

2   GARAGE

Is a garage included? ▶

Yes	No

Fig. 8.4 (*continued*)

2

3   AREA OF LAND

Is a garden included? ► **108**

	Yes	No
108	0	1

If there is more than one acre of land, please state how much land. ► **109**

| 109 | | Acres |

4   NEW PROPERTY

If the property is new please give the name and address of the builder.

_____

_____

Is the builder registered with the National House Builders' Council? ► **110**

	Yes	No
110	1	0

5   ROAD CHARGES

Have the roads adjoining the property been taken over by the appropriate Authorities? ►

Yes	No

Have the sewers used by the property been taken over by the appropriate Authorities? ►

Yes	No

6   TENURE

Indicate the tenure of the property. ► **115**

	Freehold	Leasehold	Feudal
115	0	1	2

If FREEHOLD please state amount of any Chief Rent or if FEUDAL amount of any Feu Duty. **116** £

If LEASEHOLD please state the term of years. ► **117** years

The term of years starts from (state year only). ► **118**

Amount of the Ground Rent. ► **119** £

Can the Ground Rent be increased? ► **120**

	Yes	No
120	1	0

If YES please state how often and give the amount.

_____

7   OWNERSHIP

Do you already own the property? ► **125**

	Yes	No
125	1	0

If you have a mortgage on the property, please state the present debt, the name of the mortgagee (lender) and the reason for wishing to repay that mortgage.

_____

Do you intend to purchase the property under a shared ownership scheme or do you already own the property under such a scheme? ► **126**

	Yes	No
126	1	0

8   VENDOR

Please indicate if you are buying from one of the following:- ► **128**

	Local Authority	New Town Corporation	Housing Association	National Coal Board
128	1	2	3	4

Fig. 8.4 (*continued*)

3

9 OCCUPATION OF THE PROPERTY

Do you occupy the property now? · · · · · · · · · · · ▶

	Yes		No	
130	1		0	

Will you be given full vacant possession of all the property on completion of your purchase? · ▶

Yes	No

Will you occupy the property as soon as you complete your purchase? · · · · · · ▶

Yes	No

How much of the property will you occupy? · · · · · · ▶

	Whole		Part		None	
131	0		1		2	

Will any persons who are aged seventeen or more but will not be
parties to the mortgage live at the property with you? · · · · · · · · · · ▶

Yes	No

If YES please give their full names (and present address if different from your address). They will have to allow the Society's mortgage to come before their interest in the property.

_____
_____
_____
_____

10 INSPECTION BY THE VALUER

If the property is now occupied please give the name and telephone number of the occupier.

_____
_____

If the property is unoccupied where can the key be obtained? _____

_____

11 ESTATE AGENTS

Name and address of estate agents (if any) through whom you are purchasing.

_____
_____

12 PURCHASE PRICE

Amount of Purchase Price. · · · · · · · · · · · · · ▶		£	
Where any carpets, curtains etc. worth more than £2,000 are included, state their value. · · ▶		£	
Net Price (after deducting the above stated value of carpets, etc.). · · · · · · ▶	135	£	
Add cost of any improvements or alterations you intend to make. · · · · · · ▶	136	£	
	Total	£	

13 LOCAL AUTHORITY GRANT

If you are obtaining a grant from the Local Authority please state how much. · · ▶

137	£	

Fig. 8.4 (*continued*)

C THE LOAN 4

Please state the amount of loan you require . . . . ► | 200 | £ |

Period of Repayment you prefer. . . . . ► | 201 | | years |

	Yes	No

If the property is being built will part of the loan be needed during building? . . . . . ►

	Yes	No

Do you intend to apply for assistance under the Home Purchase Assistance Scheme? . . ►

	Yes		No	

Do you require an Option Mortgage? . . . . ► | 203 | 1 | | 0 |

If YES please state countries of residence during the last 5 years if outside the United Kingdom.

	Yes	No

Are you finding out of your own money the full difference between the amount of the loan
and the total cost of the property? . . . . ►

If NO state who is providing the balance of the money and the amount.

1 METHOD OF REPAYMENT

The loan may be repaid by a monthly standing order from an investment
account with the Society, a monthly standing order from your bank
account, or payment at any of the Society's branches.

Please indicate your preference. . . . . ►

	HBS Standing Order	Bank Standing Order	Payment at Branch
204	1	0	2

2 LIFE ASSURANCE

The Society recommends that to protect your dependants, you should arrange life assurance to cover
the loan. The Society can arrange life assurance and advise you about different kinds of policies.

Alternatively would you prefer a representative from an insurance company to call to see you? ►

	Yes	No

	ENDOWMENT		MORTGAGE PROTECTION	
	Full	Low Cost	Convertible Term Assurance	Decreasing Term Assurance
Kind of life assurance required (if known) . . . . ►				

Do you already have an endowment policy or policies which you wish to use. . . . . . ►

	Yes	No

If YES please give details of the policies.

Policy Number	Company Name	Sum Assured

D CORRESPONDENCE ADDRESS

Please give the address to which letters may be sent before completion of the purchase.

501	
502	
503	Town
504	County Post Code

If you can be contacted by telephone please state the number.

Fig. 8.4 (*continued*)

5

E PROPERTY INSURANCE

The Society's Valuer will estimate the sum needed to rebuild the property in the same form if it is destroyed. The property will be insured for this amount. To allow for rising costs the insurance value will be adjusted monthly in line with the 'House Rebuilding Cost Index' which is prepared by the Royal Institution of Chartered Surveyors or some similar index. The premium will be amended yearly and it is likely to increase each year.

PURCHASERS OF PROPERTY ARE NORMALLY LIABLE FOR ALL RISKS FROM THE DATE OF THE EXCHANGE OF CONTRACTS TO PURCHASE

In the case of a private dwelling the Society will arrange a houseowner's insurance on the property when the cheque for the loan is sent unless insurance cover has been requested from an earlier date. Special arrangements will be made for other types of property where houseowner's insurance is not available. Your account will be charged with the premiums.

If you would like other insurance arrangements to be considered please give details_____

Of what materials are the walls and roof made? _____

If any business is to be carried out at the property please give details. _____

F SOLICITORS

Please give the name and address of your Solicitors.

Name or reference of the person dealing with your
purchase. . . . . ➤ | 706 |

G DECLARATION

I apply for a loan on the security of the property described in this application and declare that I am over 18 and believe that the information given in this application is correct. I accept that

1) the payment of the valuation fee shall not bind the Society to grant an advance,
2) the Society does not warrant that the purchase price of the property is reasonable,
3) the valuation obtained by the Society is solely for its own use in deciding how much to lend, and
4) the Valuer will make a limited inspection of the property which will not be as extensive as a survey.

The Society will provide you with a copy of its report and valuation but YOU ARE RECOMMENDED TO ARRANGE A MORE DETAILED INSPECTION FOR YOUR OWN PROTECTION. The Society's Valuer may be willing to do this for you for an extra fee.

Would you like to have a House Buyers Inspection Report? THIS WILL BE SUBJECT TO STANDARD PUBLISHED CONDITIONS OR TERMS OF ENGAGEMENT WHICH ARE AVAILABLE ON REQUEST. ➤ | Yes | No |

Would you like to have a separate survey by the Society's Valuer? . . . . ➤ | Yes | No |

Applicant's usual signature _____ Age _____

" " " _____ " _____

" " " _____ " _____

" " " _____ " _____

Date _____

Fig. 8.4 *(continued)*

6

For Society use only:

Valuation Fee Paid. . . . . ► £

Administration and Indemnity Fee Paid. . . . . ► £

Date Valuation Fee Paid. . . . . ►

Source of Introduction. _____

Branch	Agency
BRANCH RECOMMENDATION	AGENT'S RECOMMENDATION
Signature of Interviewer Date	
Recommended by: Date Signature Designation	Signature Date

Form 1/50004-8 (12/82)

Fig. 8.4 (*continued*)

a new house for £30,000 but find that a society values it at only £28,000. The valuation is made by a surveyor employed by the society but the prospective borrower must pay the surveyor's fee!

After the house has been valued the society will, if satisfied, offer you a mortgage. This will be for a period of up to 25 years (although sometimes it will be longer) and you will repay it monthly. Normally you would use a standing order on your current account. The value of the standing order may need to be changed periodically because if interest rates alter, the amount of your monthly repayments will also change.

You have accepted the mortgage offer. All that remains is to finalise the purchase of the house. Your solicitor will ensure that all the legal formalities are complied with; the final step is to hand over the purchase price in return for the deeds of the property (these prove you are the legal owner). At this point you have a problem! The sellers of the house will not hand over the deeds if you give them a cheque because it takes several days for a cheque to clear. If they give you the deeds and the bank refuses to honour your cheque (because there are insufficient funds in your account) the house sellers have a problem. The building society will not, however, hand over the mortgage money until they receive the deeds because this is their **collateral** for the mortgage. The problem could be solved if you paid cash but this is risky because of the possibility of theft. A much more sensible approach would be to use a '**bank draft**'. This is a cheque which is drawn on the bank. The house purchaser may be paying £3,000 with the building society paying £24,000. The purchaser gives the bank a cheque for £3,000; they debit his/her account and give him/her a bank draft for £3,000. This states that the bank will pay the seller (the name would be on the draft) £3,000. The latter knows the bank has the money to honour the cheque so it will be accepted; the draft is as good as cash but, as it can only be cashed by the person named, it is secure. The drafts from the purchaser and building society are handed over and the deeds are given to the building society.

The transaction can now take place and you will become a house owner.

Credit finance

Very soon you will want to purchase items for your house. Some of these (television, washing machine, refrigerator) are expensive. You can wait until you have saved enough money before purchasing them but you may consider buying them on credit.

One method of obtaining credit is to approach your bank manager for a **loan.** This is different from an overdraft in that you borrow a fixed sum of money to spend on a specified item or items (with an overdraft you can spend it how you like). You will have to persuade your bank manager that the expenditure is 'sensible' and prove that you can repay the loan. To cover the possibility of you defaulting (being unable to pay) he will probably ask you to provide either collateral (security) or a guarantor for the loan. If you default then the collateral will be sold or the guarantor will have to repay the sum borrowed on your behalf. As with an overdraft you have to pay interest until the loan is repaid.

An alternative is to purchase the goods on **hire purchase.** The item is purchased from the retailer but instead of paying the full purchase price you only pay a deposit (perhaps 10 per cent of the price). The remainder (90 per cent) plus interest is paid off in monthly instalments over a fixed period. Once the last instalment has been paid, the goods become your property; if you fail to pay any instalments the retailer can ask the court for permission to repossess the goods. This may be granted or the court may give you time to pay off the arrears.

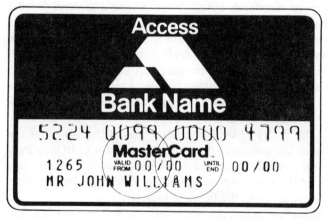

Fig. 8.5

If you have the cash to pay for the items you might decide to purchase them using a **credit card** (see Fig. 8.5) rather than paying by cheque. You hand your card to the retailer who records details of the card and the transaction and then issues you with a receipt. The retailer sends the bill to your credit card company who pay it (less their handling charge) and then send you a statement itemising your purchases at the end of each month. You check this with the receipts. Providing you pay within 21 days there is no interest payable. Why choose this method of purchasing items? You will recall that your employer benefited by paying wages directly into your current account because his money earned interest for a couple of extra days. You can do the same. By using the credit card you can delay paying for purchases for perhaps six weeks. During this period the money can be in your deposit account earning interest. If, however, you fail to pay all the outstanding bill within the 21 day period you will pay interest and this is considerably higher than the interest rates on most loans or hire-purchase transactions.

You have now set up home. Suddenly you find you have financial problems when a number of bills arrive and you discover you had not budgeted for them. The sum in your current account is insufficient to pay for them. You visit your local bank manager who agrees to an overdraft but suggests that you ought to make plans to avoid this problem in future. A **budget account** is suggested. This will help you pay bills that are regular but vary in amount such as gas and electricity. The bank will calculate your yearly expenditure on such bills and divide this figure by 12 (e.g. £240÷12=£20). The resulting figure (in our example £20) is transferred every month from the current account to the budget account so that when the bills arrive there are sufficient funds to meet them. If there is not there are automatic overdraft facilities. There are numerous miscellaneous banking services open to the individual. Find out what these are when you visit the bank to check on interest rates.

Examination questions

1. In one particular month a young couple found themselves in financial difficulties due to gas, electric and telephone bills coinciding with a repair on the car, renewal of the road fund tax, annual subscription to the RAC, and TV licence. The bank manager, have assured himself that their joint income was sufficient to meet their outgoings, advised them of two services which the bank offered which would help them to avoid this problem in the future.
   Describe the **two** most appropriate banking services to help this couple.
   (Q. 2 1977)

2. What is the essential difference between hire-purchase and a bank loan?
   (Q. 1(g) 1976)

3. A relative who is purchasing a car cannot decide between hire-purchase, a bank loan or a bank overdraft as the means of financing this acquisition. Explain each option to him giving guidance as to the advantges and disadvantages of each method of finance.
   (Q. 7 1975)

4. Explain simply what the term 'collateral' means in banking.
   (Q. 1(i) 1978)

5. *Selecting* **three** of the following pairs, explain their difference in meaning:
   (i) commercial banks and merchant banks;
   (ii) loans and overdrafts;
   (iii) standing orders and credit transfers;
   (iv) deposit accounts and current accounts.
   (Q. 5 1978)

6. A friend is able to save a pound or two each week from her wages and tells you that she is saving for another 18 months when she is due to get married. She has already saved £190 which she keeps at home in a drawer. Give her advice on **three** alternative ways she can save in a more productive and secure manner.
   (Q. 8 1978)

7. Outline the main services offered by the commercial banks and explain briefly features of their operation which distinguish them from other forms of commercial enterprise.
   (Q. 11 1974)

8. Imagine you are about to purchase your first house. You pay a visit to a building society or a bank to discuss the possibility of obtaining a mortgage. What are the likely questions the manager will want answered before granting your request?
   (Q. 2 1976)

9. How does a building society function? Why does a change in commercial bank interest rates affect a building society's deposit rate, and the interest rate charged on mortgages?
   (Q. 4 1979)

10. What is a banker's draft? (Q. 1(b) 1983)

11. Your employer, a bank manager, dictates the following letter:

    Dear Mr. Nethercott,
        In answer to your query I would recommend a <u>loan</u> rather than an <u>overdraft</u>, but in either case we will require <u>collateral</u>.
    Yours sincerely,

    Explain the terms underlined. (Q. 6 1981)

12. Describe briefly the following bank services and state how you would use them:
    (a) standing order
    (b) direct debit
    (c) deposit account
    (d) bank draft
    (Q. 7 1984)

13. During your induction course the representative from the Personnel Department explains that your salary can be paid directly into your current bank account. Explain how this can be done and the advantages to your firm, and describe the services a bank provides to holders of current accounts.
    (Q. 9 1985)

14. Describe the banking services which a college- or school-leaver might use when first becoming employed.
    (Q. 8 1986)

15. Home improvements can be expensive. What methods of financing them are available and which method would you recommend?
    (Q. 3 1986)

16. Explain the difference between a cheque card and a cash card.
    (Q. 1(c) 1985)

International trade

Chapter 9

International trade is an unfamiliar concept to most students. To help understanding, therefore, let us start off by considering a situation with which students are familiar, namely a typical household.

In our household both parents are working. The husband is an insurance broker. As you will see in Chapter 13 this involves selling insurance policies to the public in return for which the broker receives a commission from the insurance company. His wife is in business as a sole trader, selling home-made pottery. In the past they have purchased ordinary shares in a number of companies. These companies have been successful and profitable and the family's income for the current year has been boosted by the dividends received. The family has also received interest on the deposit account which they hold with a well-known bank. To assist with his job the husband wishes to buy a new car and has therefore borrowed £1,000 from his wife's parents. His own parents are retired but cannot claim supplementary benefit because they have £5,000 in the bank. They therefore give their son the £5,000 so that they can claim; he agrees to pay the £5,000 should they ever need it. The family's income could therefore be presented as in Table 9.1.

Table 9.1. Family income

	(£)
Wife's earnings	6,000
Husband's earnings	10,000
Dividends	600
Interest from bank	200
Loan from wife's parents	1,000
	£17,800
Deposit from parents	5,000

We now know where the family's income comes from. How is it

spent? Part of it goes on goods. We have already noted that the family intends to purchase a car, and other items purchased may include a washing machine or a video recorder. In addition a large proportion of the family income will be spent on food and on heating. As the family house has oil-fired central heating, oil will need to be bought regularly. In addition the husband has a number of insurance policies on his life and the premiums of these need paying as does the interest payable on a mortgage on the family home. Before the end of their financial year they discover that they have a £1,500 surplus. They spend £1,000 on a holiday abroad and decide to invest £250 in shares and place £250 in the deposit account.

From the above it is possible to list the family's expenditure as shown in Table 9.2.

Table 9.2. Family expenditure

	(£)
Car, washing machine, video etc	12,000
Food	3,000
Oil	500
Holiday	1,000
Interest on mortgage, premiums on insurance policy	800
Shares, money invested in deposit account	500
	17,800

We have already seen that when a family has a surplus, that is income exceeds expenditure, then this surplus will go into its reserves, either into a bank account, a building society account or possibly invested in stocks and shares. Where however there is a deficit and its yearly expenditure exceeds the income then the difference must be made up by drawing from the reserves. Money must be withdrawn from the various accounts or the shares which it holds must be sold. If the family is in the unfortunate position of having exhausted its reserves then it must borrow funds, either from family or friends or by obtaining an overdraft from the bank. Both of these methods of financing a deficit are short term only as loans must eventually be repaid. In the long term the family must balance its books by making its income equal its expenditure and it can do this by either increasing the income which it receives or by reducing its expenditure.

Let us now consider the financial position of a country. Where does a country's income come from? The answer is that most of the income arises from selling goods and services to other countries. Our wife earned money by selling pottery. A country earns money by selling a wide range of goods. If it is an underdeveloped country these will be raw materials, but in the developed Western world it is more likely to be manufactured goods (although in the United Kingdom the most important commodity now sold is oil). As goods can be seen they are referred to as *visibles* and when items are sold abroad they are said to be exported (the Latin 'ex' means 'out of'). Goods sold abroad are therefore called *visible* exports.

Part of the family income was derived from the husband's job as an insurance broker. He did not sell goods, he was selling a service. A country can also earn income by selling its services. Thus Lloyd's of London sell insurance to the rest of the world. It is an export but, unlike goods, there is nothing tangible to be seen, and is therefore referred to as an *'invisible'* export.

The family also derived income from dividends from ordinary shares and from interest from deposit accounts. A country has the same source of income. In the past the United Kingdom (through its citizens) may have invested funds in overseas companies. If these are successful and declare dividends then the dividends are sent to the citizens in the United Kingdom. It is also possible that funds have been invested in overseas banks and again if the interest is sent back to the United Kingdom it forms part of its income.

Our family's income for the year under consideration was boosted by the £5,000 which was given to them by his parents. It will be recalled that this money was given to the family for 'financial' reasons and because they could have been asked to repay it at any time in the future they considered it prudent not to spend it. Just as people outside the family have deposited money with the family which must be repaid at a later date, so foreigners may deposit money in a country which similarly has to be repaid. They usually do this because they can obtain high rates of interest by depositing money in UK banks or because they believe the changes in a country's exchange rate could lead to them making a profit. This cash deposited in a country increases its income but because it must be returned, a country would, like the family, be unwise to spend it.

Finally, suppose that the wife formed a company in which another party bought shares. The money paid for the shares would boost the family's income for the year under consideration but it will mean that in future years part of the income from the business will need to be paid out to investors in the form of dividends. When foreigners buy shares this again leads to an inflow of funds but, as with our family, means that income in the form of dividends will flow out in following years.

Having generated a given level of income how does a country spend it? Just as the family buys goods so a country will purchase goods from abroad (imports goods) in the form of raw materials and manufactured goods. Imported goods fall into two basic categories. The first are those which a country cannot produce for itself (many raw materials fall into this category) and secondly those which a country can produce itself, but where consumers prefer imported goods because they are cheaper, better made, etc. Most developed countries possess a domestic car industry but nevertheless many imported cars will be sold because the consumer prefers them, perhaps because of their better reputation, reliability or design.

In addition to goods, a country will purchase services such as shipping, insurance or tourism; there are its invisible imports. In the family's budget this would be the expenditure on a foreign holiday.

Funds may also leave the country as dividends to overseas investors or as interest on money which has been deposited in this country. In addition, British citizens may decide to invest their funds abroad either in stocks and shares or in bank accounts. While this is an expenditure in the current year it will generate income in the following year.

We have seen how a country may generate income and the ways in which it can be spent. We are now in a position to draw up a country's accounts. Where money comes into the United Kingdom this is clearly beneficial and hence is signified by a plus symbol. Where money flows out of the United Kingdom this is bad and hence is represented by a minus symbol.

In the accounts, similar items are grouped together which makes for ease of comparison (see Table 9.3).

Table 9.3. UK accounts

1.	Goods exported	+ 100	
2.	Goods imported	− 90	
	Balance of trade	+ 10	This is the difference between visible imports and visible exports (i.e. goods)
3.	Services exported and dividends, interest paid into UK	+ 70	
4.	Services imported and dividends, interest paid to foreigners	− 40	
	Balance of payments on current account	+ 40	This is the difference between all trade in goods and services.
5.	Investment, deposits of cash by UK citizens abroad	+ 20	Money goes out of the country
6.	Investment and deposits of cash by foreigners in UK	+ 10	
	Balance of payments	+ 30	This is the total of all transactions

The difference between goods exported and goods imported is called the balance of trade and when the invisibles are taken into account this is known as the balance of payments on current account. The final balance of payments is determined after the capital movements have taken place (items 5 and 6). The capital movements are basically the movements of cash into or our of the United Kingdom and are not directly linked with the sale or purchase of goods or services. They are primarily determined by interest rates and possible changes in the Exchange Rate.

Periodically trade figures are produced and published in the 'quality' newspapers. Two typical articles follow:

Trade sinks to £180m deficit

Britain sank into an unexpectedly deep current account deficit of £180 million in April and also experienced what is believed to be the first quarterly deficit on trade in manufactured goods for more than 100 years. News of the deficits was contained yesterday in the latest monthly trade figures.

The U.K. normally has to earn a big surplus on trade in manufactured goods in order to pay for unavoidable imports of food and raw materials. . . .

In April the U.K. recorded a deficit on "visible" trade of £360 million, a very sharp deterioration from the £384 million surplus of March. . . . But after allowing for an estimated surplus of £180 milion on "invisibles" like banking and tourism, the current account deficit came out at £180 million compared with a surplus of £564 million the month before.

Notes

The deficit on the balance of trade was £360m but the surplus on invisibles of £180m meant a deficit on current account of only £180m.

Only North Sea Oil keeps the picture respectable trade figures show decline in exports

Britain's trade performance took a severe turn for the worse last month, with further proof that only North Sea oil is keeping the trading picture moderately respectable. The latest CBI monthly trends survey, out on Monday, is likely to confirm that export order books remain depressed.

The Department of Trade's figures for August reveal a visible trade deficit of £37 million against a £166 million surplus in July. The value of exports slipped back by 3½ per cent to £4,386 million, the lowest level since January. Imports were up 1 per cent or £43 million, at £4,423 million – although the surge in car imports and certain other goods such as videos continued. The picture was redeemed by another record surplus on the oil account of £484 million, up from £401 million in july. And an estimated £200 million surplus on Britain's invisible trade pulled the current account up into a £163 million surplus last month, compared with £366 million in July.

The official figures confirm that the decline in Britain's export performance started in the spring. In the three months from June to August there was a visible trade surplus of £122 million, against £370 million in the previous three-month period – mainly due to a larger deficit in the non-oil account.

There were deteriorations in the balance of trade in food, beverages and tobacco and semi-manufactured goods of over £100 million in each category over the last three-month period. The surplus on trade in oil improved by £100 million to reach £1 billion while there was a small improvement in the balance of trade in cars, despite the predominance of imports in the U.K. market.

Notes

1. To discover who the CBI are, turn to page 16.
2. If you rewrite the figures into the format on page 118 you obtain:

Goods exported	4.386+[oil sales=484]
imported	4,423−
Balance of trade	37−
Surplus on invisibles	200+
Balance of payments on current account	163+

turn to page 16.

Let us now examine the balance of payments of three hypothetical countries shown in Tables 9.4, 9.5 and 9.6.

Table 9.4. Country A

Goods exported	+ 100
Goods imported	− 80
Balance of trade	+ 20
Services exported	+ 60
Services imported	− 40
Balance of payments on current account	+ 40
Investment abroad	− 160
Investment in UK	+ 40
Deposits of cash in Country A	+ 20
Balance of payments	− 60

The balance of payments in Table 9.4 shows a deficit of 60. Despite this, Country A's accounts are healthy. There is a surplus on trade, both visible and invisible, of 40. The reason why Country A is temporarily short of cash is that it has invested a considerable sum of money overseas while foreigners have invested a far smaller sum in it. While this may create a temporary problem, students must remember that money which is lent must be repaid. Country A is owed more than it owes. In addition, interest or dividends have to be paid on the funds lent or borrowed. This is shown in the invisible accounts the following year when Country A can expect to be in surplus.

Table 9.5. Country B

Goods exported	+ 100
Goods imported	− 140
Balance of trade deficit	− 40
Services exported	+ 20
Services imported	− 80
Balance of payments on current account deficit	− 100
Investment abroad	− 20
Investment in Country B by foreigners	+ 80
Foreign deposits of cash in Country B	+ 90
Balance of payments	+ 50

Looking at the accounts for Country B it would appear to possess no problems. In fact the opposite is true. Although the balance of payments is in surplus, this is entirely due to the considerable sums invested or deposited in Country B by foreigners. We saw with the family that they decided not to spend the money deposited with them because they knew it would have to be repaid in later years. If they had spent it then the money borrowed would have had to have been repaid out of their income. What is prudent for a family is also prudent for a country. Country B has had 170 invested and deposited in it by foreigners, but the country could be required to repay this sum at any time. Unlike our family, however, they have used this money to purchase goods and services. A re-examination of the figures will show that only 120 was earned selling goods and services while 220 was actually spent. The shortfall was made up by using the money deposited by foreigners. Country B's problems will start when they are called upon to repay this sum.

Country C (Table 9.6) has a deficit on the balance of trade and yet is still in a favourable overall position because the surplus on invisibles more than compensates for this, giving a balance of payments on current account surplus. In the past this country might have achieved a surplus on the balance of payments which has led to money being invested overseas. Interest and dividends now payable on this swell the invisible surplus to compensate for the deficiency on the balance of trade. There is a surplus on the other items but as noted above, this should be discounted because it will need repayment at some later date.

Table 9.6. Country C

Goods exported	+ 100
Goods imported	− 160
Balance of trade deficit	− 60
Services exported	+ 100
Services imported	− 20
Balance of payments on current account surplus	+ 20
Investment abroad	− 20
Investment in Country C by foreigners	+ 40
Foreign deposits of cash in Country C	+ 20
Balance of payments	+ 60

Exercise. Study the items set out below and say whether you think items listed under (a) are visible/invisible; under (b) are imports/exports.

(a) *Visible or invisibles?*

1. Cars
2. Oil
3. Tobacco
4. Money spent by tourists
5. Insurance premiums
6. Whisky

(b) *Imports (+) or Exports (−)*

7. Money spent by an American tourist in your country
8. A car sold to a foreign country
9. Oil purchased from Saudi Arabia
10. Insurance premium paid by you to a foreign company
11. Hire by you of a foreign ship
12. Purchase of Californian wine

(Answers can be found at the end of the chapter.)

It should now be appreciated that a country must achieve a surplus on its current account in the long term. Sometimes, however, a deficit or even small surplus on visible and invisibles is turned into a large deficit because of items 5 and 6 of Table 9.3 (see page 121). Where this happens the country has the same two options as a household. It can either take money from its reserves or borrow. In the family situation the latter is achieved by obtaining an overdraft or loan. The same is basically true of a country except that instead of going to a commercial bank it goes to an international bank called the International Monetary Fund (IMF). This body provides loans to a country which is experiencing balance of payments problems to give it time to take remedial action. The following article details a Brazilian application to the IMF.

Brazil seeks IMF loan of $6.7 billion

Brazil has told the International Monetary Fund it is seeking $6.7 billion of credits over the next three years, the largest sum ever sought by a borrowing country.

This emerged during preliminary talks between a three-man IMF team and Brazilian financial officials in Brasilia.

The actions which can be taken to remedy balance of payments problems are the reduction of expenditure or increasing income.

1. To reduce expenditure

How can this be done? The public could be asked to buy fewer foreign goods and firms could be encouraged to place orders with domestic producers rather than going overseas. If this fails to reduce expenditure on imported goods then the government can limit the number of goods coming into the country by using a quota. A quota involves setting a limit on the number of items imported. If 25,000 Japanese cars are sold a month, then the government may decide to fix a quota of 5,000 cars a month. This would cut the import bill by 80 per cent.

Another quotation open to the government would be to impose tariffs on imported goods. A tariff is simply a tax. If a 10 per cent tariff is put on all imported cars this automatically will raise their price by 10 per cent. This makes the items more expensive compared with domestically produced goods and so the demand for imported goods will fall.

One of Britain's leading chemicals manufacturers claims that annual sales of £10m are being lost and several hundred jobs in Scotland put at risk because of unfair competition from the French. According to BP Chemicals, its continental rivals are being protected by a tax on imports and aided by subsidies on exports. The company – part of the British Petroleum empire – has demanded swift action by the European Commission to end what it calls 'these iniquitous practices'.

While tariffs may reduce demand by increasing prices, they will also increase the rate of inflation and with both quotas and tariffs there is always the possibility of retaliation by other countries.

The government may also make imported goods more expensive without using tariffs. The same effect can be achieved by devaluing the home currency.

Devaluation means that your currency is worth less in terms of other currencies. If you live in the United Kingdom you can discover the value of the £ by looking in a daily newspaper where you will find that the £'s value is given against other currencies (see Table 9.7).

PM attacks steel curb

Mrs Thatcher, the Prime Minister, yesterday called the US Government's imposition of a new clampdown on steel imports deplorable, and said Britain would raise the issue with US trade representative, William Brock. . . .

In Washington, Mr. Brock acknowledged that some steel firms may have valid cases in their efforts to overturn the new restrictions. . . . This was because of the complexity of the steel industry and the difficulty in deciding which companies used unfair practices to capture part of the US steel market. Because of this complexity, "your net is going to catch some who are not engaged in unfair practices". . . . But the four-year schedule of tariffs and quotas announced by a Reagan Administration on Tuesday were necessary to combat unfair foreign subsidies to the speciality steel industry.

Table 9.7

Foreign exchanges	Tourist rates – Bank sells				
Austria	27.70	Greece	134.00	Portugal	180.00
Belguim	80.00	Ireland	1.265	Spain	222.00
Canada	1.835	Italy	2.350	Sweden	11.72
Denmark	14.32	Malta	0.64	Switzerland	3.20
France	11.90	Netherlands	4.42	USA	1.49
Germany	3.94	Norway	11.08	Yugoslavia	180.00

The table indicates how much of another currency £1 will purchase.

Thus £1 buys: 3.94 Deutschmarks
                    11.90 francs
                    1.49 dollars
                         pesetas
(Insert the figure and check the answer (c) on page 133.)

If the £ devalued it means that it will buy less, thus a 10 per cent devaluation would mean that it would buy 10 per cent less Deutschmarks, francs, dollars etc. Therefore:

                    £1 buys 10.70 francs
                    £1 buys 3.54 Deutschmarks
                    £1 buys 1.34 dollars
                    £1 buys   pesetas
(Insert the figure; check the answer (d) on page 133.)

What effect therefore would a devaluation of the £ (we say the £ is 'getting weaker') have on the UK balance of payments?

Firstly, it would tend to increase exports because it has made our goods cheaper to foreigners. Suppose a UK word processor cost £4,000. If a Frenchman wishes to purchase it then at an exchange rate of £1=10 francs he must give up 40,000 francs. When the £ is devalued the Frenchman only has to give up 9 francs to obtain £1 instead of the 10 which he previously had to pay. This means that to obtain £4,000 he only has to pay 36,000 francs; the devaluation in effect means that the word processor is now 10 per cent cheaper.

It follows from the above that while the devaluation will encourage exports it will tend to discourage imports by making them more expensive. Let us consider the cost of a French Renault car. This may cost 63,000 francs. On the exchange rate of 10 francs for £1, somebody in the UK would have to give up £6,300 to obtain enough francs to purchase the Renault. When the exchange rate falls so that only 9 francs is obtained for £1 then in order to obtain 63,000 francs he will be forced to give up £7,000 (7,000×9). The devaluation has therefore had the effect of making the French Renault relatively more expensive. It is therefore reasonable to assume that a number of potential Renault purchasers will be dissuaded by the higher price and will turn to buying an English car instead.

A devaluation will therefore probably result in a reduction in imports while there will be an expansion in exports. This should result in improved balance of payments figures and because there is a higher demand for home-produced goods this should result in a reduction in the numbers of unemployed.

If the £ grew stronger (i.e. it bought more of a foreign currency) then the opposite would happen. Suppose £1=12 francs (the pound is stronger in that it 'buys' more francs) then to purchase a £4,000 word processor a French woman must give up 48,000 francs (4,000×12). The word processor is now 20% more expensive and so it is likely that less will be sold abroad. The stronger pound has made exporting more difficult but it will encourage us to import goods because they will be cheaper.

A French car costs 72,000 francs. An exchange rate of £1=10 francs means a UK citizen will have to give up £7,200 to get 72,000 francs (72,000÷10) *but* at £1=12 francs she will only give up £6,000 (72,000÷12) which means a saving of £1,200. You can now see why manufacturers dislike a strong pound!

Government policy

If the balance of payments is in deficit the government may decide that devaluation is the answer and as will be seen in a later chapter a government may use devaluation in an attempt to reduce unemployment.

Market forces

These may also be responsible for a change in the value of a country's currency. What do we mean by market forces? Let us assume that there are a number of Englishmen who wish to buy French wine, while there are a group of Frenchmen who are interested in purchasing English cars. The French wine grower will want payment in francs and the English car manufacturer will want payment in sterling. The customers for the wine however only have sterling, while the French-men wishing to buy English cars will have francs. The solution therefore is for the Frenchmen wishing to purchase the cars to exchange their currency with the Englishmen wishing to purchase wine. The Frenchmen get their sterling and the Englishmen get their francs. The question remaining, therefore, is at what rate should this exchange take place?

UK citizens are buying francs   French citizens are buying
worth £100   sterling worth 1,000 francs
agreed rate £1=10 francs
(1,000÷10)

In the above example UK citizens wish to exchange £100 into francs and Frenchmen wish to transfer 1,000 francs into sterling. This can be achieved at an exchange rate of £1=10 francs. Suppose now that there is an increased demand in the UK for French wine. Prospective purchasers of wine now wish to transfer £200 into francs. The French demand for sterling, however, has remained unaltered.

UK citizens buy francs worth £200   French citizens buy sterling
                                    worth 1,000 francs
exchange rate £1=5 francs

The value of the £ has therefore fallen. Instead of purchasing 10 francs it can now only purchase 5 francs while the value of the franc has increased (this is called a revaluation). The change has occurred because the demand for francs has risen. Thus when the demand for a currency increases its value will rise. If the demand falls the opposite is true. If the demand for English cars had risen, the following might have occurred.

UK buy francs £100   French buy sterling 2,000
exchange rate £1=20 francs

The demand for sterling has risen hence the change in exchange rates and the revaluation of the £ (£1 will now purchase more foreign currency).

Where a currency has been revalued it will make imports cheaper whilst it will make that country's goods more expensive to foreigners. It becomes more difficult to export. The combination of these two elements means that the balance of payments will worsen. It is for this reason that when a country has a very healthy surplus on the balance of payments, its trading partners (i.e., those who have a deficit on their balance of payments) are likely to ask that country to revalue.

As explained earlier in the chapter a devaluation can cause inflation by increasing the prices of imported goods. For this reason a government may be reluctant to see its currency fall in value. They may therefore 'intervene' in the foreign exchange markets to support their currency. What happens is they use their reserves to buy their currency on the foriegn exchange market. This helps it to maintain its value against other currencies. Thus

UK citizens are buying francs   French citizens are buying
worth £100   sterling worth 1,000 francs
agreed rate £1=10 francs

The demand for sterling remains constant but there is a greater demand in the UK for francs to pay for increased imports. Thus

UK citizens buy francs worth £200   French citizens buy sterling
                                     worth 1,000 francs
agreed rate £1=5 francs

To avoid this fall in the exchange rate the UK government can use its reserves (which it holds in francs, dollars etc). It changes 1,000 francs into sterling. Thus

UK citizens buy francs worth £200   French buy sterling worth
                                     2,000 francs
agreed rate £1=10 francs

Such an exercise means using your reserves and this can result in them falling to a dangerously low level. In this situation a government might be forced to borrow as the following article indicates.

The French Government moved to rescue[1] the franc yesterday with a \$4 billion standby loan from international banks, believed to be a record for a commercial loan to a sovereign state. The Bank of France's foreign exchange reserves had fallen from £2.7 billion to £1.9 billion since the end of July and at the present rate would have been exhausted in two months. They are now doubled at a stroke, but at a heavy cost if the standby has to be used. . . .

The cabinet also promised a new export drive to reduce the alarming trade gap, which has threatened to increase from £5 billion to £8 billion by the year end. The government policy of stimulating purchasing power through increased minimum wages, pensions and family allowance has swollen imports without helping exports.

Note

1. i.e. stop it being devalued.

It should be clear from the above that anything which affects the demand for a currency will lead to a change in its value. Some of the factors which affect demand are:

(a) A deficit

If a country has a deficit (as in the article about France) this means that it imports more than it exports. If the UK has a deficit it follows that more people will want to sell sterling to buy foreign currencies (to pay for the imports) than will wish to buy sterling. The examples above show that when this happens the £ will become worth less and will be devalued.

(b) The price of oil

If the supply of oil exceeds demand for it then in order to sell their production the oil-producing countries will be forced to lower the price in an attempt to increase demand. A lower price will mean less income for oil-producing countries, whilst at the same time it will reduce the import bill of industrialised nations such as West Germany which imports oil. This will be reflected in the balance of payments on the countries involved. If a reduction in oil prices is imminent then the value of the mark will change (it will become worth more) in anticipation of the improvement in the German balance of payments.

(c) An election

If there is a General Election in a country and the policies of one of the parties involved is believed to be detrimental to the balance of payments or they propose a devaluation, then foreigners will be reluctant to hold sterling. Companies and individuals deposit funds in banks to earn interest (see item 5 in the balance of payments table on page 118) and where there are fears of a possible devaluation the money will be removed and invested in a country which has a strong currency. The possibility of the election of a party which wants a strong currency will have the opposite effect as shown in the following article.

Pound continues upward thrust

The pound went on upwards yesterday as optimism about inflation was piled on top of the City's buoyant belief that Mrs Thatcher is certain to win the election and follow strict policies that will please the financial markets.

(d) Changes in world interest rates

As mentioned earlier in the chapter, money is deposited in countries to earn interest. If the UK rate of interest falls in relationship to the rest of the world, then companies and individuals will remove their funds from the UK to invest them in other countries where they can achieve a higher rate of interest. They will be seeking to transfer their sterling into say francs, hence the demand for francs will rise and the demand for sterling will fall. In fact everyone will be wishing to sell sterling. Apart from affecting item 5 (see page 118) in the balance of payments this will result in 'pressure' on the £ and its value against other currencies will fall.

2. To increase income

So far in order to remedy the balance of payments problem we have been primarily concerned with reducing the value of imports. The alternative remedy is to increase a country's income by increasing the amount it exports. A devaluation may help to increase sales by making the goods more competitive in price, but there are other ways to improve competitiveness. A government might decide to expand the home economy so that companies can obtain the benefits of economies of scale. As is seen in Chapter 11 companies can gain advantages from size. The research and development costs can be spread over more items and it may be in a better position to introduce new technology. The car industry is often quoted as a good example and if a government were to reduce credit restrictions this might encourage the sale of cars on the home market. If the increased sales resulted in economies of scale this would enable the firm to be more competitive in overseas markets.

A government might also attempt to encourage domestic firms to export by giving grants to encourage research. The above relates to activities 'at home' but the government also attempts to create favourable conditions for world trade. Its representatives will attend conferences; meetings will take place at which the removal of quotas and tariffs will be discussed, and a close examination of newspapers will show that when government ministers visit abroad they are frequently engaged in selling British products and it is not uncommon for large orders to follow close on a ministerial visit.

Thus while the Prime Minister is understood to have clinched several notable orders on her visit to China, India is now looking to the Soviet Union for some projects and the Nigerian[1] market is likely to shrink to half its previous size this year following the imposition of import controls.

Note

1. Nigeria's solution to her balance of payments problems is to impose import tariffs and quotas.

To help create the right atmosphere and encourage exporters, government departments provide various services ranging from statistics on imports and exports and journals detailing trade conditions in other countries (including details of quotas and tariffs) to the provision of insurance. This enables exporters to insure against the main risks of selling overseas such as the insolvency of the buyer. Regular reports are received from the commercial attachés at the overseas embassies who, being in close contact with the local markets, can ensure that the information being provided is up to date. Once the exporter is abroad he may decide to visit the local attaché who can then provide him with more detailed information such as the names of local contacts.

The government also sponsors the British Overseas Trade Board which comprises representatives from government and industry. This body helps to promote trade by providing additional export intelligence, running trade fairs and promotions as well as offering general advice to exporters. Another method would be for the government to 'ensure' that exporters get paid.

ECGD staggers under third world debt crisis

The third world debts crisis is placing an ever increasing burden on the finances of Britain's Exports Credits Guarantee Department, the arm of government which insures British exporters against the risk of not being paid for goods sent abroad.

Figures published yesterday reveal that the department is having to draw increasingly on public funds to finance cash payments to insured clients who face default by customers in countries such as Poland, Nigeria, Brazil and Mexico.

In most cases, problems arise because overseas governments do not have enough foreign exchange to allow local importers to honour their debts.

ECGD, which was set up to encourage British exports, is expected to operate at no net cost to the public. The department hopes it will eventually recover most of the money owed by debtor countries and is currently making substantial provisions against potential losses. Even so, outsiders fear that the taxpayer may end up footing part of the bill.

Answers

(a) 1. Visible
  2. Visible
  3. Visible
  4. Invisible
  5. Invisible
  6. Visible

(b) 7. Export [+] ⎫
  8. Export [+] ⎬ money flows in
  9. Import [−]
  10. Import [−]
  11. Import [−] ⎬ money flows out
  12. Import [−]

Examination questions

1. Explain, giving examples, the term **invisible exports;** could there be **invisible imports**?
   (Q. 8 1972)

2. Why is the North Sea so important for the United Kingdom?
   (Q. 1(c) 1974)

3. What is the difference between 'visible' and 'invisible' trade?
   (Q. 1(j) 1974)

4. Examine the main advantages to be derived from international trade.
   (Q. 5 1974)

5. Is money spent by an American tourist in London, UK, a British import or a British export? Briefly explain your reasoning.
   (Q. 1(a) 1976)

6. What is the difference between a quota and a tariff?
   (Q. 1(c) 1976)

7. 'The pound has fallen against the American dollar.' Does this make our exports cheaper for Americans to buy, or more expensive? Briefly explain.
   (Q. 1(a) 1977)

8. 'Although the balance of trade is in deficit the overall balance of payments is favourable.' Briefly explain how this could be so.
   (Q. 1(b) 1977)

9. Give a simple explanation of why 'gold and foreign currency' reserves are so important to the value of a nation's currency.
   (Q. 1(h) 1978)

10. What precisely is meant by the 'Trade Gap'?
    (Q. 1(i) 1978)

11. Discuss **four** ways in which an adverse balance of payments may be corrected.
    (Q. 2 1978)

12. State two ways in which a country might finance a balance of payments deficit.

(Q. 1(a) 1983)

13. Study the following figures extracted from the Balance of Payments for the United Kingdom

	Units
Goods exported	100
Goods imported	120
Services exported	40
Services imported	110
Overseas investment in UK	140
Overseas deposits of cash in UK	160

 (a) Calculate (i) the Balance of Trade
   (ii) the Balance of Payments on current account.
 (b) If sterling were devalued by 10% what effect might this have on the figures?
 (c) If UK interest rates fell how might this affect the figures?

(Q. 5 1983)

14. Your country has a Balance of Payments problem and is seeking to:
 (a) increase exports
 (b) reduce imports
 How might these aims be achieved?

(Q. 5 1985)

15. Comlon International plc imports its cassette tapes from the USA.
 (a) Are the cassettes a visible or invisible import?
 (b) Explain the likely effect on the price Comlon International charges for its tapes of:
   (i) an increase in the value of the dollar;
   (ii) an import tariff on cassette tapes.

(Q. 6 1985)

Business organisation: I
Chapter 10

A young college lecturer is anxious to improve his/her family's standard of living and so decides to set up a business, intending to produce cassette tapes on various topics which can then be purchased by students so that they can study in their own homes. He/she will then be the sole owner of the business and therefore can retain all the profits made, and is in fact **a sole trader**.

This is the simplest type of business to start, requiring no legal formalities. Its main feature is that it is owned by one person, hence the name, although the owner may employ his own staff and a sole trader can become relatively large. They are primarily found in the retail trade, the service trades (such as hairdressers, plumbers, window cleaners and beauticians) and the professions (such as solicitors and architects).

Our young college lecturer faces two main problems in setting up in business. The first is that he/she possesses unlimited liability. This means that the owner's liability is not limited to the amount invested in the business. If the business makes a loss then its creditors can claim the owner's personal assets if the business assets are insufficient to pay the debts. Thus the owner may lose his/her house, car, furniture and other personal effects.

The other problem is also financial. Where can the finance be obtained to start the business and how can the owner afford to live until the business becomes profitable? Setting up a business costs money. In the above example, a recording studio will have to be hired, readers will have to be paid, scripts will have to be written and authors paid.

Cassette tapes will have to be purchased and facilities for their production organised. The sole trader may provide the finance or may turn to other sources, perhaps relatives or friends; or may even try to obtain a bank loan, but as you will remember from Chapter 8 the bank is unlikely to give a loan unless the debtor can provide collateral or a guarantor. The problems of raising capital mean that sole traders usually start with a limited capital and in the early days many sole traders start from their own homes. This avoids the need to purchase or rent premises and it will help if the business chosen requires little equipment. The window cleaner needs only a bucket and a ladder whereas the hairdresser will require a range of expensive equipment.

Businesses do not become immediately profitable. There is often a significant time lapse before a business produces income. The cassette tapes must be purchased, the recording studio paid and the readers' fees paid long before the tapes can be sold to the public. In this period between the capital expenditure and the receipt of income, the sole trader must live. In our example, the sole trader has a full-time job, but many have become bankrupt because they have failed to take into account the need to pay the bills before they receive any income.

Let us assume, however, that our sole trader has managed to overcome the financial problems and is now successfully trading. Rather than trade under his/her own name, it has been decided to call the business Barl Enterprises. The business has expanded and is so successful that the sole trader suddenly finds himself paying more than the standard rate of taxation; and also requires additional help to run the business and is seeking to increase the capital invested in the business so that the range of tapes offered can be expanded. The sole trader therefore decides to form a **partnership**.

A partnership consists of two or more people who join together in a business enterprise. For example, the lecturer may take on his wife as an **active partner**. This means that she plays an active role in the business. She will take the responsibility for despatching tapes to meet the orders and keep the financial accounts. She is to receive one quarter of the profits of the enterprise (the division of the profits is usually found in the Deed of Partnership), as this reduces the tax liability of her husband. Everybody is entitled to earn a certain sum of money without paying tax (in 1986 a wife was allowed to earn £2,335) and so by transferring at least this amount to his wife, he can avoid paying tax.

For the same reason he intends to make his mother a partner. She does not intend to get involved in the running of the business and therefore she is known as a **sleeping partner**. She still, however, shares in the profits and losses.

The lecturer also intends to offer a partnership to a family friend who has agreed to contribute the extra capital. This friend is, however, concerned that all partners, like sole traders, possess unlimited liability. As he does not wish to become involved in the running of the business he is worried that if the active partners make the wrong decisions (and the partnership becomes bankrupt) he could lose his personal possessions. It is therefore agreed that he should become a **limited partner**. This means that although he contributes capital and shares in the profits and losses, he can take no active part in the running of the business and therefore receives limited liability. In our example this is possible because at least one of the partners possesses unlimited liability.

Hairdressing is an area where sole traders are common. The owner of 'Panache', your local hairdressing salon, wishes to expand and purchase the adjoining shop as a beauty salon. The owner has no experience of beauty work and is unable to finance the purchase through her own resources. She therefore decides to take on a partner who is an experienced beautician and who is prepared to bring into the partnership sufficient funds for the purchase of the adjoining premises. This produces two of the advantages of a partnership: an expansion of capital and greater management expertise. Both partners will, however, possess unlimited liability and as either partner can enter into contracts which bind the other, it is important that they trust each other. Because trust is important in a partnership, if one partner dies or becomes bankrupt the partnership is automatically dissolved.

Let us return to our original example of Barl Enterprises which is now a partnership selling cassette tapes. The business has continued to prosper and the partners are now considering publishing academic text books to supplement the tapes. To determine whether this expansion would be profitable, the firm must obtain the answer to four questions.

1. Is there a market (Will people buy the books?)
To answer this the views of potential readers must be canvassed and a survey made of material already existing. The latter could be done by examining publishers' book lists and the former by issuing a survey or questionnaire to selected college lecturers and students. This questionnaire may be compiled by the firm but in many organisations it is common to use a market-research firm to perform this task.

2. Can it create a suitable product at the right price?
In our example it will be books, but it could just as easily be cars, washing machines or greenhouses. With publishing a suitable author will need to be found, the length of the book determined and the type of print and layout agreed. In addition a decision must be made as to where the book will be produced, i.e. printed. These are all factors which will affect the cost. If it is possible to produce a product which fulfils the unmet needs of the consumer the firm must then consider how the product (book) is to be sold.

3. How is the product to be sold?

Will the firm use its existing mail-order business to sell the books? Will it produce a catalogue or will it go through the more traditional outlets of booksellers and multiples such as W. H. Smith? Having made the decision, the firm must then decide how it is to distribute the books to the point of sale if the latter two are used. Does it use an outside carrier or does it deliver itself?

4. How can people be persuaded to buy the product?

It will need attractive packaging (in our example a suitably attractive cover) and will then need promoting by means of advertising and sales promotions. The choice of advertising media will depend on the size of the company and the nature of the market. With a firm selling educational textbooks, advertisements in student magazines such as *Memo* or in the professional teaching journals would produce a better response than advertising in one of the Sunday colour supplements.

The above four functions are the **marketing** functions within a company. In large organisations these will be provided within the business but smaller firms may well employ outside specialists to advise them on these points.

The importance of marketing is illustrated by the case of Clive Sinclair and the domestic computer. In the late 1970s he asked himself the question, 'Is there a market for a small home computer costing less than £100?' He decided the answer was 'Yes' and found that there was not a single computer on the market. He therefore designed a suitable product, the ZX81. He found a firm to manufacture it for him and decided to sell it by mail order. Outside specialists were also employed to do this. As potential purchasers were the educated middle classes, the bulk of the advertising was done in the supplements of the 'class' Sunday newspapers. By 1983, the company had sold 900,000 such computers and the originator of the company, Clive Sinclair, was estimated to be worth £127,000,000.

Sinclair surviving computer price war

Sir Clive Sinclair yesterday showed no signs of succumbing to the bitter price war in a business he created – the cheap home computer.

His company, Sinclair Research, of Cambridge, announced pre-tax profits of £14.03 million, just above the level he had forecast, and he said that this year too is "looking pretty good". Turnover doubled to £54.53 million (which represents about £1 million per direct employee) and the profit was up by 61 per cent. A dividend of 1p a share was announced, because of the need to reinvest profits.

The personal computer business ranges from the cheapest home models (Sinclair's ZX 81, for instance, now down to £40) to £10,000 and more for desktop "work stations". The most solid market is in the middle, and Sir Clive sees a new niche there. He said yesterday that he was developing a "professional computer", to be launched early next year. This will be well up market from the home computers but cheaper than the top business micros.

Sinclair Research, formed four years ago, is still 85 per cent owned by Sir Clive himself. Last February institutional investors subscribed £13.6 million for a 10 per cent holding. Sir Clive was the first (in 1980) to see the market for a cheap introductory computer costing less than £100. Today he has hundreds of imitators and competitors.

The importance of the marketing function is clearly illustrated if we look at the future of Sinclair's company. He failed to realise that the market was changing, found himself in financial difficulties and his computer business was taken over by Amstrad.

Why the sun set over Sinclair

In the annals of micro-history, the absorption of Sinclair Research's computer division by market minded newcomer Amstrad will be used to characterise the end of an era.

Sinclair is today a household name, he was granted a knighthood for his example to British industry, and made the oldest ever *Guardian* Young Business Man of the Year. He is credited with single-handedly master minding the home computer boom, was declared by some readers to be one of the century's greatest inventors, and lauded by the tabloids as the working man's boffin.

Now that the ink has dried on the Amstrad deal, the true influence of Sinclair and his company merits a rather more critical examination. Given that within 2 short years the profits from Amstrad's efficient computer assault could finance a neutralisation of the UK market leader out of Alan Sugar's[1] spare change, it is now clear that Sinclair Research failed in effective product development after its success with the ZX81 and Spectrum.

Sinclair's 5 year pillage of a virgin market began with the launch of the ZX80, the first micro-computer to break the crucial £100 barrier. On the mail order success to this minimalist machine was founded the ZX breakthrough into retail sales. W. H. Smith spearheaded the promotion which established the computer as a viable high street product. The Spectrum – essentially a ZX81 with more memory and colour – built upon this initial success, aided by the vast games software market that grew up on the back of these cheap machines that could do little else effectively. . . .

But David Ahl's assessment of the ZX81 could stand as an indictment to both Sinclair's ZX range and its contribution to computer literacy: "Sinclair's ZX80: with its unusable keyboard and its quirky basic this machine discouraged millions of people from ever buying another computer."

In the event the public was hooked on the concept of computer power for the home. In spite of the notorious delivery delays and appalling quality control, unit sales of Sinclair micros were measured in millions. In 1983 Clive had built up a personal fortune, and institutional investors had snapped up a 10% share in Sinclair Research. . . .

The arrival of the personal computer into business ended an era in which user expectations were constrained by the limitations of the Sinclair product. Slowly but surely, awareness of what a home computer could and should offer was defining an attractive product. The market no longer demanded teaching aids on which to learn the elements of programming but applications' terminals that would effectively tackle specific tasks. Consumers, no longer intimidated by the mystic were beginning to recognise the advantages of micros as the work horses of high technology. One of Clive's most significant mistakes was his failure to note the point at which the mysteries of computing became an impediment rather than asset to sales.

As the Spectrum's allure faded Sinclair needed a new product to keep the corporate coffers filled. . . . The debacle that followed the QL launch may have disappointed Clive's supporters but had the beneficial side effect of allowing other manufacturers to approach the maturer markets that Sinclair had failed to satisfy. It took the manufacturing and marketing skills of Amstrad, using tried and tested technologies, to break the deadlock.

The application of computer technology to provide what the consumer can really make use of – in the form of reliable hardware and genuinely useful software – is the only way in which the micro can earn an enduring place in our homes and businesses. The failure of Sinclair to make the transition from simple machines on which Basic programming could be learned, to the sophisticated tools that computers ought to be, signalled the overdue demise of an endeavour founded upon the exploitation of market ignorance.

Now that the punters have a fair idea of what they want, the financial rewards will be reaped by whichever of the industry's big players can best satisfy the demand. To date, Amstrad have proven the most effective in identifying and satisfying the emerging markets. It is perhaps fitting that Sugar's Leviathan should have taken over the name of the company which both initiated the market and then inhibited its development.

Note
1. Alan Sugar is the founder of Amstrad.

A considerable sum of money (capital) will be required to set up the publishing part of the business. The partners' personal assets are likely to prove insufficient. Where can they raise the necessary capital? They may approach the bank for a loan. Whilst this may generate sufficient funds to start the publishing venture, it will have to be repaid at some point in the future. What the partnership really requires is a permanent loan (i.e. one that does not have to be paid back). It can obtain this by becoming a company.

Company

Most companies today are created by registering under the Companies Acts. They differ from partnerships in two main ways.

First, they are said to have **perpetual succession**. In a partnership if one partner dies you will remember the firm is automatically dissolved, it comes to an end. Because the number of partners is small (there is a legal limit to the number of partners a firm can have) it is fairly easy for the remaining partners to re-form the business under the same name and operate from the same trade premises. As far as customers of the partnership are concerned it will be business as usual and most of them will probably be unaware that there has been a change in ownership.

Whilst the owners of the partnership (the partners) usually number less than twenty, the number of people who have a share in a company (the shareholders) may run into hundreds of thousands. If each time one of the company's owners (shareholders) died the company was dissolved, it would create commercial chaos because all the remaining shareholders would need to be contacted before the company could be re-formed. For that reason the company has perpetual succession which means that the company continues to exist even though owners of the company (the shareholders) may die and be replaced by new shareholders.

The second difference is that shareholders possess **limited liability**. This means that if the company in which they hold shares goes bankrupt (its liabilities exceed its assets) then the shareholders' losses are limited to the amount which they have invested in the company (their shareholding). The unpaid creditors cannot claim the personal possessions of the shareholders. This protection is necessary to persuade the public to invest in companies. With a partnership each partner usually has a say in the running of the partnership. As each partner is responsible for the decisions made it is only right that they should be responsible for the profits made or losses incurred. In a company the number of shareholders is so great that, unlike partners, they cannot be involved in the day-to-day running of the company. They elect a Board of Directors to run the company on their behalf. The former are accountable to the shareholders at an Annual General Meeting. If the latter are satisfied they can re-elect the Board but if they are unhappy with the decisions made in the previous year they can dismiss the Board and elect another in its place.

Rowton coup

Two directors of Rowton Hotels were thrown off the board yesterday in a surprise move led by the group's largest shareholder, Gresham House Estate. Mr. William Harris, Rowton's chairman, and a fellow director, Mr. Clive Eckert, were not re-elected at the annual meeting after a poll demanded by a representative of Gresham House which holds a 24 per cent stake. Earlier shareholders approved the sale of four Rowton hotels which will raise over £3 million. A spokesman at Hill Samuel, Rowton's advisers, said Gresham House was no longer confident in the board's ability to handle its investments. Shares in Rowton jumped 5p to 174p on speculation of a reshuffle yet to be announced.

Because the shareholders have no say in the day-to-day running of the business, it would not be possible to persuade people to invest in companies if they had unlimited liability. This would mean that in the event of a bad decision being made by the Board a person who held perhaps only a hundred pounds worth of shares could lose their house, car and other personal possessions. To overcome this problem shareholders therefore possess limited liability.

The features of perpetual succession and limited liability are found in both public and private companies. The main distinction between a public and a private company is that only the former may sell its shares to the public and have a quote on the stock exchange. For that reason it can raise larger sums in capital than the private company. It is however very expensive for a company to have a Stock Exchange quotation and therefore the medium-sized commercial or industrial company tends to be a private company. In our example, given the size of the capital required by Barl Enterprises, it would form a private company and it would not consider going 'public' until its turnover was quoted in millions, rather than thousands.

To form either type of company two documents must be filed with the Registrar of Companies. The first of these is the *Memorandum of Association*, which indicates the relationship of the company with the outside world. It therefore defines the company's powers, includes the name of the company (in the UK this is followed by the letters plc) with an indication that its members have limited liability. It also states the amount of capital which the company may raise. The other document is the *Articles of Association* which deals with the internal running of the company. It therefore covers such matters as the issue and transfer of shares, conduct of general meetings and the powers and duties of directors. These two documents are submitted to the Registrar who then issues a Certificate of Incorporation which brings the company into being.

As explained above, apart from the desire to obtain limited liability, the main reason for forming a company is the need to raise larger sums of capital than are available in a partnership. The amount of capital which a company may raise is found in the Memorandum of Association. This figure is the company's authorised capital. It is this sum which it is authorised to raise by issuing shares. In the case of Barl Enterprises this figure might be £250,000 and the Memorandum might indicate that this is to consist of £250,000 one pound shares. Having conducted their marketing exercise Barl Enterprises discover that it will only cost £125,000 to commence publishing. It would therefore issue only £125,000 from the authorised capital. This would mean that if it ever required additional funds it could issue shares up to a value of £125,000 (i.e. up to the total of the authorised capital). Earlier in the chapter it was stated that by selling shares the company obtained a permanent loan. Once a company has issued ordinary shares it never has to buy them back although it must distribute part of its profits to its shareholders. This creates two problems for the ordinary shareholder in a public company. First, how does the shareholder know how much his/her shareholding is worth? Secondly (as it is not possible to ask the company to redeem them) how can the shares be transferred back into cash?

How does the shareholder know what they are worth?

As the name indicates, each shareholder owns a share of the company. If there are one hundred shares and the company is valued at £1,000 then each share is worth £10. If the company's value rises to £3,000 then each share will be worth £3,000 divided by 100, which equals £30.

In business of course, we are not talking about hundreds or thousands, but about hundreds of thousands and millions. If you are a shareholder in a public company you can discover how much your shares are worth by looking in the 'financial' press.

Table 10.1 is an extract from the financial pages of the *Guardian*.

Table 10.1. Extract from the *Guardian*

Low (Wm)	274	Mgmt Ag	119 − 1
Lowe RH	a29	Mchstr Ship	141
Lucas Inds	159 − 1	Manders	141 + 1
MCD Group	47	Mang Brz	35
MFI Furn	a135 − 1	Manor Mtrs	13
MK Elec	311 − 2	Marchwiel	198 − 4
MY Dart	23	Marks & Spn	202 + 1
Macarthys	a138 − 3	Marley	a65
McC'dale	273	Marling Ind	a43
Mackay (H)	63 + 1	Marshal H	a153 + 2
McKecknie	129 − 1	Marshals Un	46 + 2
Macph'son	49 − 1	Mn-Black	219
Magnet S	a154 − 2	Martin A	46

a=ex divided

Shares are listed in alphabetical order and you can see the shares in Marks & Spencer are worth 202 which is 1p more than the previous day.

From the above the shareholder can therefore ascertain the value of the shares and whether they increased or decreased in the previous day's trading. The *Financial Times* also gives other information which helps the 'professional' to decide whether to buy or sell shares. Table 10.2 is an extract from the *Financial Times* showing shares in the retailing area; shares are grouped according to areas.

Most of the information is only for the 'professional' investors and students need not bother with it. They should note that the letters xd appear against the name of Marks & Spencer and these stand for 'ex dividend'. This means that a dividend has recently been declared which is payable to the holders of ordinary shares. The letters signify that if the share is sold, the dividend will be paid to the seller of the shares and not to the new shareholder.

The general movement of all shares is indicated by the Financial Times Index. If this is at 900 and rises to 910, this signifies a general increase in share prices. It is, however, possible for certain shares to move in an opposite direction from the Financial Times Index, thus the Index may be falling although a particular share or group of shares may have increased in price.

Table 10.2. Extract from *Financial Times*

Div Paid			Price	Last Div.	Div. Net	C/yr	P/E
June	Nov	Home Charm 10p	323	21.3	4.0	2.9	22.5
Dec	July	House of Fraser	200	4.0	7.5	1.9	12.0
Dec	June	House of Lerose	147	21.3	7.6	–	–
Apr	Aug	Jones (Ernest) 10p	78	7.3	3.9	0.3	–
Sept	–	+ Kean & Scott	53	6.68	1.0	–	–
Jan	July	LDH Group	14	2.6	–	–	–
Oct	Apr	Ladies Pride 20p	49	21.2	3.4	0.5	(41.6)
Aug	Nov	Lee Cooper	113 xd	1.11	3.02	6.7	4.2
May	Nov	Liberty	140	4.10	3.0	–	–
May	Nov	Do. Non Vtg Ord	90	4.10	3.0	–	–
Sept	Apr	Lincroft K. 10p	60½	21.2	2.0	2.4	12.6
Nov	Apr	MFI Furniture 10p	155	21.2	2.8	2.4	22.0
Jan	July	Marks & Spencer	204 xd	15.11	5.1	2.0	19.7
Feb	July	Martin News	195	31.12	5.78	3.1	8.7
Oct	–	Mellins 5p	142	Je 65	n–	–	–
Jan	July	Menzies (J)	323	15.11	5.0	–	–

Why should a particular share increase in price?

We noted above that if the company's value increases then its share price will rise. Anything therefore that will improve a company's profitability, and therefore its value, will tend to lead to a rise in its share price. If a company has a large export market and there is a devaluation to the pound this will probably result in an increase in its share price. A devaluation of the pound will make it cheaper for foreigners to buy UK goods and therefore the company should see an increase in sales. A company manufacturing washing machines for the home market may be threatened by cheap foreign imports. If the government introduces an Import Tariff (tax) or a Quota (limit on the number to be imported) this should result in increased sales for the domestic company, hence higher profits and therefore an increased share price. If there is a proposed takeover, share prices will rise, or if a rumoured bid fails to materialise the opposite will occur.

Shares of S Pearson, the Financial Times and Lazards bank group, yesterday plunged on the stock market as continuing rumours of a £1.25 billion bid by American investment banker Mr Gary Klesch were discounted by many dealers.

The F.T. Index usually rises if events occur which the 'City' thinks will be favourable to the Stock Market. Consider the following newspaper article.

Buoyant city predicts Tory win

The latest opinion polls have convinced a previously cautious City that a Tory victory is now almost a certainty, and the markets yesterday pushed the pound up sharply and left shares at a new closing record.

For the first time, shares closed above 700 on the Financial Times Index, which is regarded as a landmark in the City. The index has been above this level for brief periods during trading days but never at the close of business. It ended 0.8 up at 700.6. The pound soared because of the reassurance from the polls, closing 1.65 cents up against the dollar at $1.5855, back to the level at the beginning of the year.

Of course the opposite is also true!

Share prices in Hong Kong are poised on the brink of collapse again as fears grow within the business community that the colony's relative autonomy may not, after all, be assured following the termination of the New Territories lease in 1997.

The Hong Kong market after last summer's panic, has slowly returned to normal on the belief that last September's negotiations in Peking between Mrs. Thatcher and the Chinese Government had paved the way for a settlement which would allow the colony to retain its present structure with a degree of British administration after the expiration of the lease.

This week, however, it has now been reliably disclosed that China has already drafted laws which will transform Hong Kong into a Special Administration Region without any allowance for continued British participation.

Given the worldwide financial markets, a problem in the USA can easily affect share prices throughout the world.

Wall St 'in the grip of panic'

Deepening pessimism over prospects for the US economy triggered sharp falls in stock markets around the world yesterday. . . .

Share prices opened again sharply lower on Wall Street yesterday afternoon with the Dow Jones industrial average diving another 28 points within hours of opening. Dealing was described to be in panic conditions. This followed the biggest one day fall in the market's history on Monday, when the Dow Jones collapsed 61.87 points to 1,839.

More than £5 billion was slashed from the value of companies on the London Stock Exchange as the market opened to the overnight dramatic slide on Wall Street. Fresh worries over the faltering US economy and the weak dollar prompted the falls. These fears were reflected throughout Europe as prices on all leading exchanges dived in early trading. . . .

A total £5.47 billion was wiped off share values, making it the biggest one-day collapse this year. The last record was £4.5 billion on March 25.

How can shares be realised?

'Realising shares' means turning them into cash. The answer is to find another member of the public willing to buy them. In order to link the sellers with potential purchasers of shares, a market has developed. This is known as The Stock Exchange. Prior to 1986, members of The Stock Exchange had to be either brokers or jobbers. The former acted for clients in the buying or selling of shares and the jobbers were the 'dealers' in shares. Since October 1986 members of the Exchange do not have to decide whether to be either jobbers or brokers, they can now belong to firms which perform both functions. Since 1986 these businesses may be owned by organisations that are outside the stock market and this has resulted in a growing involvement of bodies like banks (both commercial and merchant) and unit trusts.

For the investor wishing to buy or sell shares, it is simply a matter of walking to your local bank and asking them to arrange for the purchase or sale. They will do it all for you, but of course they will charge a small commission.

Stock exchange fights off inquiry

The Government has bowed to pressure from the City and plans to intervene to stop the Office of Fair Trading's case against the restrictive practices of the Stock Exchange. In return for this the exchange has agreed to make concessions. . . .

The concessions the exchange are prepared to make are mainly in its commission system. At present it fixes the minimum commission that members charge on deals. This means that brokers are unable to compete for business on price, but instead compete by offering extensive research to attract the large investing institutions. This guarantees large pro-

fits from the brokers most successful at getting institutional business. The exchange is believed to be prepared to phase out its minimum commission regulations over a number of years. In return for this, and for some easing of conditions of entry to the Exchange, the Exchange will be allowed to keep its unique system of having separate jobbers and brokers. The jobbers deal in the shares themselves but do not deal in London directly with investors. The brokers, who do deal with the public cannot trade in shares between each other, but are forced to go through the jobbers.

Business organisation: II

Chapter 11

Size and change

Any company, if it is to survive and remain profitable, must meet the challenge of new technology. This may mean changing the method of production by using, for example, more robots as has occurred in the motor industry, or perhaps by changing the range of products which the company offers.

Barl Enterprises are a relatively small public company. It is 1987 and their range of products consists of manual and electric typewriters. In the mid 1980s there is a movement away from traditional typewriters to electronic type-writers and word processors.

What is this company's response?

1. Inaction

As a result of either inertia (the company does not want to change) or ignorance (the company is unaware of the changing nature of the market), it continues to manufacture solely manual and electric typewriters. As a result it loses its market to those companies who can offer a range of electronic typewriters and word processors. Barl Enterprises will become smaller. What are the consequences?

Falling demand for its products means the company will have to cut back on the number of typewriters it produces. It will therefore need to employ less staff. The consequence of this will be redundancy. The workers who are no longer required will be made redundant and if they have worked for long enough with the company, will be given a lump sum as a redundancy payment and leave to join the ranks of the unemployed. Before the company can make a large part of its workforce redundant, however, it must inform the Trade Union. The union may decide to recommend industrial action in an attempt to preserve jobs. Such action is unlikely to involve a strike because the object of a strike would be to stop the production of typewriters and, given the falling demand, this is unlikely to embarrass the firm. A more effective weapon might be a sit-in.

Sit-in stops factory

The Sheffield engineering firm of Firth Denhon was at a standstill yesterday after 80 workers began *a sit-in over compulsory redundancies*. They warned that they would continue to occupy the factory until five compulsory redundancy notices were lifted. Workers at the factory, which make aerospace parts, have been on short time for 2½ years, and 60 jobs have been shed through voluntary redundancies over the last 15 months.

The company's problems affect not only its work-force, they also affect the owners (the ordinary shareholders). The dividend they receive and the value of their shares depends upon the profitability of the firm. As profits fall so the dividend they receive will decrease and, as you will recall from the previous chapter, as the value of the company diminishes so the value of their shares will fall. For example:

100,000 shares   Company valued £1,000,000

Value of share $\dfrac{1,000,000}{100,000}=£10$

100,000 shares   Company valued £500,000

Value of share $\dfrac{500,000}{100,000}=£5$

100,000 shares   Company valued £100,000

Value of share   _____

Eventually the company will be forced to go into liquidation (it will be broke). In this situation its assets will be sold and its creditors paid off. Any surplus is then divided among the Debenture Holders. Any remaining sum will then be divided among the ordinary shareholders who therefore may receive nothing. If the company's assets are insufficient to pay the creditors then, because the ordinary shareholders possess limited liability, their personal assets cannot be seized by the unpaid creditors.

2. Action

Barl Enterprises is aware of the need to change. Its Marketing Department has been monitoring the sales returns from the sales representatives and conducting market research. As a result the Board of Directors are aware of the declining demand for electric and manual typewriters and the growing expansion of the electronic market. They are anxious to grasp the opportunities that are offered. The first step is therefore to assess the new consumer needs more accurately. This is another function of the Market Research Department. They will need to collect information on the type of typewriter required and, once a sample machine is produced, test it in a simple area. If the results are satisfactory the company will then arrange for a national launch. The product will be displayed at Trade Fairs and Business Exhibitions, advertised in the Trade Press and potential customers circularised.

The company will need to finance the research which is necessary before a new product can be manufactured and also the cost of setting up a new production line. Where can Barl Enterprises find the additional cash? A bank loan or overdraft could be used for temporary finance and it could re-invest profits (see earlier Sinclair press cutting), but long-term capital would probably be raised by issuing more shares. Students will recall that the Memorandum of Association includes details of the company's authorised capital. Barl Enterprises' authorised capital is £2 million, to be issued in £1 shares. In order to start trading the company only issued £1 million shares (its issued capital) and it therefore has a further one million shares which it is authorised to issue (the difference between the issued capital and the authorised capital). It can therefore raise additional funds by the issue of further shares. If, however, the company had already issued £2 million of shares, then a further issue of shares could only be made with the permission of the Registrar of Companies. Barl Enterprises decides to issue the whole £1 million in £1 shares. How can it do this? The most common way is through an offer 'for sale'. This means offering the new shares to the general public at a fixed price.

Although the company is issuing shares with a nominal value of £1 they may be issued to the general public at £1.50. When the company was originally formed it was valued at £2 million. As it could issue two million shares, each shareholder owned one/two millionth of the company, hence the value of the share was £1. The company has been successful and as a consequence its value has risen. It is now worth £3 million. There are still only two million possible shareholders, each shareholder therefore still owns one/two millionth share in the company. This share is now however worth £1.50 (3 million divided by 2 million). The original shareholders who purchased shares for £1 can now sell them for £1.50 through their brokers on the Stock Exchange. Anybody now wishing to buy a share in the company would be expected to pay £1.50, hence the new issue would be made at this price. If the offer price is too high then the public will not purchase the shares and if it is too low the company will effectively lose money.

In our example, let us assume the offer price is £1.30. The public will appreciate the shares are undervalued and therefore the offer will be over-subscribed. The public will offer to buy six million shares although the company is only selling one million. When there is an over-subscription, the shares can be allocated in a variety of methods. In our example, the company might decide to issue one share for each six applied for. Once the shares have been issued they will be quoted on the Stock Exchange. Because the demand for shares exceeded their supply, it is likely that the price quoted on the Stock Market would be £1.50, thus enabling each lucky applicant to sell each share purchased at a profit of 20 pence (the shares would be quoted at a premium of 20 pence above the issue price). Shares can be undervalued as indicated in the following newspaper clipping.

Superdrug's market debut has broken Eurotherm's record for oversubscription. Its offer for sale attracted a staggering £1,470 million so each share could have been sold 95 times. Eurotherm was 85 times oversubscribed. When dealings start next Wednesday, the shares are expected to go to a premium of 40p above the issue price of 175p a share.

Brothers Ronald and Peter Goldstein saw the shares of their Superdrug group soar to 295p on the first day of trading before falling back to 271p making their personal shareholdings worth £15.3 million a piece, and pricing their supermarket drugstores chain at £95 million. The shares were offered for sale last week at just 175p each and sure of a bargain stags offered an amazing £1.47 billion for the 8.8 million shares actually offered for sale – only 25 per cent of the total group. At least a dozen financial institutions were said to have subscribed for the entire issue, and with many applications being held up in the post the issue was 95 times over-subscribed. The share allocation was greatly scaled down.

A **Stag** (or a **Bull**) is a person who buys shares he believes are about to rise in price. When shares are purchased the buyer does not have to pay for them immediately. He must pay on 'settlement day'. This means that if a stag sells the newly purchased shares before settlement day he can make a profit without having to part with any money.

Consider Superdrug   Purchase 1,000 shares at 175p on 1 October
Settlement day 8 October
Sell 1,000 shares at 295p on 2 October
Settlement day 8 October

The Stag receives a cheque for £2,950 on 8 October from his buyer and must then write out a cheque for £1,750. He has therefore made a profit of £1,200!

A **Bear** is the opposite of a stag. He sells shares (say 1,000) which he does not own because he believes they will fall in price before settlement day. He will then buy 1,000 shares at the lower price. Thus

Sells 1,000 shares at 295p on 3 October
Settlement day 8 October
Buys 1,000 shares at 215p on 4 October
Settlement day 8 October

The **Bear** must write out a cheque for £2,150 on 8th but the buyer must write him out a cheque for £2,950 on the same day. This gives him a profit of £800.

If, however, the Bear is wrong and the share price rises (or if the Stag finds the share prices fall) he will make a loss.

Because it is important to get the issue price correct, companies offering shares to the public usually seek the professional advice of a Merchant Bank. It will advise the company on the timing of the new issue (i.e. at a time when the public want to buy shares) and the price. The company will advertise the offer in the serious Press and a prospectus will be published with an application form. The prospectus includes information on the company's history, details of the issue and profit statements for previous years. Once he has read this the potential investor will decide whether she wishes to buy the company's shares at the offer price. Apart from advising on the time and price of the offer for sale, the Merchant Bank will act as an underwriter. In the event of an offer being under-subscribed (not all the shares are sold to the public) the underwriters guarantee to purchase the unallotted shares which they will then seek to sell at some later date.

The company may, however, decide to issue the new shares to the existing shareholders by means of a Rights Issue. This means that each existing shareholder is offered one share at a favourable price (i.e. below the current market price of the shares) for each share or number of shares she holds.

Having obtained the necessary finance, the firm's management can now plan the production of the electronic typewriters. The production line for the component parts must be set up and the production process planned to avoid delays that could arise because of shortage of materials or equipment. The Personnel Department will also need to recruit additional staff and, depending on the nature of their work, train them.

The business is now producing electronic typewriters and provided it has got the product and the price right it should be able to expand. As it does so, it should become more profitable because the cost of producing each item should fall, as Table 11.1 shows.

Table 11.1

Items produced	Total cost of production	Average cost of production (i.e. total cost ÷ items produced)
1,000	100,000	100
2,000	180,000	90
3,000	255,000	85
4,000	320,000	

The reason for the fall in the average cost price of producing each item is that as the firm expands in size it can take advantage of what is referred to as the 'economies of scale'.

The first of these are the technical economies. In order to produce the electronic typewriters the business has set up a production line to make the component parts which it later assembles into the finished machines. Let us assume that the cost of setting up the production line was £100,000. This is known as a fixed cost because it does not vary with the levels of production. It remains constant. If 10,000 machines are made then each must contribute £10 towards the fixed cost (100,000 divided by 10,000). If the production increases to 50,000 machines then this figure falls to 2. As production rises therefore the fixed costs (which also includes rent and rates) can be spread over a large number of items. The increased production also enables the business to make more efficient use of its production line. If only 10,000 are being produced then one machine or one operator may be called to perform several tasks. If production rises to 50,000 machines then more specialist equipment can be used (such as robots) and the work force will also be able to specialise. This specialisation (or division of labour) enables both the employees and the machinery to be used more efficiently and therefore more cheaply. This also leads to a lowering in the average cost of production.

The second economy is marketing. You will recall that one of the functions of the marketing department is to plan the advertising campaign. This must be aimed at the potential customer. The advertising budget is therefore allocated as follows:

Advertising in trade magazines	£50,000
Stands at business exhibitions	£10,000
Sales literature	£10,000
Total cost	£70,000

If 10,000 machines are produced, then each one must contribute £7 towards the cost of advertising (70,000 divided by 10,000). If, however, the number sold increases to 35,000, then this figure falls to £2. Economies also arise in the use of the sales force. A sales representative has to be paid to cover an area and his salary could remain constant whether he sells one hundred or one thousand typewriters. You should now realise the implications this has on the price of the typewriter.

The pace of change in electronic office equipment means that the business must be engaged in research and development. They must be in a position to take full advantage of changes in technology. This will cost money. There are the salaries of the electonics engineers and the cost of designing and building the new equipment. These research costs have to be recouped from the sale of the products. If the costs are £100,000 and a thousand products are sold, each product must contribute £100. This figure will fall to £1 if 100,000 are sold. This is therefore another economy of scale.

Another advantage for the large company is that it can employ specialists. A sole trader must perform all the management functions, such as marketing and accountancy. The large organisation can employ the specialist accountant, the research engineer and the advertising specialist. Just as a company benefits from using specialist equipment so it will benefit from using specialist management.

The firm producing electronic typewriters may expand by taking an increasing share of the market. Growth may also be achieved if it amalgamates with a firm producing a similar product. This would occur if Imperial amalgamated with Canon. This would be an example of **horizontal integration**. The larger firm may be able to achieve greater economies of scale and if it has a sufficiently large share of the market it may be in a monopoly position. By being the only or one of the very few suppliers it may be able to increase profits by charging higher prices.

Our firm does not sell its electronic typewriters directly to businesses, but uses specialist office equipment retailers. With increasing competition from other firms it is worried that these retailers might promote competitors' models instead of its own machines. To avoid this situation the firm decides to **take over** (buy) Town and Country Office Supplies Limited who have a nationwide selling organisation. This is an example of **vertical integration**, which entails a company taking over firms who are involved with the prior stages in the business or, as is the case here, in the later stages. Another example would be petrol stations taking over garages or breweries controlling public houses.

A take over occurs when, as the name suggests, one business takes over another. The buying business makes a bid for the others shares and if enough of the shareholders approve, the bid will be successful. Sometimes the board of directors of the company for whom the bid is being made will recommend to the shareholders that they accept the bid, sometimes they will 'fight the bid'.

McKechnie fights off Abdullahs

McKechnie Brothers, the West Midlands plastics and metals group, was celebrating continued independence yesterday after fighting off the second hostile takeover bid it has faced this year.

Brothers Raschid and Osman Abdullah abandoned their attempt to gain control after the £160 million offer by their Evered Holdings group failed to secure sufficient acceptances by yesterday's closing deadline. Evered claimed the backing of around 43 per cent of the shares – acceptances of 27.6 per cent of the equity coming on top of the 15.1 per cent holding built up during the bid.

Defeat of the Evered offer is the third successive occasion on which a major City takeover bid has been decided in favour of existing management.

A take-over involving more familiar names occurred when Dixons attempted to take over Woolworths.

Dixons reveals plans to change Woolworth

Dixons yesterday promised a rapid transformation of the Woolworth chain, aimed at increasing the density of goods on sale, if it succeeds with its increased £1.8 billion offer for the stores group.

Dixons' revised offer document, posted to Woolworth shareholders last night, contrasts its Operation Ramrod strategy for the stores with Woolies' own Operation Focus, which Dixons' chairman, Mr Stanley Kalms has

again attacked as: "Incoherent and a hotch potch of the products where Woolworth does least badly. It is the last vestige of the old variety store concept and cannot compete."

Woolies' chief executive Mr Geoff Mulcahy, hit back by saying that the retail arguments behind Dixons' bid were "illogical". "Operation Ramrod is dangerous, costly and risky," he added.

As the cutting reveals, the Woolworth board of directors opposed the take-over and they were successful.

Sometimes two organisations may agree to join (merge) to create a more efficient business.

Next to merge with Grattan

Next, one of the high street's fastest growing fashion chains, confirmed yesterday that it has agreed a £307 million merger with the Grattan mail order house.

The marriage brings together 465 Next outlets, ranging from women's to men's wear, home interiors to mini department stores, with Grattan's extensive mail order business with millions of clients. Grattan's home shopping catalogues include Look Again, You and Yours and Streets of London, and two direct response companies, Kaleido-

scope and Scotcade.

Next's chairman, Mr George Davies, said the merger will create an exciting new retailing format which brings together Next's buying and design strengths with Grattan's mail order expertise. New catalogues under the Next name will be quickly produced to go out to an instant market. . . .

Grattan's shares had already soared last week on market rumours but yesterday added another 78p to 532p on the merger details. . . .

Both groups see considerable

scope for expansion – particularly in home shopping. Grattan has recently spent heavily on installing sophisticated computer systems to process telephone ordering and merchandise handling which Next hopes to use in its own retail activities. They also see potential to develop Next's Club 24 credit finance subsidiary with Grattan's growing number of direct mail credit customers and Wescot, the credit reference division. Next's credit card could also be used as a further list of customers for Grattan's products.

It should not, however, be automatically assumed that becoming larger means becoming more efficient. Sometimes firms that merge may find their methods of operating are so different that integration is impossible. The merger therefore fails; the problems of integration have caused more than one proposed merger to be called off.

Yorkshire and BBBS merger set to collapse

The proposed merger between the Bradford & Bingley and Yorkshire building societies is in danger of collapsing. The directors of the Yorkshire are meeting today knowing that the majority of head office staff are opposed to the merger which would have created the seventh largest building society.

A spokeswoman for the Bradford & Bingley admitted yesterday that there were difficulties. She said: 'There are differences in our business approach.' The Bradford & Bingley board has no plans to meet before July 28. . . .

The Yorkshire staff association is in continual meetings with the management about the merger. The chairman of the association said: 'There is a feeling among some of the staff that the merger might be opposed.' He blamed the incompatibility of computer systems as one reason for this. The overwhelming problem of matching two different computers was why the intended merger between the Nationwide and Woolwich building societies failed to take place.

Merger of building societies dropped

The Yorkshire Building Society yesterday confirmed that the merger with the Bradford & Bingley has been abandoned. The chief executive Mr Denis Macnaught said that the difficulties of integrating staff and systems were "too great" compared with possible future long-term benefits.

This is the second building society merger to falter because the computer systems were incompatible. Last year the Nationwide and Woolwich, the third and fifth sized societies, failed to consummate what would have been the largest ever merger because of insurmountable problems matching the computer systems.

Being large can, however, have its disadvantages. It can often result in problems with the staff. Employees who feel part of a firm are likely to work harder and take fewer days off. As organisations grow there is a tendency for them to become more impersonal and for a rift to develop between management and employees. This can result in anti-management feeling and the possible growth of a militant trade union. Management will of course attempt to overcome these potential problems by better communications with the work-force. As indicated in Chapter 3, communications are a vital tool in improving staff morale and motivation, but as organisations grow in size so the barriers to effective communications grow.

As Managing Director of the electronics firm I am concerned about the quality of the typewriters being manufactured. Many customers are now complaining of poor quality and faulty workmanship. This matter must be brought to the attention of the work-force. I know what has to be said and I appreciate that it has to be put over to the work-force in such a way that it will produce a positive response in them. In a small one-man business I can go and talk to the workers and probably solve the problem. In a large organisation the Managing Director will have a director in charge of production; he will have managers working for him and below them there will be supervisors and finally the work-force. In communicating we have already discussed the need to be aware of staff feelings. Suppose I as Managing Director call a meeting of the production workers and discuss with them the quality of the work being produced. What effect will this have on their supervisors, the managers, and the Production Director? I have by-passed them to talk directly with the work-force and this may be interpreted as a lack of confidence in the ability of the managers, supervisors, etc. Within any organisation there is a chain of communication and a failure to use this may affect the morale of those by-passed. If I do use it however then the message which I wish to have relayed to the work-force will have to pass through a number of people. This increases the chance of the message being distorted or not passed on. It is in a situation like this that 'send reinforcements' becomes 'send three and fourpence'.

It is not only internal communications that may be adversely affected. Size may also make communication between the firm and its customers more difficult. Bureaucracy and red tape are often a feature of size. The potential customer who phones up to place an order may often be passed from department to department as nobody wishes to take the responsibility for making a decision, or fobbed off with the excuse, he will phone you back (pyb!). Unable to get a satisfactory answer the potential customer may become frustrated and turn to the small firm where he can soon be put into personal contact with the appropriate person and possibly a decision can be made over the telephone.

Large-scale production, while technically efficient, demands specialisation by employees which we noted earlier was called division of labour. Each employee does one task and it is claimed that constant repetition makes him quicker and more efficient. It is also likely that the job will become boring and tedious. The employee will become frustrated. Below are the views of a car worker, taken from a newspaper article.

Let us look at the example of one production worker. Bill has never been particularly enthusiastic about working on the production line. He worked out of duty to his wife and two small children, because he wanted to buy his own home, and because he thought dole money should go to those who couldn't get a job, not those who would simply rather not.

This year though, he applied for voluntary redundancy because he could no longer face a job which had become 'monstrous' over the last two years. But he was too late – he had been left behind in the rush.

He works two weeks of five nine-hour days, then two weeks of four nine-hour nights. He gets 20 minutes' break in the morning, 25 in the afternoon and 30 for lunch – 'just time to get indigestion, after you've queued to change a note because you've got to have the right money, and then queued again for the food'. With 4,500 workers in the body plant alone, you can imagine those queues.

He is paid a flat rate, with no bonuses and takes home about £80 a week after deductions. 'You work because you have to. No one wants to. It's a monstrous job. You can't move around. Imagine someone giving you a hammer every day and telling you to stand and tap three times, pause, tap three times. All day.

'Imagine this absolutely huge place, with everything in one colour – grey green, with all the cars going through, all grey, with no wheels or engines, in straight lines where you're not supposed to encroach on anyone else's space so you shouldn't have two people working on the same car at the same time. If you look up and see a gap in the line where there isn't a grey car, it's like heaven.'

Production lines anywhere at any time are just as bad. Management, he says, is interested only in production levels and results and to that end the men are chained to their work, treated like children, having to ask to be excused, or worse, like cheats, when after they have clocked on the foreman takes a tally later to see they are all there.

In addition to the possible human problems, large-scale production may be particularly vulnerable to changes in demand. If the firm is producing a large number of electronic typewriters and there is a revolutionary discovery which enables word processors to be sold at a quarter of their existing price, then the market for electronic typewriters is likely to fall dramatically. We have seen above how the large production run is beneficial in terms of advertising and research costs but the change in demand now means closing down a production line, which would have been very expensive to set up (the bigger you are the harder you fall). Even if the demand for such machines remains constant the large firm is more vulnerable to industrial action from small groups of key workers. It was noted above how the division of labour can improve profitability. It also means that each group of workers is reliant on others in the chain. If one group of workers goes on strike or there are production problems, the whole factory may close down. Students will be aware from reading newspapers and listening to the news that a strike of a small group of workers can close down a whole car plant.

Examination questions

1. Is a rise in the Financial Times Share Index favourable to the investor? Briefly explain your answer.

(Q. 1(c) 1977)

2. In which financial institution would you find a bull, a bear, and a stag?

(Q. 1(j) 1976)

3. Why may large organisations be able to produce more cheaply than small ones?

(Q. 12 1975)

4. Name **two** of the documents which must be submitted to the Registrar of Companies when setting up a Limited Company.

(Q. 1(a) 1980)

5. Explain how each of the following could raise *additional* capital:
   (a) sole trader or partnership
   (b) limited company
   (c) state-owned industry.

(Q. 9 1984)

6. The profits of Comlon International plc have, to the dismay of shareholders, fallen since their takeover of another company. Instead of obtaining economies of scale, costs have actually risen.
   (a) What is a takeover? Give examples of types of takeover.
   (b) Explain why costs could have risen.
   (c) What action could the unhappy shareholders take?

(Q. 7 1985)

7. Comlon International plc are considering an increase in their production and they wish to enter the market for video cassettes as well as audio tapes. This will require substantial initial finance. How can this be raised?

(Q. 10 1985)

8. (a) What is the distinction between vertical and horizontal mergers? Give examples to explain your answer.
   (b) What are the advantages and disadvantages of a merger?

(Q. 2 1986)

9. What are the consequences when a share issue is over-subscribed?

(Q. 1(h) 1986)

Public sector
Chapter 12

Two senior Conservative Cabinet Ministers said,

'It remains our purpose, wherever possible to transfer to the private sector, assets which can be better managed there.'

'It must be right to press ahead with the transfer of ownership from the state to private enterprise of as many public sector businesses as possible.'

These quotes apparently reinforce the view that many students hold, that the Conservative Party is opposed to the public sector (i.e. that part of the economy owned by the state and controlled by the government) and wishes to see everything in the private enterprise sector, while the Labour Party holds the opposite view. This is not the case. In the UK we have a mixed economy consisting of both public and private enterprise. Both parties accept this. Labour does not want to nationalise everything: the Conservatives do not wish to privatise (denationalise) everything. In *some* areas the two parties actually agree!

Areas of agreement

Some of the arguments for public ownership are accepted by all political parties.

Unprofitable services
Certain goods or services are 'essential' but they would not be provided by private enterprise because it would be unprofitable. Consider public lavatories in a seaside resort. They cost money to build and run. If they were to be profitable 'clients' might need to be charged 25p. With the sea in close proximity the public might find cheaper ways of relieving themselves! The argument of profitability also covers the provision of parks, swimming pools and libraries. On a national level

the argument would apply to the provision of electricity. Supplying it to large towns is profitable and private enterprise would be happy to be involved. Supplying it to isolated villages is not, hence if it were left to private enterprises small communities would be without electricity.

Essential services
Certain goods or services are so 'essential' to a country's well being that they must be provided free (or almost free). Consider education and health. A country's work-force needs to be educated and healthy. If the provision of education and health were left to private enterprise there might be parents too poor (or too indifferent) to be able to educate their children properly, and sick people who might be unable to afford treatment. The 'basics' are therefore provided by the government (of course if you are prepared to pay, you may obtain better education or better health treatment). The parties may of course disagree about what is 'basic'!

Charges plan for council services

A scale of charges for some school activities, and passing on the cost of fire and library services to the user are being considered in a government review of the fees collected by local councils. Councils would no longer be compelled to provide many services, which would be available on payment of a locally decided fee to cover all or part of the costs. This could include school activities deemed to be outside the normal curriculum, such as piano and violin lessons or field trips. Fire services might recover the cost of attending fires from insurers. Libraries might charge for borrowing fiction or even using the reference section – an idea which has already been canvassed by some Conservative councils.

Large size and doubtful profitability
Some projects are either so enormous that no private company could finance them or the potential profits are so dubious that private enterprise would not be interested. The atomic energy programme is a good example.

National security
Certain 'industries' are best controlled by the government for reasons of national security. Atomic energy would also fall into this category as would defence. Very few people would like to see private armies!

Areas of disagreement

A principal area of political disagreement is between those who advocate private ownership and those who advocate public ownership of certain enterprises.

For example where an industry possesses numerous small firms there may be duplication and harmful competition. If the government organises the whole industry it can rationalise, obtain economies of scale and therefore offer a better deal to consumers. Nonsense, say the opponents. Competition is healthy. The inefficient go bankrupt while only the efficient survive. Profit is the spur. If the government controls an industry it creates a monopoly (only one firm) and because there is no competition it can charge what it likes and be totally inefficient. Managers become complacent because they know if there is a loss the government will just pump in money; there is no likelihood of bankruptcy. The pro-nationalisation lobby would deny this and claim that monopolies exist in private enterprise and exploit the consumer. If the monopoly is state-owned this can be avoided. Which argument you accept depends on your political views. Thus Labour believes industries such as British Telecom, Britoil, British Airways and British Gas should be part of the public sector while the Conservatives want them in the private sector.

Privatisation dispute worsens as employees are bussed in

The executive of the Post Office Engineering Union yesterday agreed to intensify its campaign to prevent the sale of British Telecom.

The union intends to black maintenance work on the telecommunications equipment of more commercial institutions. It refused to specify its targets until it has consulted with union branches, but the general secretary, Mr. Brian Stanley, said that the action would begin this week.

The union is taking industrial action against the sale of BT and the establishment of an alternative private telecommunications network, Mercury. BT management has suspended more than 2,200 union members because of the action.

The union action failed. British Telecom was privatised.

Share perks for gas workers

The 90,000 employees of British Gas were offered free shares perks worth £54 million yesterday when the government confirmed its carefully leaked financial plans for the stock market flotation of the corporation later this year. All employees will be given £70 worth of shares plus £2 worth for each year of service. Those able to invest up to £2,150 will be given £500 worth of extra shares free. The 50,000 living pensioners of British Gas will each be given about £75 worth of free shares. The Energy Minister said that the deal amounted to a £600 offer to the average employee – more generous than the £470 perk offered to British Telecom's 130,000 employees. . . . The sale of British Gas in one fell swoop is the biggest and most sensitive disposal of a state asset yet attempted.

When it is decided an activity should be in the public sector it will usually be run as either a nationalised industry or by the local authority.

Nationalised industries

These are known as public corporations (not to be confused with public companies which are in the private sector), are technically owned by the public and their general policy is determined by the government through the appropriate minister. The minister appoints a board to look after the day-to-day running and it submits an annual report to Parliament who (if they have time) will debate it. This is one method of public accountability; the other is through Consumer Councils who act as a watchdog on behalf of the consumer.

The finance for nationalised industries comes from:

- revenue from the sale of its goods and services.
- selling stock on the Stock Exchange
- government subsidies and grants

It is this last area that is politically most sensitive because the government subsidies come indirectly from the taxpayer and therefore mean higher taxation.

The National Coal Board yesterday offered union leaders of 190,000 mineworkers an increase on the basic rate of 5.2 per cent and told them that it was the 'last word' in the present wage bargaining round. . . . It is clear that the industry will sustain a heavy loss this financial year. . . . The main problem is that we are simply producing much more than we can sell and the over production is, in the main, from heavily losing collieries.

The opponents of public ownership claim subsidies prove the 'inefficiency' of the public sector. The validity of such an argument depends on whether such losses would still be incurred if the industry was run by the private sector. Some services (such as electricity to isolated communities) can only be provided at a loss! Any profits (and many nationalised industries are profitable) will probably go to the government to finance its spending elsewhere.

Local authorities

They provide services such as education, police, fire as well as recreational facilities. Elected councillors are responsible for broad policy but leave the day-to-day running to paid full-time employees. The finance for local authority undertakings comes from:

- revenue from the sale of services, e.g. charges to enter a swimming pool.
- grants from central government.
- local rates. Each piece of property is given a rateable value and the local authority annually fixes a rate in the pound. This is multiplied by a property's rate value and that is what the occupier pays.

Example

Rateable value	Rate in the £	Payable
£200	50p	£100
£300	40p	£120
£400	80p	£320
£500	50p	
£600	25p	

- borrowing from the public. Local authorities issue fixed interest stocks which the public can buy. They are for a fixed period; on the expiration of this they must be redeemed (i.e. repaid).

Aims of public sector organisations

Organisations in the public sector do not exist solely to make profits; their political masters may use them to pursue 'political' objectives and these may conflict with the objective of profit maximisation.

Minister turns down MacGregor

Mr. Ian MacGregor, chairman of the British Steel Corporation, has advised the government to close the hot strip mill at Ravenscraig in Scotland. With over production in the industry this is essential if it is to become viable. . . . Mr. Patrick Jenkin the Secretary for Trade and Industry has insisted the mill be kept open because it is in an area of already high unemployment.

£700m BA order may go to USA

British Airways is planning to purchase up to £700 million of aircraft engines from America in preference to UK-made Rolls-Royce engines. BA officials have stated a clear preference for US-built General Electric engines in a straight choice against Rolls-Royce.

A final decision will be taken in the summer, and there will be a political–industrial row up to Cabinet level if BA picks the American engines. . . .

The airline's preference for the US-made engines will publicly test the Government's policy of exposing it to more commercial pressures in the run-up to the proposed privatisation next year. On purely commercial grounds the airline would plump for the General Electric engines. But the likely widespread hostility especially amongst Conservative MPs suggests that the Cabinet will ultimately be called upon to settle the row.

Tory backbenchers have shown increased opposition to government privatisation and industrial policies affecting BL, British Shipbuilding and Westland. The row is further complicated by a government commitment to sell Rolls-Royce into private hands some time next year. . . .

The emergence of BA's clear preference for the General Electric engine coincides with the start of a nationwide campaign by the trade unions to oppose the planned privatisation of Rolls-Royce. The campaign, led by the Confederation of Shipbuilding and Engineering Unions, is founded on the belief that short-term commercial considerations will operate against the ability of Rolls-Royce to maintain its long term research and development programme into new engine products.

Rolls 'may still win'

Mrs Thatcher fought back yesterday in the row over British Airways' bid to buy £700 million worth of aircraft engines from America. She insisted that the Government would impose no pressure on the airline to purchase British made Rolls-Royce engines.

Mrs Thatcher, responding to widespread criticism over the potential loss of work to UK factories, said in the Commons that Rolls-Royce had to win. She insisted that it was wrong to protect industries if they were inefficient and Downing Street sources said later that the Government still expected Rolls-Royce to win the order.

Another example would be keeping open an uneconomical coal-mine because it is in an area where there is already high unemployment.

To sum up, Table 12.1 offers a comparison of the public and private sectors.

Table 12.1. Comparison of public and private sectors

	Public sector (e.g. nationalised industries or local authorities)	Private sector (public companies)
Sources of finance	Various, including support from government	Sale of shares to public
Control: policy	Elected representatives (e.g. Minister/Councillors)	Board of Directors
Day to day running	Paid officials (e.g. board of nationalised industry)	Senior Managers
Profits	Available to government/ local authority	Available for distribution to shareholders
Pricing	May not be able to maximise profits because of social and other objectives	Aims to maximise profitability
Responsible to	Public through their elected representatives or through Consumer Councils.	Shareholders

170 Section A

Examination questions

1. What is the main purpose of the Annual General Meeting of a Public Limited Liability Company?

   (Q. 1(a) 1977)

2. In terms of ownership, to whom are the Directors of a Joint-Stock company responsible?

   (Q. 1(h) 1976)

3. What special difficulties face the small private firm which wishes to expand?

   (Q. 10 1976)

4. Briefly explain the kind of information contained in:
   (i) The Memorandum;
   (ii) The Articles of Association.

   (Q. 1(d) 1975)

5. If Public Limited Companies are accountable to their shareholders, to whom are the nationalised industries accountable?

   (Q. 1(i) 1975)

6. What are the main differences between Public Limited Companies and Public Corporations?

   (Q. 10 1975)

7. Describe any **two** of the following forms of business enterprise:
   (i) The sole proprietor
   (ii) Partnerships
   (iii) Private companies
   (iv) Public Limited Liability Companies

   (Q. 12 1978)

8. Consider the strengths and weaknesses of the small business unit in today's economy.

   (Q. 4 1978)

9. What are the principal ways in which business enterprises in the private sector are owned and controlled?

   (Q. 5 1973)

10. State the difference between authorised and issued capital.

    (Q. 1(c) 1983)

11. Mr Jackson has inherited £20,000. He decides to commence business as a sole trader.
    (*a*) What business problems is he likely to face?
    (*b*) Apart from retailing, in what areas might you find sole traders?

    (Q. 7 1983)

12. What is meant by limited liability?

    (Q. 1(a) 1981)

Business insurance
Chapter 13

Imagine you have just been appointed secretary to one of the managers in a large insurance company. Your manager controls a section which deals with business insurance. When you arrive at work on your first day, you are told that there is a three-day induction course. You will recall from Chapter 4 that there are three main features of an induction course. One will deal with the personal aspects of employment (information on company pay, safety, positioning of toilets, canteen, etc.), another deals with the overall picture of the company and involves describing the product or service which it provides, while the final part relates to the job the new employee is expected to perform.

Let us now consider each of these in turn.

The personal aspect
This is influenced by matters such as the layout of the building and students should revise this aspect before continuing.

The company and the service
The company which employs you supplies insurance and is therefore an **underwriter.** It is a public company and its shares are quoted on the Stock Exchange (see Table 13.1).

Table 13.1

Britannic 5p	398	Legal & General	396
Combined Int. $1	£22½	Pearl 5p	612 xd
Comm. Union	154	Phoenix	330
Eagle Star	408	Prudential	384
Equity & Law 5p	643	Refuge 5p	360
Gen. Accident	433	Royal	530
G.R.E.	450	Sun Alliance £1	£11 7/8
Hambro Life 5p	352 xd	Sun Life 5p	472
Ins. Cpn. of Ireland	272 xd		

It is owned by shareholders and if the company is successful and makes a profit this will be distributed to them in the form of dividends. Not all insurance companies however are owned by shareholders. Some are owned by the **policy holders** (the people who are insured) and these are called **mutual companies.**

Having given a brief history of the company, the induction programme deals next with the nature of insurance. This is best explained by using an example.

Assume Barl Limited are a private company that manufacture small personal computers. It is a family business which started as a partnership but was formed into a private company to obtain the advantages of limited liability (in the event of bankruptcy the shareholders' liability is limited to the sum they invested in the business). The factory premises and equipment cost £100,000. The family know that it is possible, although extremely unlikely, that the factory could be burned down. As all their assets are tied up in the factory this would mean the end of the business. They therefore approach a company and ask them what the likelihood is of the factory being burned down. They are told that there is a one in ten thousand possibility. Expressed in another way, the odds are ten thousand to one.

The insurance company therefore calculates the risk that the factory *will* be burned down and charges a premium of £10. As the likelihood of this happening is ten thousand to one, the other company will agree to give them £100,000 (ten thousand times £10) in this eventuality. This pleases Barl Limited. But what about the other company (which is the insurance company)? The insurance company will offer similar odds, ten thousand to one, to all other factory owners wishing to insure against fire. Let us assume that ten thousand factory owners each pay £10 to the company. This would mean the company received £100,000. There are ten thousand businesses and given the odds of a factory burning down of one in ten thousand then only one factory will burn down. The company willl receive one claim for £100,000. Thus its expenditure equals its income. Of course, in reality, an insurance company seeks to make a profit. In our example, the likelihood of a factory burning down is probably eleven thousand to one, therefore the company would receive £110,000 from eleven thousand customers but, as only one factory is burned down, it would only pay out £100,000 leaving a surplus of £10,000. The vast majority of those taking out insurance do not have to claim but the money they have paid to the insurance company gives them peace of mind. Those policy holders who suffer the misfortune insured against (burglary or perhaps fire in their factory) are, however, compensated (indemnified) to the extent of their loss.

The job

The final part of the induction programme attempts to familiarise the new employee with the job. The employer will spend a considerable amount of time out of the office and the new employee will therefore be expected to deal with customer enquiries (these can come directly from the public or via their agents (brokers)). The enquiries can take various forms, for example an enquiry from a potential customer (who is referred to as the proposer) asking for details of the various policies that would be appropriate for a business person. The training must therefore include instruction on the various types of policies available. A list of policies and details of the cover provided can be found in Fig. 13.1.

BUSINESS POLICIES

Basic Cover

Property

Your stock, machinery, plant, furniture, fixtures and fittings all receive essential protection against such events as fire, flood, or theft following forcible entry into or exit from the premises.

Additionally, you can cover your buildings, or, if you are a tenant, you can include in the insurance the portion of the structure and interior decorations for which you are responsible.

We will pay the cost of repair or replacement as new for your buildings or machinery.

Loss of Gross Profit

This covers you if your gross profit is reduced following interruption to your business from events covered under the Property section of this policy.

Money

Money lost or stolen from your premises, home or during transit is included. Also, if you or your employees are injured by thieves, we will pay compensation for the injury caused.

Legal Liability

If you are legally liable for injury or damage we cover your liability to
* **Your employees**
  — with no monetary limit.
* **The public**
  — up to £500,000, including your liability arising out of the sale of goods.
In each case legal costs and expenses are also included.

Optional Covers

Glass

Accidental damage cover to your external glass, sanitaryware, neon and other fixed signs or any other glass is available.

Temporary boarding up costs are covered as well as damage to alarm foil and the removal of fixtures and fittings.

Goods in Transit

Your property can be covered against loss or damage whilst being carried in your own vehicles or despatched by road, rail or post anywhere within the British Isles.

Personal Accident

Compensation is provided for death or disablement for you and your employees following accidents at work or elsewhere.

Office Machines

Accidental damage to your office machines such as typewriters, calculators and franking machines is catered for on a full replacement basis.

Book Debts

Loss of outstanding balances due to damage to records and books of account by any event insured under the Property section is covered.

Fidelity Guarantee

You are covered for loss of money or other property following fraud or dishonesty involving any employee.

There will be other insurances which you may need according to the nature of your business.

Fig. 13.1

Commercial Union Assurance

Business Policy

Proposal Form

Agency

Branch and Agent No.

Policy No. UB

Period from   to

Due date

Please return completed proposal form to:—

ASSURANCE

Commercial Union Assurance Company plc.
Registered Office: St. Helen's, 1 Undershaft, London EC3P 3DQ.
Registered in England No. 21487.

Printed by Group Supply Department of Commercial Union Assurance

JANUARY 1982

G1729

Commercial Union Assurance Business Policy

Provides you not only with wide 'Basic' cover against fire, flood, theft and malicious damage, but also cover for those other unexpected things that can happen. Like payment for your lost gross profit if your business is unexpectedly closed or impaired, or compensation to your employees or members of the public if you are legally liable.

To this you can add a number of optional extensions to obtain the most suitable cover for your particular business needs.

For example: replacement of glass broken accidentally; compensation if you or your employees are accidentally injured or disabled whether at work or elsewhere; and payment for loss or damage to your goods in transit.

You could say it's many policies in one.

Please see the CU Business Policy prospectus and your Broker, insurance adviser or CU office for further details.

Two special advantages

Discount:
If you agree to renew your policy for three years, and the combined sums insured for Property and Loss of Gross Profit exceed £50,000, you are eligible for a 5% discount off the total premium.

Time to pay:
If you prefer, the annual premium payment for the cover you select can be spread over 5 payments by CU Credit.

Please ask for details

Fig. 13.2

Business Policy Proposal Form

Please answer questions in BLOCK CAPITALS

Full Name

Postal Address

Postcode | Telephone No.

Full description of business

Year established

Risk address if different from above

Postcode | Telephone No.

Description of Premises e.g. store, warehouse, factory

If only part of the building is occupied by you state a) which part:

b) the nature of the business of the other occupants:

For summary of covers, please see prospectus

Basic Cover comprising:
Property, Loss of Gross Profit, Money and Liabilities insurance

Information on your business and assets — When writing in values against the various headings, please ensure they are sufficient. They should include an allowance for inflation and growth during the period to be insured; please see prospectus for guidance.

1. Buildings — the rebuilding costs including walls gates and fences plus an amount for Architects' and Surveyors' Fees, shoring up and removal of debris. — either £

2. Interior decorations, improvements and that portion of the structure for which you are responsible as tenant. — or £

3. Machinery, plant, trade and office furniture, fixtures and all other contents owned by you or your responsibility (excluding landlord's fixtures and fittings). — £

4. Stock and materials in trade EXCLUDING jewellery, watches, furs, precious metals, precious stones, tobacco, cigars, cigarettes, non-ferrous metals and explosives. — £

   If any of the excluded property is to be insured, please list these separately below with sums insured applicable.

i)	£
ii)	£
iii)	£
iv)	£

5. Estimated annual gross profit. — £

6. Estimated wages/salaries, other than clerical, of all employees and any payments to self-employed sub-contractors:
   i) for work at your premises — £

   ii) for work away from your premises — £

7. Estimated annual turnover. — £

Fig. 13.2 (*continued*)

Variations

The basic cover can be extended to meet your special requirements. Complete only if variations are required.

Loss of Gross Profit

1. If you wish to extend the indemnity period beyond 12 months to 18 months or 24 months, please indicate
   a) Period, and | Months |
   b) Estimated gross profit for this period | £ |

2. Do you wish to add loss following damage to:
   a) Surrounding property preventing access to your premises? | YES/NO |
   b) Suppliers' premises? | YES/NO |

Money

1. If you require cover in excess of £2,000 for any one loss for money in your premises during business hours, in transit or in bank night safe, please state:
   a) Amount required, and | £ |
   b) How many employees will accompany the maximum amount in transit. | |

2. If you require cover in excess of £1,000 for any one loss for money in your locked safe outside business hours, please state:
   a) Amount required, and | £ |
   b) Details of your safe, below

Make, Model and Serial Number	Is it anchored	If anchored, how?
	YES/NO	

Liability

1. Do you wish us to consider cover for exports to the U.S.A. or Canada? Please see General Question 5. | YES/NO |

Optional Covers Please complete the sections required, otherwise leave blank

Glass

Do you require cover for:
1. External glass, comprising all fixed external glass in doors and fanlights and windows excluding glass in rooflights? | YES/NO |

2. Sanitaryware comprising fixed sinks, wash basins, lavatory pans and cisterns? | YES/NO |

3. Neon and other fixed signs? If YES, state total value. | £ |

4. Any other glass? If YES, please provide description, position and measurements.

Description	Position	Height	Width

Goods in Transit

1. **By own vehicles**
   Maximum value of goods carried at any one time. | £ |

   Number of own vehicles used for the carriage of goods. | |

2. **By other means** Please state:

	Road Hauliers	Rail	Post
Max. value of any consignment	£	£	£
Estimated annual carryings	£	£	£

Fig. 13.2 (*continued*)

Optional Covers (cont.)

Personal Accident

Name of person(s) or class of persons to be insured	Full duties of person(s) to be insured	Date(s) of birth	State number of units required (Max. of 5 units per person)

Is each person proposed to your best knowledge and belief in good health and free from physical defect? | YES/NO |

Office Machines – Accidental Damage

State the total value of all Office Machines to be insured.   £

Describe below any item exceeding £5,000 in value or which is not within the description in the prospectus.

	£		£
	£		£
	£		£

Book Debts

Maximum amount of Outstanding Debit Balances likely to be outstanding at any one time, including a suitable allowance for expansion of business, seasonal variations, inflation and V.A.T., but deducting an allowance for bad debts. Maximum sum insured £20,000.   £

Fidelity Guarantee

If NO, give details

1. Have you always been satisfied with the honesty and general conduct of all employees to be insured?

   YES/NO

2. Does your system of obtaining references and of supervision correspond to that stated in the prospectus?

   YES/NO

Other Covers

Your business could be affected in other ways.
Please indicate if you require details of the following:

Commercial vehicles or motor cars.	YES/NO
Machinery and Plant — Accidental damage, breakdown and inspection.	YES/NO
Machinery and Plant — Consequential loss.	YES/NO
Computers.	YES/NO
Cargo — Imports and exports.	YES/NO
Key people.	YES/NO

You may require additional cover for individual employees or higher limits than provided under the CU Business Policy. Do you wish to receive details for the following:

Personal Accident?	YES/NO
Fidelity Guarantee?	YES/NO

A separate proposal will need to be completed in each case.

Fig. 13.2 (*continued*)

General Questions

1. Please state
   a) whether premises are built other than of brick, stone or concrete with slate, tile, metal, asphalt or concrete roof. If YES, give details.　　　　YES/NO　　a)

   b) condition of repair of buildings.　　　　b)

   c) method of heating premises if other than by　　c)
      i) low pressure, hot water or steam,
      ii) fixed electrical appliances or
      iii) fixed oil or gas fired space heaters, where the fuel is fed through fixed metal pipes and with an external flue.

2. Describe:
   a) work undertaken and　　　　a)

   b) goods supplied, installed, erected, repaired, altered or treated by you.　　　　b)

3. Have you entered into any agreement assuming a liability for injury, illness, loss or damage for which you would not have been liable in the absence of such agreement?　　　　YES/NO　　If YES, please supply a copy of the agreement.

4. Do you undertake operations outside the United Kingdom? If YES, give full particulars, including countries concerned, nature of activity, wages and expenditure.　　　　YES/NO

5. a) Do you import any goods?　　　　YES/NO　　a)

   b) Do you export any goods?　　　　YES/NO　　b)

   If YES, give full particulars including countries concerned. If you export to the U.S.A. or Canada state gross turnover.

   c) If you have previously exported goods to U.S.A. or Canada give full details.　　　　c)

6. Do you supply goods for use in the nuclear, aircraft or marine industries? If YES, give full particulars including turnover. (N.B. Separate insurance may be necessary.)　　　　YES/NO

7. Are any of the following used in your business? If YES, please give details.　　　　YES/NO

   a) asbestos, silica, or any other substances involving a health hazard.　　　　a)

   b) radioactive substances or other sources of ionising radiations.　　　　b)

   c) power driven machinery.　　　　c)

   d) flame cutting or welding plant or other heat producing plant or processes away from your own premises, by you or your sub-contractors.　　　　d)

Fig. 13.2 (*continued*)

General Questions (cont.)

8. Are you aware of any situation where noise may be impairing hearing ability? If YES, give full details. — YES/NO

9. In connection with the insurances for which you want cover, have you:
   a) ever been refused insurance or had any special terms or conditions imposed by any Insurer? — YES/NO — a)
   b) during the last 3 years sustained any loss or had any claim made against you? If YES, give details. — YES/NO — b)

10. Are you at present insured or have you ever proposed for insurance in respect of any of the covers to which this proposal applies? If YES, state Class of Insurance and name of Insurer.

Class of Insurance	Insurer

Any other facts known to you which are likely to affect acceptance or assessment of the risks proposed for insurance must be disclosed. Should you have any doubt about what you should disclose, do not hesitate to tell us or your insurance adviser. This is for your own protection, as failure to disclose may mean that your policy will not provide you with the cover you require, or may perhaps invalidate the policy altogether.

Declaration:

I declare that the foregoing statements and particulars are true and complete and that this proposal shall form the basis of the contract with Commercial Union Assurance Company plc.

I agree to accept Insurance subject to the terms and conditions of the Company's policy and that the insurance will not be in force until the Proposal has been accepted by the Company.

Signed

Date

Space for further information if required

Fig. 13.2 (*continued*)

If the proposer is interested in one or more of the policies outlined, then he/she must be sent a **Proposal Form** (see Fig. 13.2). The information provided on this enables the company to calculate the premium (money) which the customer must pay to obtain the insurance. In the example given above, the chances of a factory burning down were quoted as ten thousand to one. In practice, the likelihood of a fire occurring will vary depending on the nature of the building and its location. A wooden building will be more likely to burn down than brick one and a factory in the middle of a large town is at greater risk than one sited in the countryside. The more likelihood of the fire occurring the higher will be the premium.

The proposal form therefore seeks to elicit the necessary information from the proposer. The form will also ensure that the customer has an insurable interest in the property which is to be insured. This simply means that the person seeking the insurance must possess a financial interest in the risk being insured, thus the owners of the factory could insure it against fire because if it burned down they would suffer a financial loss. If a competitor tried to insure the factory there would be no insurable interest and the policy would be void. It would have no legal effect.

Having been satisfied that there is an insurable interest and once the premium has been calculated (where there is a standard policy there is a standard premium and it will not be re-calculated for each policy), the party seeking insurance can be informed of the annual premium to be paid and sent the appropriate form for payment. Although insurance premiums may be paid in cash or by cheque it is more common to ask the insured party to pay by means of standing order or direct debit.

Some insurance policies have a fixed premium. This means the annual premium remains constant. A standing order would be suitable for this type of payment. If a building is being insured against fire, then the sum insured will rise every year to take inflation into account. Thus if a building is worth £100,000 and there is a 10 per cent rate of inflation, the policy would need to be increased to £110,000 the following year as this will be the sum necessary to rebuild the factory. For this reason, premiums also increase annually. A direct debit is a more suitable method of payment. It enables the bank to send varying amounts to the insurance company at the latter's request. An insurance policy needs to be 'inflation proofed' because if the sum insured is less than the value of the item you may not recover your losses.

Example:

Property worth £100,000
Insured for £75,000
Insured can only recover ¾(100,000÷75,000) of any losses
therefore fire causes £40,000 damage
Sum recovered £30,000

Once the customer has returned the appropriate forms, the policy can be issued. In most companies it takes several days and even weeks to issue the policy. The secretary will therefore, in the meantime, issue a **cover note** to the insured. This states that the premium has been paid and the insurance cover exists. It is proof of the contract until the policy is actually issued. The latter document will contain all the terms of the contract. As stated above, most premiums are paid by means of standing order or direct debit but, where it is paid annually by cash or by cheque, the secretary will have to send out a **renewal notice** to the insured.

The final function of the secretary will be to deal with queries concerning claims. If the factory burns down Barl will wish to claim on their insurance policy. The secretary will send them a **claim form** (Fig. 13.3) and when this is returned the damage will be assessed by a third party employed by the insurance company called an **adjuster.** The extent of the loss will be calculated and this sum will be paid out by the insurance company. Although Barl have insured their building for £100,000 it may not be totally destroyed by fire. It may only have caused £70,000 of damage. As insurance compensates the policy holder for losses incurred, Barl can only claim £70,000. Once the insurance company have paid the claim they then take over the rights of the insured under the doctrine of **subrogation.** The equipment in the factory may have been severely damaged by fire and the owner compensated. The equipment then belongs to the insurance company who are entitled to sell it off as scrap. If, having been paid the value of the machinery, Barl were entitled to sell it for scrap they would then make a profit out of the insurance policy and the aim of insurance is to compensate, not to give the insured a profit. For this reason, the claim form which Barl complete will ask if the property is insured with any other insurance company. It is possible that Barl may have fire insurance with two separate companies each for £100,000. In the event of a fire causing £70,000 of damage they are not entitled to claim this sum against each insurance policy. They are entitled to only £70,000 compensation and therefore each company would pay £35,000.

Commercial Union Assurance

Business Premises Claim Report

ASSURANCE

Please return to:

ГРУ**АТЕ HOUSE**
ГЛ*ЛЮ* **D ROAD**
ГЛЯТЕ
EX1 1PY

Please answer all questions on this page as fully as possible
and relevant sections on other pages.

* delete as required

Claim No. _____ (Office Use Only)

Insured

Policy No. _____ Renewal month _____

Insured's name _____

Address _____

_____ Postcode _____ Tel. No. _____

Business _____

(a) Is the Insured registered as a taxable person?   YES/NO*

(b) If the Insured is registered for V.A.T., is full remission of input tax obtained?   YES/NO*

(c) If only partial remission of V.A.T. is obtained, state last annual adjusted percentage of tax recoverable _____ %

The Event

Date _____ Time _____ am/pm

When and by whom discovered _____

If known, state name and address of person causing the loss or damage _____

_____

Address where the event occurred _____

_____ Postcode _____ Tel. No. _____

State rooms or area affected _____

State fully what happened _____

_____

_____

_____

_____

If illegal entry, which windows or doors were forced? _____

Were premises occupied at the time?   YES/NO*   If "NO" state date and time they were last occupied

Date _____ Time _____ am/pm

State date police were advised, name of station and officer's number _____

(Inform police at once if the claim is for articles lost or stolen or maliciously destroyed or damaged)

Fig. 13.3

The Property Lost or Damaged

Are you the owner?   YES/NO*   If "NO" state name and address of the owner

Name and address _____

_____

Give name(s) of any other party having an interest in the property _____

_____

Are there any other insurances on the property?   YES/NO*

If "YES" give details (including name, address and policy no. of other insurers) _____

_____

State total value of insured property (**Not for Glass Claims**)

Building £ _____   Stock £ _____   Other property £ _____

State nature of occupancy of premises _____

Are you responsible by agreement for the property?   YES/NO*   If "YES", please forward copy of the agreement

Have you ever before made a claim of this nature on any insurance company or underwriter?   YES/NO*

If "YES", give details: Nature of claim _____

Name of Insurers _____ Amount paid £ _____

Breakage of Glass
Details of Claim

Size_____ Type_____

Was glass sound previous to breakage?   YES/NO*

Do you require the reglazing deferred until further notice?   YES/NO*

Situation (e.g. door, window, showcase, etc)_____

Buildings (including boundary walls where specially insured)
Details of Claim

Specify separately each room or building damaged or destroyed and how occupied	Age of building or damaged fixtures/ fittings, water tanks, etc.	Date when last decorated (each room or part damaged)	Amount of tradesman's estimate **Please attach estimate**	Adjustment for previous depreciation alterations or improvements	Net amount of claim
			£		£

If necessary continue on a separate sheet

Fig. 13.3 (*continued*)

Contents
Details of Claim

(mark an X in the last column if articles are on loan, hire or belong to a customer)

Description of articles (attach estimates for articles repairable)	From whom obtained (name and address)	Date acquired or manu- factured	Cost (net of profit & V.A.T.) price	Value of salvage	Net amount of claim less deprec- iation, salvage, profit & V.A.T., etc.	V.A.T. if claimed
			£	£	£	£

If necessary continue on a separate sheet

Fig. 13.3 (*continued*)

Property in the open

Describe fully and state situation	From whom obtained (name and address)	Date acquired or manu- factured	Cost (net of profit & V.A.T.) price	Value of salvage	Net amount of claim less deprec- iation, salvage, profit & V.A.T., etc.	V.A.T. if claimed
			£	£	£	£

Contract Works

State form of Contract (e.g. R.I.B.A., I.C.E., etc.) _____

Any special terms?   YES/NO*

Period of contract from _____ to _____

State value of whole contract   £ _____

Declaration

I declare that these particulars are true to the best of my knowledge.

Signature _____   Date _____

Commercial Union Assurance Company plc. Registered Office: St. Helen's, 1 Undershaft, London EC3P 3DQ. Registered in England No. 21487
Printed by Group Supply Department of Commercial Union Assurance.

FEBRUARY 1981

GSF769(d)

Fig. 13.3 (*continued*)

186 Section A

Examination questions

1. Why is an insurance company better able to afford risks than is a firm seeking insurance cover? Give two examples of insurance cover a firm might seek.

   (*Q. 4 1976*)

2. What is meant by an insurable risk?

   (*Q. 1(h) 1975*)

3. What are the main principles underlying insurance agreements?

   (*Q. 11 1975*)

4. Imagine you are an insurance agent trying to 'sell insurance' to a small business. Explain the main insurances you would recommend and the reasons why you think they are needed by this business.

   (*Q. 6 1978*)

5. What are the chief risks that the owners of a small factory might insure against?

   (*Q. 10 1974*)

6. As part of an internal training course an insurance firm is providing a list containing definitions of insurance terms. Suggest suitable definitions for the following words: proposer, premium, cover note, subrogation, fidelity guarantee.

   (*Q. 3 1983*)

7. You join an insurance business as a secretary. During the training programme there is a section on Insurance. What would you expect this talk to contain?

   (*Q. 10 1984*)

The government and the economy

Chapter 14

Of what relevance is this topic to the potential secretary? In the first place it may affect the employer.

Imagine you are a secretary employed by a firm manufacturing electronic typewriters. How would your employers be affected by:

1. An import tariff on electronic goods?
2. An increase in domestic interest rates?
3. A strong domestic currency?

If there is an import tariff (tax) on electronic goods this will increase the price of imported electronic typewriters. This would improve the sales of your firm because your competitors' machines are now more expensive. You are working for a more profitable firm and are therefore less likely to be made redundant and more likely to receive a pay increase. If there are high interest rates this will have the opposite effect on the profits of your employers. They would almost certainly have borrowed money to start up in business and will now have to pay higher interest on this. In addition the higher interest rates may discourage firms from investing in new equipment and this could mean reduced sales for your employers. If your firm is making less profit it will need less staff; your job could be at risk. Finally, if the domestic currency is strong this will make imported goods cheaper and it will make the goods you sell more expensive to foreigners. There is more competition on the home market and it will be more difficult to export. This could mean fewer sales for your firm with the unpleasant consequences that will follow.

Just as the decisions which the government makes may affect your future employer, it may also affect you as an individual.

Suppose that you intend to buy a Japanese car on hire purchase. How would you be affected by:

1. An import quota on Japanese cars;
2. The tightening up of hire purchase restrictions?

187

If there is a restriction on the number of Japanese cars that can be imported you may well find it difficult to buy a model and because they are scarce the price may rise. The tightening of hire purchase restrictions may mean that instead of putting down a deposit of say 10 per cent of the cost of the car, you may be required to put down a 20 per cent deposit. The effect of both of these may mean that you are unable to purchase the car you wanted.

When the government gets involved in the economy it affects you. Why does the government get involved?

Provision of services

The government has to provide certain services and it needs the money to pay for these and Table 14.1 gives an indication of how the government spends its money.

Table 14.1. Government expenditure

	Expenditure (£ billion)	Percentage
Defence	17.0	13
Education	12.6	10
Social Security	37.2	30
Social Services	15.4	12
Law and Order	4.9	4
Housing	2.5	2
Roads	4.4	3
Miscellaneous	30.0	26

The amount spent will vary depending on the political party which happens to be in power. Some parties believe in considerable state involvement in the economy while others believe that the state should only be involved in providing the minimum of services. It is important to appreciate that no politicial party has ever claimed that no services should be provided by the government. Some services are so crucial that they cannot be left to private enterprise; for instance, one of the largest elements of expenditure is defence and all parties agree that it is the responsibility of the state to pay for this. Again, there is political agreement that education, social services and the police should all be provided for by the state, although there may be disputes as to the amount of private enterprise that should be allowed in these areas.

Given the need to provide these services the government must raise sufficient funds to pay for them. It can do this in two ways:

Taxation

Finance can be raised by levying direct or indirect taxes on the citizens or the companies within a country. Direct taxes are collected by the Inland Revenue and are levied directly on the individual or the company that has to pay them. They include income tax and corporation tax. Thus income tax is paid directly (which is why it is called a direct tax) by the taxpayer to the Inland Revenue. It is deducted from your wage packet by your employer.

Indirect taxes are collected by the Customs and Excise and, unlike direct taxes, they are not collected directly from the taxpayer. Thus VAT, which is an indirect tax, is levied on goods or services. The consumer buying a washing machine may pay £150; of this £120 may go to the retailer and £30 may be destined for the tax man. The consumer is not really concerned with this, but is mainly interested in the purchase price, £150. Once the retailer has collected the money he remits the appropriate amount to the Customs and Excise. The consumer is therefore paying the tax indirectly.

Taxation is not, however, used solely to raise revenue. It can be used by the Chancellor of the Exchequer to achieve social or political aims. Consider how the Chancellor should use taxation to:

1. discourage smoking
2. encourage firms to adopt new technology
3. re-distribute income from the wealthy to the poorer groups within society
4. affect the retail price index

(The answers can be found at the end of the chapter.)

Borrowing

Where government expenditure exceeds the revenue obtained from taxes then the deficit must be made up by borrowing.

The choice of where to raise revenue and how much should be raised has both political and economic implications. Suppose you are the Chancellor of the Exchequer and you calculate government expenditure will be £100,000,000 but you decide to collect only £90,000,000 in taxes and to finance the other expenditure by borrowing £10,000,000. What effect will this have on the economy? As can be seen in Fig. 14.1 the government expenditure of £100,000,000 ultimately finds it way back to the consumer in the form of wages and dividends. The public therefore have £100,000,000 to spend but they have had to pay out only £90,000,000 in taxes. The net result therefore is that there is an additional £10,000,000 to buy goods and services (the public have lost

£90m, but gained £100m). This may well have the effect of stimulating the domestic (home) economy. The consumer has more money to spend and therefore will require more goods. If the consumer buys home manufactured products then in order to produce these the manufacturers will have to purchase more equipment and take on additional labour; this reduces unemployment. The additional labour will be paid and they will use this money to purchase more goods, this in turn will create further employment. When a Chancellor therefore wishes to stimulate (expand) the economy he may well decide to bring in a deficit budget, which is the technical name used when expenditure exceeds the amount of revenue raised from taxation.

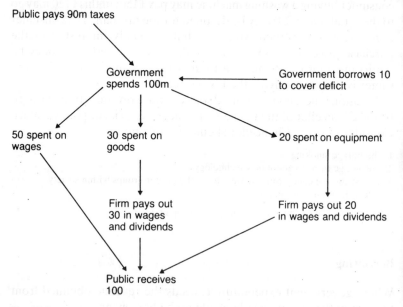

Fig. 14.1

Economic objectives

The government wants to obtain the economic objectives that it has been elected to achieve.

Although the policies which political parties may follow vary, most parties seek to obtain four main objectives.

1. Full employment

This does not mean that everybody must have a job but merely that the rate of unemployment falls within an acceptable figure. What is acceptable will depend on the political party.

2. Low inflation figures
This is an essential prerequisite of some of the other objectives. A high domestic inflation rate can affect a country's competitiveness in overseas markets and have a damaging effect on the balance of payments. Given an exchange rate of £1=10 francs consider the following:

Cost of car in UK £5,000
Cost of car in France 50,000 fr.

Financially it makes no difference whether the UK citizen buys a car here or in France. Suppose:

Inflation in UK 10 per cent
Inflation in France 5 per cent
Cost of UK cars £5,000+10 per cent=£5,500
Cost of French car 50,000+2,500=52,000 which at £1=10 francs means it will cost 52,500÷10=£5,250.

The UK citizen now finds it cheaper to purchase a French car, hence imports will rise and the balance of payments will deteriorate.

3. Economic growth
It is a natural human reaction to want to be better off. This is not automatically achieved by higher wages as the increase may be offset by the rise in inflation.

Example:
Salary £5,000   Expenditure on food, heating, etc £5,000
Salary increase 10 per cent=£5,500   Prices rise by 10 per cent

Therefore salary buys the same amount of food, heating, etc. The wage earner is no better off.

Economic growth means that the country is producing more and therefore there is more to go round. Everybody may therefore have a higher standard of living.

Example:
Salary £5,000   Expenditure on food, heating, etc. £5,000
Salary increase 5 per cent=£5,250   Inflation 1 per cent=£50

Therefore the wage earner only needs £5,050 to buy equivalent amount of food, heating, etc. The earner has £200 remaining to purchase additional items and is therefore better off. Your standard of living only rises if wages increase faster than inflation.

4. A stable balance of payments
This is a prerequisite of achieving the others. If the balance of payments falls into deficit and the country is forced to borrow or draw on its reserves, then it may be forced to take remedial action to improve the balance of payments. This could have a detrimental effect on its economic growth and levels of employment.

It is extremely difficult to obtain all four objectives.

Earnings up as jobs fall

The Government's economic hopes were hit yesterday by official figures showing a further underlying rise in unemployment and continued earnings growth well ahead of the dropping inflation rate set to fall tomorrow below 3 per cent for the first time since the first oil shock.

Those in work have now enjoyed the largest spurt in living standards since Labour's pre-election boom in 1978–9. But if earnings growth continues at the rate of 7.5 per cent inflation is bound to pick up again unless the Government puts a new squeeze on the economy – and hits growth and jobs.

Obtaining economic objectives

To obtain the objectives detailed above the government may use: fiscal policy, devaluation; high interest rates.

1. Fiscal policy (taxation)
One already mentioned would be a budget deficit (see Fig. 14.1 on page 190).

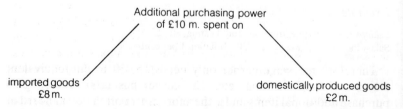

Additional purchasing power
of £10 m. spent on

imported goods
£8 m.

domestically produced goods
£2 m.

Fig. 14.2

The budget deficit results in an increase in purchasing power within the community. If this increased purchasing power is spent on domestically produced goods there will be an increased demand for labour and a reduction in the unemployment figures. As Fig. 14.2 indicates, however, part of the additional spending power may be spent on imports. This may then lead to a balance of payments problem. As we saw in Chapter 9 this may result in a weakening of the domestic currency. If this happens it makes imported goods more expensive and where a country imports raw materials or foodstuffs this will result in higher prices for the consumer and inflation. Even if this does not occur and all the increased purchasing power is spent on domestic goods, a time may arise when there is insufficient productive capacity at home to meet the demand. This will mean imports will be purchased and the demand for domestic products will force their prices up, again resulting in inflation. A budget deficit may therefore achieve economic growth and full employment while at the same time causing inflation and an unstable balance of payments.

2. Devaluation

From Fig. 14.3 it can be seen that following a devaluation the domestic currency will be worth less in terms of other currencies, thus instead of £1 being worth 10 francs, £1 would only buy 8 francs. The reader will remember from the chapter on international trade (Ch. 9) that as a consequence of a devaluation exports will rise because domestic goods will be cheaper to foreigners (in our example British goods will be cheaper in France). At the same time because the domestic currency will buy less foreign currency, foreign goods become more expensive. It therefore follows that imports should fall. Given that exports rise and imports fall there will be a balance of payments surplus and an increased demand for British goods both here (because the goods of foreign competitors are now more expensive) and from abroad. This will necessitate an increase in production to meet the increased demand which should result in additional workers being required. Thus the devaluation should achieve a balance of payments surplus, less unemployment and economic growth.

There is a problem, however. As we have seen above, imports become more expensive and we have therefore assumed that people no longer buy them and turn to British produced goods. In some cases, however, this will not be possible. Britain, like most countries, lacks certain raw materials and is forced to import these. In addition, certain foreign products may not be produced in this country or may be so popular that people still require them, even though the cost has risen. The cost of importing foreign goods has risen and this will be reflected

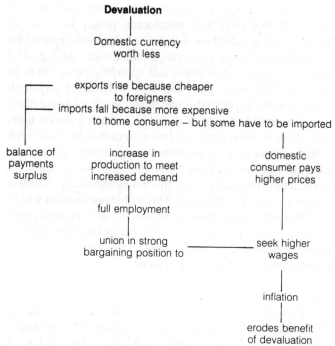

Devaluation

Domestic currency
worth less

exports rise because cheaper
to foreigners
imports fall because more expensive
to home consumer – but some have to be imported

balance of
payments
surplus

increase in
production to meet
increased demand

domestic
consumer pays
higher prices

full employment

union in strong
bargaining position to — seek higher
wages

inflation

erodes benefit
of devaluation

Fig. 14.3

in the prices which retailers charge in the shops. It follows that the domestic consumer will therefore be forced to pay higher prices, and in consequence is likely to seek higher wages. As was seen in Chapter 1 this is one of the functions of the union and because there is full employment, the union will be in a strong bargaining position. Employers will be anxious to recruit staff to cope with the increased demand and are more likely therefore to agree wage demands rather than risk damaging strikes. Because the demand for goods is high they will feel confident that they can pass on the higher wage costs to the consumer in the form of higher prices. This of course will lead to inflation. As domestic prices increase so the value of the devaluation will lessen (as explained above) and a point will eventually be reached where British goods are more expensive than imported goods, at which point the balance of payments will go into deficit and unemployment will increase. If devaluation is therefore to work it is essential that wages do not rise to compensate for the higher prices which the devaluation must bring.

Sterling plunge halts drop in interest rates

The pound yesterday plunged downwards against most important currencies for the third day running, wiping out hopes that interest rates will start falling again soon. . . .

The Government is standing by to intervene by raising interest rates if the snowball effect in the foreign exchange markets gets out of hand. But it has so far accepted an overall devaluation of sterling approaching 4 per cent in the last three days. . . .

The decline threatens to raise retail prices, but it will be good news for many exporters. . . .

The sudden weakness of the pound threatens to reinject some inflation into the economy, because each 1 per cent fall in its average value increases the retail price index by 0.3 per cent over a year. Whitehall is stressing that only a part of this comes through quickly, in prices such as oil. But with a 3.8 per cent fall in sterling's average value this week, more than 1 per cent will be added to the RPI [Retail Price Index] over a year.

3. High interest rates (Fig. 14.4)
If there are high interest rates, then foreigners will wish to invest their money in the UK to take advantage of these (as explained on page 118). There will be a healthy demand for sterling and the £ will be 'strong'. This means the opposite of devaluation. Thus instead of an Englishman obtaining 10 francs for £1 he will obtain 12 francs. It follows from this that British goods will be expensive to foreigners while the price of foreign goods (imports) will be cheaper. This means that manufacturers will pay lower prices for their raw materials, hence price rises should be kept to a minimum. This will therefore achieve a low inflation rate. Given however that it makes exporting difficult and reduces the price of imports, it is likely to have an adverse effect on the balance of payments. In addition there will be a lack of demand for UK goods both at home (because we will import goods) and abroad (because they will be more expensive than those of our competitors). As a consequence, British firms are likely to produce less. The decision to produce less is reinforced by the high interest rates which makes it very expensive for industry to borrow money to re-equip or to carry stocks of goods. If a firm produces goods which are not sold it must carry them in the warehouse and if the goods are worth, say,

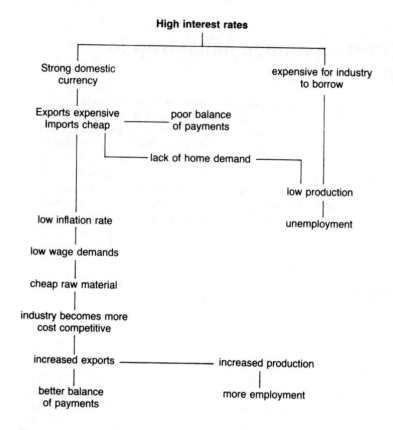

Fig. 14.4

£1,000,000 then it has this sum of money tied up. If interest rates are 15 per cent the cost of tying up £1,000,000 in stock is £150,000. Manufacturers will therefore reduce production and this results in unemployment. Clearly, then, three of the objectives, balance of payments, employment and economic growth, are not achieved in the short term. In the long term, the low inflation rate caused by the strong currency should result in lower wage demands. Industry therefore has the benefit of low cost for raw materials and lower wage rises than its competitors. It is anticipated that this should make industry more efficient. As it becomes more efficient it is therefore able to sell its goods overseas which improves the balance of payments and to increase domestic sales at the expense of imports. The net result of the increased sales both at home and abroad should lead to full employment. If the objectives are therefore to be achieved through a strong domestic currency, it is crucial that British industry takes advantage of the low cost to become more efficient vis à vis the rest of the world.

Examination questions

1. The government controls the economy in a variety of ways. Distinguish by examples between fiscal and monetary policy.
   (Q. 1(i) 1977)

2. Give: (i) **one** example of a direct tax; and
   (ii) **one** *example of an indirect tax.*
   (Q. 1(d) 1976)

3. Name a reason (other than the raising of government revenue) why tax is levied.
   (Q. 1(c) 1975)

4. There are various ways in which governments can fight inflation. Explain the way in which your government has attempted to reduce inflation or maintain it at a low rate.
   (Q. 10 1982)

5. Explain ways in which a government could:
   (a) discourage consumption of a product
   (b) restrict imports which compete with home produced articles
   (c) encourage the efficiency of exporters.
   (Q. 2 1984)

6. As a wage earner how might you be affected by the following?
   (a) An increase in interest rates;
   (b) A decrease in the rate of direct taxation;
   (c) A fall in the value of your currency.
   (Q. 11 1984)

7. Apart from taxation, explain one way a government can obtain large amounts of money.
   (Q. 1(j) 1986)

Answers

1. Raise VAT on cigarettes. This would make them more expensive which might discourage people from smoking them. The tax of course will generate income. A Chancellor who wanted 'energy saving' measures to be introduced into houses might 'encourage' householders by taxing gas, oil and coal. This would provide an incentive to reduce consumption.
2. Give grants to firms or agree to waive corporation tax on the profits for one year.
3. A progressive tax (i.e. one where the rich pay a bigger percentage of their income than the poor) is one way of achieving this.

4. A change in VAT will affect prices and hence the index. If VAT is reduced by 5 per cent prices will fall. If it is increased the index rises. The retail price index is one factor influencing wage demands. The higher it is the bigger increase the unions will claim. If the government wishes to raise revenue but does not wish to see the index rise it will increase the rate of income tax. Although an employee's take home pay (salary less deductions such as tax and national insurance) is reduced, prices will not rise.

Section B

Starting up

Chapter 15

Dennis Kay is the South Western Sales Manager for an organisation supplying office equipment. The company wish to move him to the North East, but because he and his family are happy living in Devon, he decides to resign and set up in business on his own account. Given his business background, he is considering opening a shop in Plymouth. He employs a market research firm to conduct a survey into consumer needs. The questionnaire they devise produces a positive response and he therefore decides to go ahead.

To establish himself in business he will require premises, but before he can look for these he must make arrangements to obtain the necessary finance.

Finance

Given that Kay is setting up on his own account, he will be a sole trader and you will remember that he has to provide the finance himself, either from his own resources or by borrowing the money from friends or the bank. If he chooses to take somebody else into the business as a partner, then the capital must be found by the partners (a public company would be able to raise funds by issuing shares to the public up to the value of its authorised capital). Once he is satisfied that he has sufficient capital to start the business, Kay will need to find premises.

Premises

In order to purchase premises Kay decides to take out a mortgage. This is a loan but differs from a bank loan in that it will be for a long period, often up to 25 years. He can obtain the mortgage from a building society, such as the Halifax, or one of the commercial banks, such as the Midland or the National Westminster. The security (collateral) for the mortgage is the property to be purchased. In the event of Kay being unable to make the mortgage repayments, the building society or bank will be able to sell the property and use the funds obtained to pay off the loan, any surplus being given to Kay. The legal formalities involved in the purchase will be dealt with by Kay's solicitor and the purchase will be completed when the solicitor hands over the banker's draft (cheque drawn upon the bank) for the appropriate sum.

Having purchased his premises, Kay will need to engage and train his staff.

Staff

The recruitment of staff in a large company would be the function of a Personnel Department. They would arrange for the appropriate advertisement to be placed in a local newspaper, for the application forms to be sent out to interested parties and for the selection interviews to be held. In a small company it is not possible to have specialist managers and so these functions will be performed by Kay.

He decides to start with a staff of two. Once the staff are engaged he will then have to organise their training programme. He intends to offer a word processing service to small firms and therefore both his staff need to be competent on the Xerox word processor he has purchased. There are short word processing courses at the local College of Further Education. Should he send the staff on these? The answer is, almost certainly, no. It is important that his staff learn to operate a Xerox word processor, whereas those in the local college are Bitsy Secretaires. Manufacturers, aware of the training programmes, will undertake when they sell a word processor to train one or two operators free of charge before the machine arrives, or immediately on its delivery. It is, therefore, almost certain that the company delivering the Xerox word processor will arrange for the staff to be trained.

Once the word processor is installed what happens if a member of the staff who has been trained leaves? What is the most appropriate method for teaching the replacement how to use the machine? A college course is out, for the reason outlined above, and letting the replacement learn by sitting next to the other operator is not desirable for a number of reasons. Firstly, the other employee, although a competent operator, may be a poor teacher and unable to teach the proper skills and if he/she has developed any bad habits these will be transferred to the new employee. Secondly, the word processor will be in use and it will not therefore be possible to plan the teaching so that the new employee is taken through the procedures step by step. In addition, the pressures within a busy office may not be conducive to learning. For these reasons it will be better if a new employee receives off-the-job training away from the normal working environment, and may therefore be sent on a course organised by the manufacturers of the machine.

It may however have been possible to recruit a new member of staff who already has the necessary skills, who may have attended a full-time course at the College of Further Education where, although the new employee may have learned on another machine, will have the basic word processing skills and should be able to transfer these relatively easily by reading the manual and talking to the experienced operator. Or the new employee might have received instruction through one of the courses organised by the Manpower Services Commission. This may have been a course for mature applicants or one of the courses designed for unemployed school-leavers, which consists of a period of training supplemented by a period of work experience.

Kay also wishes to train both his new staff on the switchboard. Given that both have a suitable telephone technique, this type of traning is probably best done on the job and given to employees in the normal working situation. The employee to be trained will sit next to somebody who can use the switchboard, watch and then use the switchboard under supervision. Once competent, the trainee will then be allowed to work without supervision.

If the business expands, Kay may wish one of his staff to undertake more accountancy work. In order to acquire the necessary skills he/she may be sent away to the local college on a day-release scheme to take the examinations of one of the accountancy bodies.

The engagement and training of staff are two of the personnel functions which Kay must perform. He will also have to perform one of the functions of the Accounts Department, the calculation and payment of staff wages. From their gross wages, sums will be deducted for National Insurance and income tax (which you will recall is a direct tax) and the remaining sum will be paid to the employees. If they agree, the sum will be paid directly into their current accounts at the bank. They can then draw out any sums they require by writing out cheques or using their cash cards.

Only one thing remains to be done before Kay can set up in business and that is to buy the equipment.

Equipment

The equipment which Kay requires (word processors, computers, photocopiers etc) is expensive. A word processor, for example, might cost £6,000. Once it has been purchased and installed it may generate an income of £100 per week; this means that it will take approximately 60 weeks before Kay has recovered the initial cost. He may be able to finance their purchase from the capital which he or his partners initially contributed, alternatively he may approach his bank for a short term loan (the income produced from the equipment purchased should be enough to repay the loan within two years). Before giving him the loan the bank will require security (collateral). This may be the equipment purchased or anything else which the bank could sell in the event of Kay failing to repay the loan on time.

Instead of seeking a bank loan, Kay may decide to purchase the equipment on credit. With hire purchase he would pay a deposit on the item and then agree to pay the balance, plus interest, over a fixed period. The advantage of this scheme would be that the machines would produce sufficient income to cover the monthly instalments. When the final instalments have been paid Kay would become the legal owner of the goods. Until that point they will remain the property of the sellers who can, with the court's permission, re-possess them if Kay fails to pay his instalments.

Kay can now start trading once he has taken out the necessary insurance policies.

Let us assume that Kay's business has expanded and he is now writing and developing computer programs. Being based in Plymouth he is also considering exporting these to France, especially as the pound is weak against the franc. The computer expansion is costly because it involves new premises and equipment and exporting to France means establishing premises there. Kay requires additional finance.

A large public company could raise additional long term capital by issuing shares to the public. However, the cost of becoming a public company is considerable and it is uneconomic to raise less than £500,000 in a share issue. Kay must obviously look to other sources of finance.

He has already had an overdraft from his bank to pay bills when he was starting up and the bank manager is now prepared to offer him a loan. Unfortunately this will only provide short term finance whereas Kay needs finance for a longer period.

It is possible that retained profits could be used but in Kay's case these have already been re-invested in the business. He therefore approaches a merchant bank. Unlike the commercial banks (those you see in the High Street) which deal with both the public and businesses, merchant banks deal only with businesses.

He may be successful in obtaining funds from the merchant bank because they specialise in providing 'venture capital'. This is money invested in a small business which has little collateral but where the potential profits are considerable (as in the case with the 'new technology'). In return for the investment the bank obtains part of the business. Although the investment is risky one success will offset numerous failures.

Not only will the merchant bank provide capital, it will also advise Kay on potential export problems. It will advise him on the currency situation, exchange controls and problems of insurance.

Saving for a house
Chapter 16

Most people hope at some time to be able to buy their own house, and the sources of finance to would-be house-owners have been described earlier. It was also remarked that the banks or building societies would not provide a mortgage for the whole of the purchase price. It is normally a percentage of the valuation and this is usually less than the purchase price. You may be buying a house for £30,000 but it is likely that the building society surveyor will put a valuation on it of say £28,000, leaving the would-be purchaser to find £2,000, as well as the legal fees and the cost of the surveyor's report. Before embarking on house purchase, therefore, you will need to have saved several thousand pounds.

Being aware of this, you and your partner decide to save £20 per week from your salaries. In less than three years' time you will have saved £3,000. You allocate £2,000 for the deposit and £1,000 for other costs. This, of course, pre-supposes that the property you are after will still cost £30,000 in three years' time. It is likely, however, that house prices will rise in the next three years because of inflation.

If there is 10 per cent inflation, then

Year 1   £30,000 plus 10%=£33,000
Year 2   £33,000 plus 10%=£36,300
Year 3   £36,300 plus 10%=£39,930

The amount saved, £3,000, was to be 10 per cent of the purchase price (£30,000). Given inflation, at the end of the three years the sum required has risen to £3,993. If your savings had been left in a **current account** on which no interest was paid, then you would have to save an additional £993. It is therefore crucial that when you save money it is invested so that it will increase in line with inflation.

One possibility is to ask your bank to open a **deposit account.** You could arrange for your bank to transfer £20 a week automatically from your current to your deposit account, where it will earn interest. Some banks will guarantee its depositors a mortgage. The capital in the deposit account is secure, but the interest payable may be below the rate of inflation.

Alternatively, it may be decided to open an account with a building society. This is similar to a deposit account in that interest is paid and the capital is secure. It also gives depositors priority when seeking a mortgage. There are different types of accounts with building societies but it would be unwise to select one which involved leaving the savings untouched for a period of years as you may require the money before the end of this period if a suitable house is found.

The choice of bank or building society could therefore depend on which offers the higher rate of interest. Since 1985, both organisations' rates are quoted net of tax. What this means is that when you receive interest you do not have to pay tax on it; the tax has already been paid.

As stated above, both of these investments are secure, but if the rate of inflation is 10 per cent and the interest you receive (after tax has been paid) is 5 per cent, then it follows that your capital is not increasing as fast as the rate of inflation.

In an attempt to find an investment which will rise faster than the rate of inflation you may be tempted to look at **stocks and shares.** The **Financial Times Share Index** (which monitors the general progress of stocks and shares) will rise over the long term to compensate for the rate of inflation. If there is high inflation, it means that companies are charging higher prices to the consumers and this should ultimately be reflected in increased profits for the company resulting in higher share prices. The difficulty for the investor is that, although this is a long term trend, there are times when the **Financial Times Index** may actually fall, although prices are rising. If you are buying a house then you may wish to sell your shares (realise your assets) at a time when share prices are actually falling. You may find that the £1,000 you invested is now only worth £900. Of course, if share prices are rising, the investment might be worth £1,200. A further complication for the small investor is that shares in individual companies may not follow the general trend of share prices. Thus the **Financial Times Index** may be increasing but the shares of British Leyland may be falling because there is a serious industrial stoppage at BL which has brought production to a standstill. Conversely, a successful introduction of a new car might cause the share price to rise although the FT Index is static or even falling. Interest, of course, is not paid on shares (the shareholders receive dividends which depend on companies' profits) but the main reason for not investing funds in stocks and shares is the risk involved. You may however decide at the end of one year to leave £800 of your savings in the deposit account or with the building society and to invest £200 in shares, hoping that you make a speculative gain.

Rather than selecting an individual company you might choose to invest in a **Unit Trust**. This means giving the funds to an investment manager in return for units in the Trust. You will not own shares in companies but part of the trust. The investment manager will then invest the funds in a variety of shares. The total value of all the investments will determine the value of the fund and therefore the value of the units held. The investment manager is a specialist who will buy and sell shares on behalf of the fund in an attempt to make a capital gain (profit) for the unit holders. By entrusting the funds to a specialist who can invest them over many securities it is therefore hoped to minimise the risk.

Example

A trust has 1,000,000 investors each contributing £10.

£10 = 1 unit

Trust Capital £10,000,000

Invested in 1,000,000 shares, current value £10,000,000

Each unit holder owns $\frac{1}{1,000,000}$ of the trust.

Shares owned increase in value to £15,000,000

Each unit held now is worth £15 $\left(\frac{1}{1000,000} \text{ of £15,000,000} \right)$

It is also possible to invest money in **gilt-edge securities.** These are issued by the government for a fixed period of time and because the government guarantees them, there is no possibility of investors losing all their money (unlike stocks in companies where, if they go bankrupt, investors do lose their money). They are therefore a more secure investment than ordinary shares, but their value can change. To understand this, let us assume that the government has issued a number of certificates and has promised that it will pay the holder of each certificate £5 interest annually. If I pay £100 for one of these certificates then the rate of interest payable is 5 per cent (£5 on the £100 investment). Like stocks and shares these certificates can be traded on the Stock Exchange so that investors may realise their assets. Let us now assume that interest rates have risen to 10 per cent; the holder of one of these certificates will still only receive £5. A prospective purchaser will only be willing to buy the certificate if the interest (£5) is equivalent to 10 per cent of the sum invested, i.e. the price paid for the share. It therefore follows that the purchaser would only be prepared to pay £50 for the certificate (£5 is 10 per cent of £50). If interest rates rise therefore the value of gilt-edge securities on the stock market will fall. Conversely, if interest rates fall then the value of gilt-edge securities will rise. If interest rates were to fall to 2½ per cent, then the holder of a certificate would expect to sell it at £200 because £5 paid on a £200 investment is 2½ per cent.

You will appreciate that the value of gilt-edge securities depends on the movement of interest rates, therefore investing in gilt-edge securities is best left to the experts.

Organisation and the large business

Chapter 17

Throughout this book, reference has been made to the various functions of a business. Mention has been made, for example, of marketing (page 137), personnel (page 48), and the roles of company officers such as directors and the company secretary have been described. It is now time to pull together all the various pieces so that the full picture can be seen.

An organisation chart usually shows the main functions and how they are organised. The one shown in Fig. 17.1 is typical of a manufacturing business but students must appreciate that talking about a 'typical' organisation chart is like talking about an 'average' person. Neither exist. When writing your project you will almost certainly find that the organisation chart of your business differs from the one included here.

The chart on the following page, as well as indicating the main functions of the business, also illustrates some of the vertical channels of communication. As mentioned in Chapter 2, effective communications are vital for an efficient business and the chart clearly indicates the lines of authority from top to bottom. The chart will be supported by job descriptions which expand on the roles of the staff involved.

An organisation chart also illustrates any individual's 'span of control' (or 'span of responsibility'); this indicates the number of staff for whom the individual is responsible. Thus the head of personnel has a span of control of three, the head of marketing a span of four and the buyers five. Calculate the span for the works manager and for the foreman. It is generally agreed that there is a limit to the number of staff you can effectively control. If you are made responsible for too many people, then there will be insufficient time for monitoring them; communications will suffer and performance deteriorates. The ideal span of control varies with the nature of the job but, as an example, it is usually felt that at the higher levels of management, a span of six is enough.

The number of levels of management is also reflected by the chart:

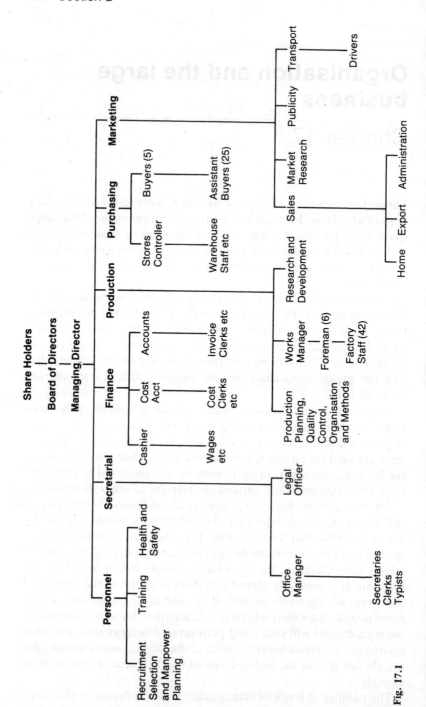

Fig. 17.1

the more layers, the more likely communications will be distorted or slowed down. It needs emphasising, however, that communications depend very heavily on people and if the 'right' type of organisation possesses staff who lack communication skills, there will be problems and vice versa.

Referring back to Figure 17.1, we find the shareholders at the top. They own the business, having acquired their shares either when the company was formed or through the Stock Exchange. They effectively exercise their right of control by electing directors at the Annual General Meeting. If they are unhappy with the performance of any of the existing directors they can replace them at this meeting.

The board of directors are responsible for running the business on behalf of the shareholders (and are accountable to them at the AGM) but normally delegate the day-to-day running to the managing director who is the company's chief executive and normally appoints the senior managers and is closely involved in making all the major decisions.

The major functions of the company are as follows.

Personnel

In a large company a personnel department will probably be divided into sections covering the main areas of work. The training officer is responsible for organising and assessing the success of the company's training and will also place staff on outside courses where this is appropriate.

Health and Safety often includes staff welfare and this involves areas such as the sports and social club, canteen and, of course, meeting the requirements of the Health and Safety at Work Act. The third section deals with recruitment, selection and the keeping of staff records (often on a computer!).

Secretarial

This is controlled by the company secretary who is usually qualified in law and/or accounts. The company secretary has certain legal (statutory) duties including holding the register of shareholders, minute books of company meetings and the books of account. As well as involvement in the legal and financial areas of the business, the company secretary, as the name suggests, is responsible for general office administration, and in the large organisation this function will be delegated to an office manager(ess).

Finance

This is usually controlled by a qualified accountant assisted, in a large business, by section heads responsible for all receipts and payments, wages and petty cash (cashier); monitoring the costs of running the business and analysing the costs of production (cost accountant); general financial management from keeping the accounts through to credit control (general accountant).

Production

Headed by the production or works director, this function only exists in a manufacturing business. The head has overall responsibility for the factory and the duty to ensure that the right goods are available at the right time. This involves planning methods of production (including purchasing and replacing equipment); liaising with purchasing to ensure that the raw materials are available and with personnel to ensure that sufficient trained staff are available and working conditions are appropriate. The head is also responsible for meeting the financial target set by finance.

In our chart we have included the Research and Development section within production and their role is to carry out, as the name suggests, research and development into new materials, methods and products.

Purchasing

Under the supervision of the chief buyer, the department is responsible for buying all materials and equipment and for their storage. It is the responsibility of the head buyer to purchase goods of the right quality and the right quantity for delivery at the right time, and to ensure they are available when required by the other departments.

Marketing

The marketing or sales function has already been examined on page 137. While the role of the marketing department is the same in any company, the actual structure of the department will vary considerably. Some businesses may conduct their own advertising while others may use outside agencies; some businesses sell abroad and need an export section but this is superfluous for a producer limited to the home market.

No single department can exist independently of the others. If the production director is concerned about safety within the factory, liaison with personnel on training will be needed; liaison with finance in the preparation of budgets; and also communication will be needed with purchasing to ensure that raw materials are available. The same interdependence applies to all other departments. For example, personnel must be aware of the staffing requirements of all the departments, and the marketing and production departments need to work closely together to ensure that the results of market surveys are reflected in the goods being designed or manufactured.

Efficient organisations depend on the close co-operation of all the departments, hence the importance of an effective communications system.

Examination questions

1. Using the organisation chart (readers should refer to the 1987 examination paper) explain who would be on the board of directors.

(4 marks)

2. Using the organisation chart (readers should refer to the 1987 examination paper) give **two** examples of vertical communication.

(4 marks)

3. What does the 'span of control' mean?

(4 marks)

4. How do shareholders exercise their right of control?

(4 marks)

5. Briefly outline the job of the 'works director'.

6. Describe the role of the personnel department.

(20 marks)

An industrial dispute
Chapter 18

A multi-national car firm manufacturing cars in the UK is in the process of automating its production line using robots. It hopes that this will produce cost savings which will enable it to compete more effectively. It is particularly concerned about overseas competition as there is a strong pound which has made it more difficult to export, while at the same time making imported cars cheaper to the domestic purchaser. The sales at home and abroad have therefore fallen and, coupled with the growing use of robots, the company needs fewer employees. The need to reduce the wages bill is made more urgent because the company has a large overdraft at the bank and interest rates are at present very high (this is one of the reasons why there is a strong pound).

As a result of the falling profits the Board of Directors have instructed the Personnel Director to put the staff on to short-time working. This means that the employees will work only four days a week. The Personnel Director decides to inform staff by putting notices on the notice board and into all the pay packets stating simply, 'As from Monday 14th, all staff will work a four-day week and the factory will be closed on Fridays'. Within one hour of these notices being read the shop stewards ask to see the Personnel Director.

In communicating this information to the staff, the Personnel Director has made several serious mistakes.

(a) What has been said is incomplete. There has been no attempt to explain to the staff the reason for this decision.

(b) An inappropriate method of communicating the message has been chosen. Both the notice board and the written notice to the staff are one-way communications. They do not enable the staff to ask questions to clarify any points of confusion. As a result of defects within the formal channels of communication the informal channels (the grapevine) have taken over. The problem with these, as far as management are concerned, is that they have no control over the information

being passed down. In this situation one member of staff, having seen the notice, has assumed that this is a prelude to staff being made redundant (losing their jobs), has communicated this fear to a colleague and within minutes the work-force are talking about redundancies. To make matters worse the rumour has spread that the reason for these redundancies is that the firm is transferring production of one of the models to a new factory that it is building in Spain.

(c) The union are upset because the Personnel Director has not gone through the formal channels of communication. Within any organisation there are formal channels and where people are bypassed they are likely to resent this as they may believe it implies a loss of status. The shop stewards are concerned because the Personnel Director has chosen to go directly to the staff over their heads. They are convinced there was some ulterior motive for doing this.

There is a meeting of the Joint Shop Stewards' Committee which consists of the shop stewards from the three main unions involved in the plant. There is a white-collar union representing the managerial and clerical staff. A craft union representing a small group of electricians and the general union (which is the largest) representing 80 per cent of the employees. The committee has elected a Chief Shop Steward who can act as a spokesman for all the unions. The demands of the committee, which includes no short-time working, are put to the Personnel Director who rejects them.

Following the unsatisfactory meeting with the management the committee meets again to decide on the action to take. They consider a work-to-rule and a strike. As the effect of both of these will be to reduce the number of cars produced they reject them, feeling this would be playing into the hands of management. As they consider the issues involved to be extremely serious, however, they recommend to their members that the local branch should refer the matter to the Regional Committee with a recommendation that if the Regional Officers cannot obtain a satisfactory response from the management, the matter should be referred to the National Executive. Following further fruitless negotiations this is eventually done. The National Executive Committee is responsible for putting union policies into practice and it is headed by the union's senior full-time official, the General Secretary. The Executive discusses the problem of the car workers and decides that there are both short-term and long-term problems involved. The short-term problem is how to avoid any redundancies or short-time working. They therefore instruct the General Secretary to inform the firm's management that if there are any redundancies or short-term working, they will organise a strike at the car firm's other UK plant. This is working at full capacity producing a new model which has captured a large share of the UK market. The union realise that if production of this plant is halted it will have a disastrous effect on the firm's profitability. To stop the car firm (which is multi-national) switching its production to plants overseas, the General Secretary is instructed to have talks with union colleagues in other countries to gain their support. Such talks have already been held on other issues as indicated by the following article:

Fight for car jobs to cross borders

Union leaders representing more than 100,000 Ford workers throughout Europe have pledged to fight the company's rationalisation plans.

A three-day meeting in Valencia ended on Sunday with a promise of "international solidarity by Ford workers to prevent one group of Ford workers in one country being played off against another".

The meeting, which was attended by representatives from seven countries, also promised "to resist any attempts by the company to improve the status of Ford's Japanese partner, Toyo Kogyo, at the expense of Ford's existing operations". . . .

Steve Broadhead, convener at the strike-hit Halewood body plant, attended the meeting and said yesterday: "It became apparent during our discussions that the company's claim that other plants in other countries have accepted Japanese-style working practices is simply not true." . . .

The Ford UK delegation, led by Dagenham convener Bernie Passingham, promised to support their Belgian colleagues, who today begin annual pay negotiations. Last year Belgian Ford workers narrowly voted against a strike in pursuit of a 39-hour week.

The long-term problem is to improve the competitiveness of UK industry. Because this involves many unions, the Executive asks each General Secretary to bring it up at the appropriate committee of the Trade Union Congress. At this committee the whole matter is discussed and the TUC decides to make representations to the government to modify their economic strategy. In particular, they request:
1. A reduction in interest rates. This will have the two-fold effect of reducing the operating cost of UK industry and weakening the pound (because foreigners will no longer wish to deposit their money in the UK) which will result in exports being made cheaper.

2. Devaluation on the pound. This makes exports cheaper while making foreign cars more expensive to the UK consumer.
3. Import tariffs and quotas. This will reduce the number of imported cars that can be sold in the UK. If you read the following article you will realise this is true to life:

Car unions unite to fight for import controls

Trade unions throughout Britain's vehicle and car components plants are to unite to campaign for selective import controls. . . . At a meeting in Coventry yesterday more than 100 senior shop stewards set up a committee to co-ordinate the fight against foreign imports, which they say are slowly strangling the home car trade.

The campaign involving unions at BL, Ford, Vauxhall, Lucas and other companies, will seek protective legislation from Parliament. There will also be more immediate direct action, possibly with picketing at docks.

Mr. Bernie Passingham, a senior shop steward at Ford, who chaired the meeting, said yesterday that the time for "pussy-footing around" had gone. If jobs were going to be saved, only strong and unified action could do it.

The pressure group, called Campaign for Import Controls Committee, will be based in the Midlands. It also plans talks with unions in the steel and textile industries, which could affiliate to the campaign.

While negotiations with the government are continuing there are strikes at the two factories because the management have refused to given an undertaking that there will be no redundancies. To help solve the dispute the parties utilise the services of the Advisory Conciliation and Arbitration Service (ACAS). This body cannot recommend a solution, although it can arrange arbitration and its function is to act as conciliators, persuading the parties to consider every particular solution. Following ACAS's intervention the strike is called off when the management promise there will be no compulsory redundancies and the unions agree to negotiate with the management about voluntary redundancies among the work-force.

As a result of the production lost because of the strike, the firm shows a substantial loss in its UK car plants and as a result no dividend is issued to shareholders. Some of the large investors are extremely unhappy about this and therefore, at the next Annual General Meeting, they intend to use their powers to seek the removal of some of the Board of Directors.

Car unions unite to fight for import controls

Section C

Model answers
Chapter 19

Careful consideration needs to be given to answers for 'short-answer' questions and 'long-answer' questions in examination papers of the Background to Business and Business Administration papers of the Secretarial Studies Certificate and Certificate in Office Technology.

Students frequently spend too long on the short answers. The model answers given in the first section below show you how much (or how little) needs to be written.

The second section covers 'long-answer' questions. In it there are a number of essay-type answers to the questions. The answers are not 'models' and are given merely to show what would be sufficient for a good 'Pass' in the examination.

1. Short answers

Students are required to answer five of the twelve questions.

(a) What is the difference between a sleeping and an active partner?

An active partner is involved in the running of the business, shares in its profits and losses and possesses unlimited liability. A sleeping partner also possesses unlimited liability, shares in the profits and losses but plays no part in the running of the business.

(b) How would a devaluation affect the balance of trade?

The balance of trade is the difference between visible imports and exports. A devaluation would improve it because it would make imports more expensive while making our goods cheaper to foreigners.

(c) The French franc is about to be devalued. What effects will this have on a UK holidaymaker?

If the franc is devalued UK holidaymakers will get more francs for their pounds. It will make their holidays in France cheaper.

(d) State three reasons for a rise in British Leyland shares.

Any factory which would improve the profitability of British Leyland would cause its shares to rise, e.g.
Successful launch of a new car
Devaluation of sterling (it would make exporting easier)
Import tariffs on foreign cars.

(e) Give an example of a 'communication' you would not use a notice board for. Explain why

I would not use a notice board to discipline an employee because it would be seen by the rest of the staff. This would upset the employee.

(f) A newspaper article commented that 'White-collar workers will exercise greater economic strength in the future'. Who are white-collar workers?

White-collar workers are employees who perform clerical and professional tasks. They are called white-collar because they wear suits rather than industrial overalls. Their unions include APEX and ASTMS.

(g) What is meant by arbitration?

Arbitration is used when the parties cannot solve a dispute and call in a third party. He is the arbitrator and he will recommend a solution which both sides will accept.

(h) In communications what is meant by the grapevine?

The grapevine is an informal method of communication and consists of gossip and rumour.

(i) In terms of ownership to whom are the directors of a joint-stock company responsible?

The directors are answerable to the shareholders at the Annual General Meeting (AGM).

(j) State the main difference between a commercial and a merchant bank.

The former deals with the general public whereas the latter offers services to businesses.

(k) Explain simply what the term collateral means in banking.

Collateral is security for the loan. If the borrower defaults it can be sold.

(l) Is a rise in the Financial Times Index favourable to the investor?

The index reflects all share prices so a rise is generally favourable although your shares could fall in price while all other shares were rising.

(m) What is a premium?

A premium is the payment the insured makes for his insurance policy.

(n) What is the difference between a quota and a tariff?

A quota is a limit on the number of goods that can be imported and a tariff is a tax.

(o) Give (i) one example of a direct tax
(ii) one example of an indirect tax.

Income tax is a direct tax and VAT an indirect tax.

2. Long answers

Requiring traditional essay-type answers.

1. Describe some of the problems a sole trader might face in setting up in business.

The first problem for the person starting in business is to raise sufficient capital which will be needed to set up the business; he/she will need to buy or rent premises, purchase equipment and perhaps engage specialist staff, and may borrow from friends or relatives or perhaps the bank.

Although sufficient funds can be raised to start the business, the financial problems are not over. A new business is unlikely to make much profit in the first year. Even if there is a market it will take time to find customers and during this period bills must be paid. Unless sufficient profit is made to cover these (or the initial start-up capital was large enough) bankruptcy will ensue.

Having survived the financial hurdles, the sole trader cannot relax.

Staff may be employed (being a sole trader simply means owning the business) but the sole trader is responsible for decision-making, and is the management. This will involve working long hours, finding it difficult to take holidays, and also being forced to work when feeling ill.

Underlying all these problems is the problem of liability. The sole trader has unlimited liability. This means that if the business debts exceed the business assets, creditors can take all the sole trader's personal assets (house and car). The price of failure is very high.

2. Give examples of the types of training provision which might be provided by:
  (1) Employee's own company
  (2) College of further education

The most common training provided by the firm is induction training. This is given to all new employees and consists of telling them about the company and its products, company facilities and rules, the nature of the job and finally giving them a tour of the firm. Once employees have been 'inducted' they may be given on-the-job training. This might involve learning how to use the various pieces of equipment such as photocopier or switchboard. Once an employee has learnt her job, training does not finish. There might be changes in technology which require retraining, e.g. a typist learning how to use a word processor. Promotion may be gained and this might involve learning new skills, and all the time the company may be running short courses to improve performance.

The retraining for word processing might be done at the local college, but the college is mainly used for other types of off-the-job training. This could be for existing employees in the form of day release (this is common in apprenticeships) or it could be training of individuals so they acquire the necessary skills before they start work. This would be the situation of a secretarial course in a college. Colleges also offer short courses for employees who wish to acquire qualifications to improve their promotion prospects.

3. Describe the advantages and disadvantages of putting money into
  (i) Stocks and shares
  (ii) Deposit account
  (iii) Building society account.

The advantages of stocks and shares are that they can rise in value, perhaps faster than inflation. This means that if you invest £500 it might become worth £1,000. While you own the shares you will receive income in the form of dividends, provided the company is making profits. The big disadvantage is that you can lose all your money. If the company makes a loss you will not receive a dividend and if it goes bankrupt you might lose all your £500.

A deposit account in a bank is secure. If you invest £500 you know you can withdraw £500 at any time. You will be paid interest on your deposit but the disadvantage is that your deposit grows slowly. If inflation is high, although you can withdraw your £500 it may be worth less than when you invested it.

A building society account is just as secure as a deposit account and also pays interest. It may also fail to keep pace with inflation. The advantage of this account is that it gives the saver priority when seeking a mortgage. There are a variety of accounts and you can choose one that suits your method of saving. You can have one that allows instant withdrawal or one that requires you to leave in money for some years. This pays a higher rate of interest.

4. Describe two ways in which an adverse balance of payments may be corrected.

An adverse balance could be cured if a country reduced its imports. It could do this by imposing tariffs or quotas. The first is a tax on imports and this causes their price to rise. This, it is hoped, will discourage people from buying them. A quota is a limit on the number of items that can be imported. If the government devalues the pound this will also reduce imports because it makes them more expensive.

A devaluation means foreign citizens can buy more pounds for their currencies and so it makes it cheaper for them to buy UK goods. This should improve our export performance. Exports can also be encouraged by the government granting subsidies to firms or by marketing UK goods through foreign fairs etc. The government can also help exporters by trying to persuade other countries to revalue their currencies (which has the same effect as a devaluation of the £) or to remove trade barriers.

The above answers provide an indication of what will prove acceptable in an examination. Just to show what a student can achieve the following answer was written by an ex-student in a mock examination. It is uncorrected.

Q. A car firm has a poor industrial relations record and senior management believe this is caused by poor communications at factory level. In what ways might the communications be defective?

The communications in this car firm could be defective for many reasons. One of the reasons for this might be that the management aren't going through the factory supervisor and therefore the factory supervisor is upset because he wasn't consulted so he makes trouble for the management by stirring up the factory workers and telling them that it is a bad idea etc.

Another reason for bad communications could be that the management put up notices on the notice board telling the workers what they have decided and what they want the workers to do, this creates bad feeling as nobody has been consulted. This type of communication, one-way communication, means that they cannot discuss or compromise and management don't see the reactions and feelings of the employees until it is too late to do anything.

If they did get the workers together it could be that they shouldn't have got them altogether at once as this causes the workers to come together as one to argue their points of view.

It could be that the management don't talk to the workers on their level, or that they give the workers too much information to carry out at once causing friction between the two levels. Bad timing is another, if the workers are given instructions or information at the end of the week.

If the management explained the situation, the problems, ideas, they could discuss it and look at each person's point of view and try to sort it out agreeably or compromise, thus make for much better relations.

An example of bad communications is British Leyland over the cutting out of washing up time.

The communication in this ... either could be detected, for these reasons. One of the reasons for this might be that the management are going through the recent supervisor and therefore the factory supervisor is upset because he wasn't consulted so he makes trouble for the management by stirring up the factory workers and telling them that there is a trouble etc.

Another reason for the bad communications could be that the management put up notices on the notice board telling the workers what they have decided and that they want the workers to do, but this could be treating as nobody has been consulted. The type of communication ... one-way communication means that they cannot discuss their problems and management don't see the reactions and feelings of the employees until it is too late to do anything. ...

If they did get the workers together ... or in before they should? ... ... them together once a month to discuss the workers become together ... are to argue their points of view.

It could be that the management don't talk to the workers or their levels or that they give the workers ... too much information to carry out a correct communication between the two levels. Here things happen that if the workers are given instructions or information across end of the ... we ...

If the management ... explained the situation, the problems, ideas, they could discuss it and look at each person's point of view and try to sort it out amicably or compromise, thus make for a better relationship.

As example of bad communications is ... which I read over the coming out of washing up time ...

Section D

The project which accompanies the written examination is important because, if well done, it makes passing the examination easier. Students and lecturers often seek guidance from the LCC as to the standards required for each grade. Model projects are available from the LCC but **two** model projects which have been moderated by the LCC follow. It is hoped these will indicate to students the level they should seek to attain.

Project – grade C
Chapter 20

An investigation into . . .
Luminol Research Centre

A project report required in the Background to Business Section of the London Chamber of Commerce Secretarial Studies Certificate June 1983.

Contents

Report compiled
by
Examination
Number
Name of College
Date completed

Introduction

I have chosen the Luminol Research Centre because I think it plays a large and important part in the lives of so many people in all walks of life, not only for people buying petrol for their cars, but for other uses for domestic, factory and testing purposes.

I was able to gain information from a friend who works there and who lives close by. I also went on two weeks' work experience in a Division of the Centre and was able to do some work on my project whilst I was there, being accessible to information in the office in the form of booklets, leaflets and brochures, and asking staff certain questions on particular subjects I was studying.

I was interested to find out the different experiments the Centre carries out, and how they affect people in the community and the country.

The Luminol Research Centre makes new additives to serve the petroleum industry. It is not a refinery, an office, or anything else, but purely a research establishment for finding new and improved methods for the petroleum industry, although the Centre does have many administrative offices, and other offices in which the staff and scientists work.

The Centre has a great deal of confidential information, and spends very large sums of money in their research programmes. They derive much information and develop new ideas which are of substantial value to the parent company. This information would, therefore, be of great value to competitors and potential competitors.

History and development

The company began in 1888 and has been very much a part of social and economical development in Britain. The importance of oil is now so great that no one can live without it.

In the 1930s, the first research establishment was set up in the UK. The laboratories were concerned with product quality control work on behalf of companies operating in Europe.

From the beginning, the work of the laboratories was continually expanding and when the Second World War arrived, the company accelerated rather than slowed down.

Because of the dangers of bombing during the war, there was lack of space for expansion in London so new equipment was installed on an estate in the country.

When the war had ended, there were more facilities for research there so it became necessary to move the administrative offices, records, library, etc. out of London.

After the war, the laboratories were set up separately under the name Luminol Development Ltd.

Later, the name was changed to Luminol Research Ltd, the name it has today.

Luminol House was originally called Milford House, and during the war, served as evacuation accommodation for head office.

The company sold the building to a group of stationers who used it for training purposes.

A new building, which also contained offices and the library, replaced several of the prefabricated buildings which had been used for the previous ten years in the late 1950s and it was opened by a Member of Parliament.

Gasolex Corporation

Gasolex Research and Engineering Company is the oldest and largest research organisation within the corporate structure. Its main objectives are research, development and engineering activities.

It was founded in 1919 as a wholly-owned, but separately incorporated subsidiary of Gasolex Corporation and is responsible for finding, testing and developing ideas of technology to meet most of its needs in petroleum, refining, transportation and marketing.

Before the Gasolex Company was formulated, another organisation called the Development Centre was formed at a local refinery.

About 2,000 scientists and engineers, and a similar number of support personnel, work under the Company's management at facilities in the USA.

Research, development and engineering expenditure by the Gasolex Company amounted to more than $5 million in 1982. The main funds came from the Corporation and its affiliates. It was responsible for engineering work on more than 50 major projects. The 12 largest of these involved $11 billion in capital expenditures.

The Luminol Research Centre

(i) The function of the establishment

The Luminol Research establishment is located in a country position on the edge of the Downs. It is the largest research laboratory of its kind in Europe with 250,000 square feet of laboratories etc spread over a 60 acre rural site. It is estimated that the buildings and equipment are worth £25 million.

Luminol Petroleum and Luminol Chemicals are two separate companies which deal with different aspects of the oil industry, and within the Centre, there is friendly rivalry between the two groups, but which join together at the top.

The main aspects of the Centre's work is concerned with extensive academic, governmental and industrial research. There are many well-equipped general purpose laboratories together with analytical, engine test and pilot plant laboratories in which research is carried out. Subsequently, tests go on into the factories of customers, into ships, into fleets of cars and trucks so that the new products are fully tried and tested before they are branded and available for customers to purchase.

Here are some examples of items that are tested within the Centre:

Additives are one of the Centre's specialities. Work on enhancing oil products by means of theoretical calculations and practical tests at the laboratory bench and pilot reactors. Experimental investigation into how additives work is followed by extensive testing in bench rigs (apparatus designed to simulate parts of an engine), in test engines and in the field. For example, motor oils contain a dispersant, a detergent, a viscosity modifier, and an anti-oxidant.

1. *Dispersant.* Solid, sooty particles which are produced as a result of combustion remain in suspension in the lubricant rather than being deposited in the oil channels.
2. *Detergent.* Prevents the formation of carbon and varnish-like deposits on the pistons or within the cylinders.
3. *Viscosity modifier.* Ensures that the motor oil remains thick enough to maintain lubricating film between surfaces when hot, but thin enough under cold conditions to minimize drag on engines or by restricting variations in viscosity.
4. *Anti-oxidant.* Helps to prevent the oxidation of hot oil by the oxygen from the atmosphere.

The Centre also has many workshops, garages, a printing plant, a photographic studio, meeting rooms, library, offices and a fully equipped cinema/lecture theatre. For the evaluation of automotive products, there is a high speed test track.

The Research Centre exists to provide technical help for Luminol companies and through them for their customers. The staff work very closely with the staff of other affiliated laboratories, particularly with those in Europe, and with the refineries, marketers and through them with their customers.

The Centre provides technical assistance for Luminol Petroleum Company Limited and Luminol Chemicals Limited, and it specialises in many different aspects of petroleum knowledge needed for operations, worldwide, of Luminol and Gasolex. Luminol is now a company specialising mainly in engine lubricants of all types, in gasoline, distillates, aviation fuels and in gas. There are numerous laboratories that specialise in many other areas of the research.

The Centre, is mainly aimed at producing new additives for lubricants, and this, which is completely separated from the lubricants research activity, enables the maximum possible use to be made of the many widely used engine tests and analytical facilities of the Centre. It also includes the Performance Chemicals Group who are involved with the development of chemicals to aid crude oil production.

Over the past five years, £11 million has been invested in the erection of new, modern facilities. The laboratories now contain the largest engine test house in the organisation. In 1981, as part of the investment programme, improvements were made to both the inspection and blending facilities on the site.

Environmental monitoring programmes are a regular feature of the Company activities with technical advice from the Research Centre.

North Sea oil

Britain's energy has greatly changed since the discovery of oil and gas beneath the North Sea. The nation's economy has changed and so the balance of payments has risen. The Government has provided the opportunity for further investment of coal, nuclear and other energy sources.

The North Sea is one of the most difficult areas the oil industry has to face—deep water, rough seas and very bad weather. Successful development requires huge sums of money, new technological ideas and excellent management skills.

Cost of development
The deepest North Sea projects can cost around £5 million each for each well dug and a drilling ship up to £30 million. Luminol has invested £2.1 billion in North Sea development by 1980 and this has risen to nearly £3.5 billion by the mid-1980s.

The oil

North Sea oil is light and relatively free of sulphur and is of high quality. It is not altogether suitable for the manufacture of heavy fuel, lubricating oil and bitumen, so in order to maintain supplies of these products, some higher value North Sea oil is sold abroad and cheaper, heavier crudes are imported.

(ii) Number of staff

Altogether, there are 475 members of the Research Centre staff, most of whom are connected with the Luminol Petroleum Company. The members either work on petroleum research and technical service or on general Research Centre services. A smaller number of the staff are employees of Luminol Chemicals Limited and they are concerned with chemicals, particularly additives. Research and technical services are carried out in this section and Performance Chemicals activities.

Other employees are engaged in the Lubricants Division of Luminol and also in the Fuels Division. These divisions deal with research into fuels and lubricants and also technical service work. Technical support is provided by the Engineering Division, the Analytical Division, and the Information Division. Administration services for the site as well as Safety and Security for the buildings and equipment and personnel fall within the Analytical and Information Division. A few staff are employed to oversee the Employee Relations and University Liaison activities.

Of the staff, approximately 200 are graduates, mainly in chemistry, chemical engineering and engineering. Many skills are represented in the support staff for these graduates.

Apart from the chemical and engineering technicians working in the 50 laboratories of the Centre, there are secretarial, reprographic, electrical, library and many other staff, all essential to the completion of the technical work of the Centre.

The role it plays in the local community

The Luminol Research Centre donates useful equipment such as chairs to scouts and any suitable items with which they have finished in the laboratories or any other buildings on site. They may aid local charities, and staff in the Centre are encouraged to do voluntary work.

The Centre provides jobs for the local people, especially in the scientific field. As this area is scientifically nucleated with the Oxford colleges, Harwell, Rutherford, Culham and Jet all being research centres, there are more jobs available in this field. It will also provide work for administrative and secretarial workers but mainly for personnel with a scientific bias.

Other offices around the country will also provide jobs for people to work at the refineries and on the rigs in the North Sea.

The Luminol Research Centre provides a Nature Reserve in the grounds of the Centre which is managed by the local Naturalists' Society. One of the aims is to encourage wild life preservation and the Society makes great efforts during winter months to protect the animals.

In the early 1970s, the Luminol Research Centre provided five and a half acres of the Centre's ground to the local Naturalists' Society for use as a nature reserve and a study centre.

This area used to be part of the Milford House estate. The reserve consists of mainly man-made features such as parkland, an old orchard and a copse. However, there has been a natural invasion of wild animals and plants which has made the reserve an interesting place to study.

A large area has been dug out to form a pond, and over 100 flowering plants have been identified.

Members of the public are welcome to visit the reserve but they are asked not to pick flowers or disturb the wild life.

One of the items donated by the Centre is a spectrometer presented to a chemistry department of a University.

An event took place as part of the celebration of two years without a time loss injury at Luminol, a safety Poster competition was held for local children. Prize winners received gift vouchers and all entrants were given some form of prize.

The Luminol Research Centre also made a series of environmental studies using new equipment in order to test water, and air pollution. This survey work of air and water pollution was directed towards maintaining a better awareness of environmental matters.

The Centre also provides jobs on a temporary basis for school-leavers wishing to gain experience or for graduates who are employed at the Centre but, at the same time, attend a course at college to learn their skill more thoroughly.

Young people can also join the Centre on a Youth Opportunity Programme for a period of time to gain experience in any of the skills covered by the Centre, such as administrative work, engineering, technical and secretarial. These young people then leave the Centre and usually most find good jobs in the skills they have been *practising* within a very short period of time.

Conclusion

Gasolex is a multi-national organisation which has different incorporated companies all over the world. The UK company has connections worldwide although it is a very close-knit community with people working at Luminol from numerous places, all members contributing to worldwide research.

The advantage of Luminol as a large company compared to smaller companies is that it is recognised all over the world. Staff are mostly permanent, e.g. there is not a great deal of staff turnover, so it remains open and does not lose money. If it did start to lose money or support, then assistance would automatically be fed in from the Gasolex Corporation in the form of funds, staff or equipment.

On the other hand, small companies are not so easily recognised because of lack of support from parent companies so could easily be closed through lack of funds etc.

Project – grade E

Chapter 21

Report on
Bidwell Laminates Limited
(*as a result of work experience*)

Contents

Introduction

Bidwell Laminates is a firm on a local trading estate. The firm is in a good position for trading as it is situated near to the by-pass making the transport of goods by road easier and much quicker. The goods are sold all over the country and some go abroad.

Structure of the firm

The firm has a working Board of Directors who each have an office in Factory One. The directors are responsible for all the final decisions which are made within the firm. They also draw up all the plans for the firm in the future such as exploring new markets abroad.

The Accounts Department are responsible for recording all financial transactions of the firm such as purchase of materials for the production and the sale of the finished products. There are two reasons for keeping records of this description within a firm. Firstly the directors wish to know if the firm is making a reasonable profit or making a considerable loss. They wish to know exactly where money is being made and where it is being lost. Using this information the firm can change methods of production to suit the needs of the market. Secondly the firm is legally obliged to keep records of its finances. Every year an auditor visits the firm and checks all its financial records to see if they are correct and complete.

The Sales Department are responsible for marketing the products of the firm. It is their job to get new customers who will regularly make large orders. The firm has names and addresses of all their customers. Every so often to push up sales, circulars are sent out to them advertising big discounts for a limited period. This usually encourages bulk buying by the customers.

The Drawing and Design Department are responsible for the drawings required on the factory floor and in the directors' offices. The drawings are very detailed and show all the various measurements of the products. They have to be very accurate because if they are wrong in any way the result is a completely different product is produced to what is required by a customer. This results in unnecessary waste of materials, time and perhaps most importantly money.

Factory One

Factory One manufactures translucent sheets on an automatic production line which requires only a small group of workers; a worker to clean the wooden moulds after use which is quite a messy job; a worker to monitor the mixing of the polyester resin which is sieved to remove any lumps to prevent spoiling the finished product. The resin is reinforced with glass fibres. The sheeting is then moulded into the required profile by drawing it through the wooden dies, within a heated oven. The sheeting is then cooled down with water which is sprayed onto it. Finally the sheeting is cut into the appropriate lengths to suit the roofing requirements of the customers. Two or three workers monitor this final process of cutting and stacking up the sheets ready for transporting. The construction of the sheet provides considerable strength which enables the sheeting to be fixed and handled without the fear of it shattering.

The sheeting is produced in a natural translucent finish which provides natural light for factories, warehouses, agricultural buildings, canopies, car ports, swimming pool covers, vertical glazing, suspended ceilings and partitioning. It is also produced in a colour-tinted finish. Green or blue tinted sheeting is particularly suitable for use overseas in reducing glare in countries subject to bright sunlight.

The sheeting is available flat and can be corrugated in a large range of profiles. Each of these profiles is designed to match in with most types of asbestos cement, aluminium and steel roofing.

Double Skinned Units provide thermal insulation too. Other types provide water absorption, flexibility and hardness depending on the needs of the customer.

Below are some examples of the translucent sheeting

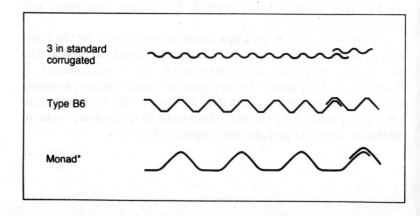

| 3 in standard corrugated |
| Type B6 |
| Monad* |

Factory Two

Factory Two manufactures reinforced plastic poles, e.g. telegraph poles. These poles offer various advantages over the conventional wooden or steel ones. They have a neat appearance and smooth exterior which cannot be attacked by insects or fungi. Indeed they are highly resistant to marine tropical and industrial environments with chemicals in the ground such as sulphates which can rapidly affect steel and concrete. Also when a vehicle crashes into one of these poles the occupants are less likely to be injured or killed and the vehicle is less likely to be damaged. These poles are produced on an automatic spinning machine.

Reception

The reception area was very pleasant with comfortable chairs and fresh green foliage. The staff from the general office deal with the reception area, clients visiting the firm could be helped quickly without leaving the office by sliding back a glass partition. The glass partition was very useful because it enabled the switchboard operator positioned next to it in the general office to deal with clients the other side of it and on the telephone simultaneously.

The general office

The general office was situated next to the reception. The office was quite small but very well organised. Every available space was used to its best advantage.

There were four large desks. One for each of the two secretaries and one for the sales assistant. Each desk was situated in a light, airy position next to a window. Strong sunlight could be blocked out by blinds.

There were filing cabinets and a large three-tier rotary file for information and past invoices which are kept on their customers. There was also a card index containing the names and addreses of their suppliers. These were kept handy for typing invoices and circulars.

Typewriters

There were two electric typewriters in the general office. The typewriters were in constant use. Most of the time they were used to type order sets.

Orders were usually phoned through by the customer and written down on special printed order forms. The printed forms had to be typed up correctly on special order sets as quickly as possible so the factory could start production. The order sets consisted of four coloured sheets, white, pink, blue and green, with carbon sheets between them.

The two secretaries would type up the order sets which were then placed to one side ready for checking by the sales assistant or the sales manager. This is to ensure the production team produce the correct type of sheeting which the customers have ordered. Errors cost money and private firms cannot afford unnecessary waste of labour, time or materials.

The secretaries in the general office were also responsible for typing the circulars sent out to their customers.

The switchboard

The switchboard was situated next to the glass partition for reception. It was quite large and modern with four lines available for use at any one time. It had sixteen extensions and all of these were in use. The bottom line of switches seemed to be generally used for ringing up the extensions. Calls were generally switched through on the three top lines to avoid cutting in or cutting off any conversations which were taking place. To help in the selection of vacant switches were red lights which glowed opposite them.

A lot of the firm's business was done by the telephone. Clients would phone through orders easily and quickly. The operator had a very important position because she would be the first person clients telephoning would be in contact within the firm. So a good first impression was needed to be made by being polite and helpful and speaking in a clear, well-spoken voice. The operator's main aim was to put calls through, whether incoming or outgoing, as quickly as possible because people left hanging on telephones tend to get very annoyed.

The operator had to have a wide knowledge of the firm's products and clients because on rare occasions information had to be given to clients, usually when the sales assistant or sales manager could not be contacted within the firm for some reason.

The outgoing mail

All outgoing mail was checked in the general office before posting. Unsealed letters were sealed with a damp sponge. The letters were sorted into two sorting trays. One tray was for mail going to another part of Great Britain and the other tray for mail going overseas. The overseas mail could then be sorted into mail which was going to the same country.

The incoming mail

All incoming mail had to be sorted out to see if there was a number of letters going to the same person or department. Then it was promptly delivered by one of the secretaries to the right addresses. Quick delivery of the mail was important because the information in it might be urgent and need the quick attention of the receiver.

The franking machine

All outgoing mail had to be franked using a franking machine. The letters were pulled through automatically. The stamp or stamps were printed on the envelopes. When inserting the letters you had to check they were up the right way and the correct way round for franking. Thick or large envelopes could not be passed through the machine. Stickly labels were passed through the machine and then fixed to the envelopes in the correct position. Mail was franked according to where it was to be posted. The appropriate cost could be looked up on a special wall chart. The chart showed costs of sending mail to every country in the world.

The weighing machine

The weighing machine was used to weigh thick or large envelopes and all parcels in the outgoing mail. This is because items such as these cost more to send depending on their weight and size. The electric weighing machine calculated the cost when the item was placed on its scales.

The supply room

The supply room was situated next to the reception area. It housed the telex machine and the photocopier because of the lack of space for office equipment in the general office. There were two large floor to ceiling cupboards which held various bits of office equipment such as duplicating paper for the photocopier in various sizes and also much smaller items such as pens, pencils, rubbers, rulers, elastic bands, paper clips, staples, liquid paper.

The telex machine

The telex machine was quite an old and noisy model which was due to be replaced by a modern and much smaller model which could be kept in the general office. The new model would also be much quieter so it would not disturb the staff working in the office.

The machine was in use quite frequently during an average working day. Messages were sent to the clients and suppliers in Great Britain and those overseas. Sending telex messages is very expensive so the messages have to be as short and accurate as the operator can make them. The messages were recorded on perforated tapes and then sent out. This was to prevent any mistakes being made in its transmission such as wrong prices for goods. The operator using this method can check his/her work thoroughly before it is sent out to the receiver.

Messages can also be received on the machine without the operator being present. An incoming message was indicated by a loud buzzing.

The photocopier

The photocopier was very modern and had various controls in use in the operation of it. The copies could be made light, medium or dark according to which you required. The machine could produce up to ninety-nine copies at one time.

The factory workers often used the photocopier to produce copies of drawings for use on the factory floor. For these drawings A3 duplicating paper was used. The office staff used the photocopier for duplicating letters and plans. Also used for producing circulars to be sent to clients.

Microfilming

All the microfilming was done in the Accounts Department. All the company accounts except very recent ones were on film to save valuable office space. When a past account needs to be consulted for some reason it is far easier and much quicker to find it on film than in a large filing cabinet of paper documents. The accounts were all on film in date order.

The computers

There was a main computer room near the general office. Here a new computer was soon to be installed to control the other computers within the firm. The firm already had several Apple computers. One of these computers was in the Accounts Department and stored on floppy discs such information as the rate of pay of every person working within the firm. Such information had a secret code which had to be typed into the computer before it appeared on the VDU. This was to prevent unauthorised persons looking up confidential information on the computers.

Section E

Press cuttings
Chapter 22

The syllabus specifically states 'Candidates as well as demonstrating knowledge and understanding (of the syllabus), will be expected to be aware, through newspapers etc, of current events affecting the business world. Questions on this background reading can be expected.'

It follows you should read newspapers. Students often fail to do this. You should read a quality newspaper once a week, cutting out articles that are relevant. You will soon get into a routine and acquire an improved knowledge of current business events. The following are articles taken from newspapers. Each is followed, where necessary, by explanatory notes.

You should adopt the same practice because by referring to the main text to make the notes, you are 'revising' throughout the year. By reading the articles you are, of course, revising!

Bank base rate cut

Bank base lending rates are expected to come down by ½ per cent to 9½ per cent today or tomorrow after a clear signal from the Bank of England yesterday.

The prospect of lower interest rates boosted shares and the Financial Times index closed at an all-time high, up 4.2 at 721.3. But the pound fell back, because lower interest rates will make it less attractive for investors to hold.

The immediate reason for the fall in interest rates is the recent strength of the pound. There is a suspicion that the Government's motive is to get sterling down to a level more acceptable to exporters.

Notes

1. Interest rates are determined by the Bank of England which acts for the government.
2. The Financial Times Index is a general indication of movements in share prices. If it rises and you hold shares this means your investment is probably worth more.
3. If the pound is weaker it makes our goods cheaper to foreigners and therefore makes exporting easier.

A nasty little nudge to expectations

The rise in retail inflation to 4.6 per cent was hardly unexpected, but it does not come at the best time for the Government. This is exactly the point in the year when many unions are first turning their attention to pay claims, and the cost of living is bound to be a factor. Nevertheless, the rise in inflation from its summer low does look, in the short term at least, as if it will be modest. The chances are that the year-on-year rise by Christmas will fall slightly within the Government's budget forecast of 6 per cent. What happens thereafter will itself depend crucially on the wage round, since wages and salaries still account for some 70 per cent of business costs. The depressed state of demand and output suggest that there is likely to be a small further fall in wage increases compared with last year.

Notes

1. Wage claims are related to inflation.
2. Prices manufacturers charge are related to their costs of which wages are the most important.
3. Because demand for products is low manufacturers do not require labour. Union's negotiating strength is therefore reduced which is why wage increases might be low.

Saudi foreign trade plunges into the red as oil sales fall

Saudi Arabia's foreign trade plunged into the red for the first time in more than a decade during the first quarter of the year as a direct result of the slump in the kingdom's oil exports.

Figures released yesterday by the Saudi Ministry of Finance and National Economy show that visible trade was $290 million in deficit in the first quarter, compared with a $14.6 billion surplus in the corresponding period last year. Exports, which are almost 90 per cent reliant on oil, dropped by over 40 per cent between the last quarter of 1982 and the first quarter.

The Saudis have seen their oil production plummet from a zenith of more than 10 million barrels a day to about 4 mbd currently, while imports have been growing to fuel successive development programmes. A number of leading industrialised countries – including Britain – now have considerable trade surpluses with the kingdom.

Note

1. Visible trade consists of items you can see (e.g. oil) and the fall in oil exports has resulted in a deficit on the balance of trade (i.e. visibles).

UK travel account back in the red

Britain's travel account was still in deficit in March – but the number of European tourists rose considerably and the account was back in the black for the first quarter of the year.

Latest official figures show that 750,000 visitors came to Britain in March, 16 per cent more than in the corresponding month last year. But some 1,140,000 British travellers went abroad, 3 per cent up on the level for March 1982, and spent £210 million compared with the £200 million spent in the UK by overseas visitors.

British tourist authorities are now anticipating an increase in the number of American tourists – which is likely to be fuelled by the advent of the new People Express cut price transatlantic flights. However, this could be counterbalanced by a drop in French visitors because of the new currency restrictions.

Notes

1. Tourism is an invisible export when foreign tourists visit the UK. Money flows into the UK.
2. France has made it more difficult for its citizens to travel abroad in an attempt to improve its balance of payments.

Respite for textile industry

Negotiations to secure a cut-back in textile imports into the EEC got under way in Brussels yesterday amidst Third World charges that the Common Market was adopting an increasingly protectionist trade stance. But despite these protests it seems that enough Asian and Latin American textile producers are willing to come to terms with the EEC to ensure that the Common Market will get its way.

Note

1. The EEC is imposing a quota (limit) on the amount that can be imported.

Brazil seeks new loan

Urgent negotiations took place in Washington yesterday to try to raise an additional $2.5 billion in western government loans to save Brazil from bankruptcy. This would be in addition to the $4.5 billion loan agreed with the International Monetary Fund over a three year period and a further $4.5 billion new money from commercial banks in this year alone.

Notes

1. Brazil has a massive balance of payments deficit which it has to finance by borrowing.
2. The IMF has already lent money to Brazil.

Banks in accord on shopping terminals

Deep disagreements between clearing banks over the way to bring in electronic shopping have been resolved and the top executives of a dozen banks have agreed to go ahead with point of sales terminals in shops by 1986.

This follows a long debate among the banks about how to bring in electronic funds transfer in shops. It will allow customers to use plastic cards which instantly debit their bank accounts and transfer the money to shop's account using computerised tills.

The banks said yesterday that trials of the new system could start in 1986 and there could be live tests by the end of 1985.

Note

1. This change in technology could result in banks requiring fewer employees.

Factory without people opens

Britain's first unmanned factory was opened yesterday by the Industry Secretary, Mr. Patrick Jenkin.

It is a £3 million small batch production line at Colchester producing a variety of shafts, gears, and discs in steel, cast-iron and aluminium. The products made by the robots and the computer-run machine tools are genuine, but the factory is initially operating only as a government-sponsored showpiece.

Pilot projects in peopleless factories were begun nearly a decade ago in countries ranging from Japan to Bulgaria. The British version has taken five years to emerge.

Sir Jack Williams said yesterday, that the factory produced finished components – untouched by hand – over a three day cycle. The old manpower heavy methods involved 10 to 12 weeks of work and about 50 separate handlings of the different small batches of orders.

Future of London as port in balance

The future of the Port of London now rests on the ability of an independent inquiry, meeting tomorrow to find a solution to a seven-week-old pay dispute involving 2,000 Tilbury dockers.

The independent inquiry, under the auspices of the conciliation service, ACAS, and chaired by Professor Sir John Wood, has to find a way of resolving the dockers' claim for parity with white-collar workers.

The PLA chief executive Mr. John Black, has claimed that the strike has cost the port £5 million and that the London docks will never fully recover from the effect. The Transport and General Workers' Union is officially backing the strike and the strikers are not due to meet again until Thursday.

Notes

1. ACAS is appointing the arbitrator in the dispute.
2. The union are using the strike as their form of industrial action.
3. The union involved is a general union.

Metal Box to shed 470 jobs

Metal Box revealed the loss of another 470 jobs yesterday with the closure of its loss making plastic container factory at Bromborough, Merseyside.

The Wirral factory, which makes thermo-formed plastic containers for the dairy and margarine industries is to shut early next January. Metal Box, still Europe's largest packing group, blamed the losses on the highly competitive UK thermo-forming market burdened with excess capacity. A spokesman said considerable efforts had been made to improve productivity but forecasts for future trading were that losses would grow.

Talks are being held with the four unions involved – USDAW, the shop workers union, ASTMS, the AUEW and EEPTU and in line with group policy all redundancy payments will be more than government requirements. Rowntree Mackintosh, the sweet makers, also announced redundancy plans yesterday, with the loss of 200 jobs out of the 850 maintenance workers at its York factory. Further proposals are under way among 5,000 production workers and 800 office workers which will be announced shortly.

Notes

1. Job losses involve both industrial and white-collar staff.
2. The unions include industrial (USDAW), craft (AUEW), and white-collar (ASTMS).

Post Office Engineers widen action against sell-off

The Post Office Engineering Union spread its industrial action against privatisation outside London for the first time yesterday.

The Union also said that its work-to-rule, begun on Monday, by more than 1,000 engineers maintaining international telephone services, was already having an impact. The work-to-rule is affecting three exchanges at Mondale House Upper Thames Street, Stag Lane in Burnt Oak, and Wood Street near Tower Bridge.

After one day of action the union reported 900 faults at Mondale House – 6 per cent of total circuits. Stag Lane and Wood Street are said to have faults on 5 per cent of circuits.

Mr. Keith Simmons, organiser of the union's international servicers branch, said: "We have 100 per cent support within the branch and increasing signs of congestion in international traffic circuits." Management has not taken any action against those working to rule, but it is widely thought disciplinary action will begin soon.

The union has committed itself to a campaign of industrial action against government and big business telecommunications in an attempt to prevent the sale of BT.

Notes

1. The industrial action being used is a work-to-rule.
2. The government is attempting to 'denationalise' British Telecom by selling shares to the public. This is the reason for the dispute with the union.

Spectacular rise

Mr. Rodney Bickerstaffe, the 38 year-old general secretary of the National Union of Public Employees, has been elected by the TUC as one of its six representatives on the National Economic Development Council, the body which brings together Government ministers and the two sides of industry.

His elevation yesterday to the "Neddy Six" completes a remarkably rapid rise through the TUC hierarchy since he became NUPE general secretary last summer and a member of the TUC general council last September.

Notes

1. NUPE is a type of industrial union; everyone in the public sector can belong.
2. The TUC is the body representing all unions.
3. The general secretary is the 'head' of the union.

Abbey National breaks home loan cartel

The building societies' long established system of a single mortgage rate for all home owners has been shattered by a decision by the country's second largest society, the Abbey National, to withdraw from the scheme.

The building societies' joint agreements on mortgage and savings rates have been under threat for the past few years, since the incursion of the High Street banks into the home loans market and increased competition for personal savings have breached the near monopoly position the societies previously enjoyed.

Notes

1. The competition from the banks has resulted in the Abbey National leaving the building societies' 'association' so that it can be more competitive.
2. Interest rates offered by building societies to investors and borrowers will now vary between societies.

Rights issue raises £48 m

The rapidly growing financial group Exco International is raising £48 million through a rights issue and using £17 million of it to gain overall control of Telerate, the booming New York firm which supplies computerised data to dealing rooms around the world. Telerate is a rival to Reuter's Monitor service.

Of the rest of the two shares for nine rights issue proceeds, £17 million will be used to wipe $25 million off Exco's US debts and the remaining £14 million will be to broaden the group's capital base to take account of a larger business and further expansion.

Note

1. One method a public company can use to raise finance is by selling new shares to its existing shareholders (this is called a 'rights issue'). In the above, existing shareholders can purchase two new shares for every nine they already hold.

More jobs go to chips

At least 80,000 jobs have been lost in British industry over the past two years alone as firms have turned to microchips for their production processes. The rate of attrition outlined in a new report from the Policy Studies Institute, is three times faster than that seen in the previous two years.

According to PSI, the bulk of the job losses have been achieved through natural wastage, and men have suffered more than women. The report confirms that unskilled workers have been losing their jobs far more quickly than skilled workers, and PSI believes that

more new jobs will be created among skilled staff in the coming two years.

The study shows that bigger factories have cut back on staff more readily than smaller ones, and the firms losing labour because of the introduction of microchips include those in the electrical, instrument engineering, chemicals and metals industries.

The report observes that Scotland, the North and North-West have suffered the largest reductions, with the South-East, South-West and East Anglia faring the best.

PSI also found that opposition

from shop floor trade unions was rare, affecting only 5 per cent of 1,200 companies questioned, and that foreign-owned companies in Britain were using microchips in production more than UK-owned companies.

On the brighter side, PSI concludes that the expected "massive job losses" have not so far materialised and the current reductions seem "on the whole to have been acceptable" in the working places where they have been achieved through natural wastage.

The report warns that the continued acceptance of job shedding cannot be taken for granted, particularly as the use of more advanced microchips is likely to accelerate the pace of change.

Prestel now gives information on work-related courses

Over 5,200 short work-related courses and training opportunities are now available on PRESTEL, thanks to an extension of the PICKUP Short Course Directory.

Also available on the original microfiche, the directory is continually being developed to help employers who need to find out the 'where, when and how much' about short courses for their workforce.

It also tells them which colleges, polytechnics and universities can develop tailor made courses when off-the-shelf courses are not immediately available or suitable to their precise needs.

Index